KINTUI

KINTUI

Vision of the Inca's

*The Shaman's Journey
to Enlightenment*

JESSIE ESTAN AYANI Ph.D.

**1995
Heart of the Sun, Inc.
P.O. Box 17296
Minneapolis, MN 55417**

First Edition
First Printing 1995

Ayani, Jessie Estan.
    Kintui: Vision of the Inca's, The Shaman's Journey
to Enlightenment / Jessie Estan Ayani - 1st Heart of the Sun Edition
        ISBN# 0-9648763-0-2
        1. Shamanism. 2. Spirituality. 3. Medicine Wheel.
4. Q'ero Indians. 5. Inca Mythology. 6. Psychology, Self Help.

Cover art: "Inti", by Michelle Bové

Cover design: S. John Hagenstein

This book is printed on recycled paper.

For more information about workshops, lectures, and seminars by the author write to the author in care of:

Heart of the Sun
P.O. Box 495
Mount Shasta, Ca 96067

TABLE OF CONTENTS

ILLUSTRATIONS

*To Inti Tayta, Pachamama and all that lies between.
May fire and wind, in an act of co-creation,
purify and open the hearts of all human beings.*

PROLOGUE

Prior to the Spanish conquest, the Q'ero Indians of South-central Peru sequestered themselves on the inaccessible high plains beneath the holy mountain of Ausangate. In this region of Q'ero, where the legends say the first Incas appeared, they have kept an ancient knowledge from the dilution and distortion of Western rational thought. The Q'ero shamans, direct descendants of the Inca nobility, believe it is time to share the wisdom with those who would become the caretakers of the earth, who would keep the ancient wisdom alive.

Their expectation is not that we drop out of society and live in rugged isolation, but that we bring a communion with earth and sky into our everyday lives. The teachings are simple. They could be stated on a single page of this book, but their integration into the world as we know it is an awesome task. The purpose of this book is the expansion of our own awareness, lifting our own consciousness, and nothing more. Because all of life is connected like an infinite web, when one individual is able to raise his or her own consciousness, the collective consciousness of the entire planet is raised. The cosmos reverberates with heightened awareness and we touch the divine vibration with love and light.

KINTUI

In the Inca cosmology, our time upon earth is guided by a few basic principles which penetrate all aspects of life. One of these pearls of wisdom is *ayni*, reciprocity. *Ayni* is gifting to the sun and earth, the mountain spirits, all of nature and to our fellow humans in order to sustain a relationship that brings abundance and balance to our lives. *Ayni* is based on the circular flow of energy that sustains unconditional love rather than the one way, self-centered road of greed. It makes sense.

Kintui, the multifaceted principle of the trinity in the Inca tradition, holds treasures of universal importance. It must be noted that the term Inca is not a reference to the Indian people of Peru, a common assumption, but to the noble line of descendants of *Inti*, the sun. Inca means child of the sun and to be an Inca was to shine with a brilliance unmatched among men. In other words, an Inca had fully embodied the Divine on earth. Historically, there was one Inca at a time who ruled with his co-creative partner as king, prophet and realized human being. The Inca was depicted with a headdress of three feathers, the *kintui*. *Kintui* represents the three highest attributes of man, will, wisdom, and love. The Inca, descendant of the sun, embodied all three. He shone like the sun because he had followed the wisdom path in his life and was a fully embodied spirit, an enlightened being.

The Inca was surrounded by those who sought enlightenment and was the role model for all who looked for more in their lives than the human drama. His lineage contained the healers, medicine people, high priests and master shamans who served the people with divine calling. *Kintui*, the will, wisdom, and love, applies not only to the individual potential, but to the human race and all of creation, the microcosm and the macrocosm. In short, it brings together the ability to manifest, the wisdom which must be made manifest, and the open heart from which the manifestation flows.

We are being called to embrace *kintui* in our own lives now, to manifest a new reality. In this book, you will find reference to many of the world's wisdom cultures. We can bring all we have to the mountain, but we cannot manifest our destiny without the open heart, and that is the gift of the indigenous people.

SHAMANISM

As this work unfolds, you will see another dimension of *kintui*, that which reaches outside of time, which challenges our reality. When I first became involved in shamanism, I was told there were three worlds in which the shaman worked: the lower world, the middle world and the upper world. In the lower world, one met the power animals and sought advice and kinship from them. The middle world, this reality, was used to facilitate the retrieval of lost pieces of ourselves from past. The upper world was the world of spirit and there we encountered our teachers and guides in the spirit world. This shamanism had overtones of psychology but was primarily based upon anthropological and experiential investigations of indigenous people. I expected it to mean more than that and eventually drifted away from this approach.

I read shamanic adventure stories, many centering around the *ayahuasca*, a psychotropic jungle vine. These stories had an emotional and dramatic appeal, but did not speak to shamanism and spirituality. Since I had not engaged in mind-altering drug use in the 60's, a part of me was concerned that I would eventually have to explore drug use to work with shamanism. Some wise inner voice urged me to keep digging into shamanism anyway for it seemed a familiar and inviting road to me.

What I have learned from the Q'ero are two sides to shamanism, the magical and the mystical. *Ayahuasca* definitely works from the magical side and it has a great appeal to the warrior for it takes you to meet your death. This can be mythic or actual depending on how well you prepare and who takes you out there. It can be the hero's journey or the last drink you ever take in this life. Risk and adventure, after all, are hallmarks of the good warrior. This book is written from the mystical side and though the magical is forever present, the overriding intent is the spiritual quest.

There *are* three worlds through which the shaman navigates: the lower world, the middle world and the upper world. This is also called *kintui*, the three realities or levels of consciousness. To the Q'ero, the lower world is known as the *ukhupacha* and is the world of interior shadows. The middle world is the *kaypacha* and is this reality, based upon linear time. The upper world is the *hanaqpacha*, the world of spirit. Though the lower and upper worlds exist outside of time, we approach them from this reality because we lack the flexibility, at this point, to move beyond causal thought. Granted, this is what *ayahuasca* and other psychotropic drugs can do for you, but we are looking for something beyond hallucination that will integrate into and sustain the lives we lead right now.

One of the tasks has been to bring home the Q'ero wisdom and magic from a place outside of time and make a smooth re-entry into this reality. This has been an age-old problem for wisdom-seekers who cross cultural and geographic boundaries in their search. A second task has been to integrate it with key elements of planetary wisdom to delineate a spiritual path for the twenty-first century. This seems especially important at a time when the last of the world's wisdom is being scattered to the four winds.

It has been a challenge to adapt the Q'ero teachings to a way of life that bears no resemblance to their own. The key to this has been simplicity, extracting the ageless wisdom while holding the people, the culture, and the land in a place of love and utmost respect. By far the most difficult aspect of these tasks has been to find a way to walk this path myself, largely by trial and error through intent, and to adapt it to a model which embodies the essential characteristics of a wisdom path to those seeking this same spirituality.

THE MEDICINE WHEEL

The basis for any wisdom path is the path itself, its landmarks made familiar to you by those who walked the way before you. For the most part, it is difficult to find a true path, let alone authentic role models, in our society. This is, no doubt, the reason we have reached out to the Orient, and, more recently, to the indigenous people in our current search for the sacred. Since we fancy ourselves self-made human beings, we have approached this quest as we have all things in life, like a mountain to be climbed, conquered, owned. Not only is this hierarchical, it is linear, outcome-oriented and, therefore, not enduring. It is the relationship we have had with the earth, assuming all things were created for our consumption.

The most difficult task of the spiritual quest is to understand that it exists outside of time and is circular. Instead of climbing the mountain, we embrace and become the mountain. This is the essential message of shamanism and since the path is outside of time and history and knows no geographic or cultural boundaries, it has the potential to connect the hearts of all people to their divine and timeless self.

Devoid of hierarchy, the path has only levels of consciousness. It acknowledges the world of the *ukhupacha*. but is not trapped within it. It asks us to lift our consciousness towards the sun, the light. Like most indigenous people, the Q'ero relate the landmarks to the four directions. Because polychronic time is circular and hierarchy does not exist in council circles, the model of the medicine wheel can be adapted to these teachings. Whether or not there exists an Andean Medicine Wheel is irrelevant. What is important is that the model works in the transformative process. We can call on the elements and the archetypes of each direction for assistance with our movement around the wheel. Since it moves outside of linear time, spiritual shamanism contains all other wisdom paths. It is the quintessential path for uniting heaven and earth in the fully opened heart.

You will see, as we move through the three worlds of *kintui*, that it is necessary to explore all aspects of life. We need the spirits of nature and the grounding as much as we need the esoteric wisdom. If our spiritual quest is stuck in our intellect, we will never know the joy of bringing the divine vibration onto planet earth. By the same token, if we cannot free ourselves of human bondage, we will never move past our suffering. There is only one way to approach this path, as a spirit drawn into the earthly experience because it is like no other. We want to engage the game of life and have fun doing it. This is our destiny and our birthright as children of the sun and earth. If we seek to walk in paradise, in balance between father sky and mother earth as fully potentialized human beings, we have some challenging work to do.

PLAYING THE GAME

There is a spirit appropriate to playing the game of life. In the Andean traditions, all relationships evolve in three stages. The first encounter is the place where instinct and spontaneity reign. This is followed by a kind of sparring where one is tested and either wins or loses. In our culture, we can assume that everyone wants to win, but in the Andes, the third part of the relationship requires that the winner teach all that he knows to the loser. This, more or less, takes the hierarchy out of any relationship. There is as much to be gained by losing as winning. We would like to have this kind of relationship with the medicine wheel, to engage the spiritual path with this give and take.

We will build on this medicine wheel as we pass through the three worlds of *kintui*, the *ukhupacha*, *kaypacha* and *hanaqpacha*. In our own spiritual work, we are generally approaching the *ukhupacha* from this reality, the *kaypacha*, because we lack the full awareness of these shadowy realms, and often hold them in a place of fear. But it is necessary to fully expose the *ukhupacha* so that we know its landmarks and the depth of its shadows. If you have been involved with deep psychoanalysis or transpersonal psychology, this territory of the unconscious mind will not be altogether unfamiliar to you. It is a side of us to be approached with respect. As we walk the *ukhupacha* medicine wheel, we must understand that it represents the raw material with which we will do our work. We created it that way. We need to be honest in describing it and our entrenchment in it, but not allow feelings of hopelessness to enter our energetic field. To the Q'ero, it is both the shadow side of the human experience and its greatest illusion. It is a reality we can either sustain with unconscious activity or acknowledge and release with fully conscious living. I suggest that you read this book through the first time experiencing the three worlds or levels of consciousness. Then, on a second reading, work with the four directions, exploring each direction on the three levels of consciousness.

In the *kaypacha*, we will find the path which allows us to clear and move beyond the *ukhupacha*. This is the difficult work of healing our lives and we go no further on the medicine wheel until it is finished. It is at the end of the *kaypacha* journey that we touch our souls and begin the conscious ascent to the divine. This path is about raising consciousness and bringing enlightenment into everyday life. You will see that, somewhere along the way, it throws off the yoke of shamanism, culture, gender, and all the operational belief systems which form our human experience. It stands alone, as light, energy, the sun itself.

This is exactly what a wisdom path ought to do for you, but it has to begin as something you feel comfortable with, are attracted to. For me, the earth, the elements, the ancient aspects of the knowledge and the luminous presence of Q'ero elder, Don Mariano Apaza, riveted me to the path. For me, surrender was not an issue. Integral to my journey were the teachings of my friend, brother, and master shaman Américo Yabar who has been a bridge to the Q'ero.

I have had many wonderful teachers in my life. The spirit of their teaching drifts among these pages. I, too, have manifest the joyful task of teaching what is a part of me, and have been blessed with incredible students. Together, we have explored the dimensions of this path in a prototypic two-year program, have supported each other in life transitions, and most importantly, have tried to approach this work with love and laughter. I wish, for you, the same deep connection to the work. Above all, keep a light heart, use the glossary, and form a traditional relationship with it: encounter, engage, and share your victories with someone on the path behind you.

Jessie Estan Ayani, 1995

PART I

THE *UKHUPACHA*

In the cosmology of the Incas, the universe came into being with a great explosion of the Creative Forces. A ray of Creation extended itself outward, creating our galaxy and planet earth where the rocks and mountains were called into being. In those early times called the naupapacha, the earth lay in darkness with a gaseous atmosphere fit only for the Naupamachu, the transparent beings who inhabited the earth. These creatures engaged in ritual and aligned themselves with the dark and violent forces.

When the god Rual, who guided the destiny of the earth, announced that Pachakamak, cosmic father, deemed it necessary for a new reality, a cosmic transmutation to occur, he offered the Naupamachu the leadership of the new order. They refused to align themselves with Rual, certain that their knowledge was greater, and fully embraced the forces of darkness.

At this time, the great serpent mother, Sachamama, keeper of knowledge, took fire and crawled within the center of the earth to hide. To manifest the new reality, the god Rual created the sun, Inti. Inti caused the gases of the earth to change and the sky to clear. When Inti came into being there was light. Neither light nor air could be tolerated by the Naupamachu and many were destroyed. Those who remained crept between the cracks and crevices of the rocks and made their new homes within the interior of the earth. This place, the ukhupacha, is the dark, interior world of shadows.

The serpent used the fire to warm the earth from within and made it hospitable for life. Plants appeared, followed by many forms of creation, and the wind blew clouds around the mountain tops.

The apus, the mountain spirits, were happy, but missed the transparent creatures for their lives were interesting to watch. The god Rual, hearing the thoughts of the apus, gifted the earth his highest creation, the Rhunakuna, human beings. The Rhunakuna pleased the apus and in many ways participated in creation, but they were somehow caught between worlds, living partly in the world of darkness, the ukhupacha, and partly in the light of the sun, Inti.

1

SOUTH:
SUFFERING

The *Naupamachu*, or transparent beings, are elemental forces that live within each of us. The *ukhupacha*, or dark, interior world of shadows, is the unconscious mind and also the primitive brain, which prompts action without thought. *Sachamama*, the serpent mother who holds the knowledge, is the latent kundalini, the key to awakening the soul. Until the serpent is awakened, we slumber in the world of shadows. Rather than being masters of our own destinies, we find ourselves slaves to the elemental forces; suffering, violence, negative emotion and judgment.

Since we do not live in a wisdom culture, we do not grow up with an awareness of the *ukhupacha*. In the process of awakening, we typically find it so distasteful that we do not explore the full extent of its shadowy depths. But if we are not fully aware of the *ukhupacha*, we cannot completely extract ourselves from it. We are enslaved by it.

The gates of the *ukhupacha* are guarded by *Huascar Inca* a mythic archetype reminiscent of the gate guardians of the Japanese temples. *Huascar*, a frightening figure with a heart of gold, beckons us to meet our fear and step outside the *ukhupacha* forever. He will take us in there to the dark interior world of shadows to meet our fear and the symbolic death of the self. Like the *Rhunakuna*, we are caught between the world of the shadows and a reality we do not understand. Since we are more comfortable with this in-between reality, we tend to dip into the *ukhupacha* when our need for healing outweighs our fear of the shadows.

Shamanism, approached as the spiritual path, requires us to fully comprehend the *ukhupacha*. We must free ourselves from it and understand the landscape to assist those who wish to free themselves. We can draw upon the ancient wisdom, hidden from us only by the degree of our entrenchment in the *ukhupacha*. Much like meeting the mountain, to master the *ukhupacha* and move beyond it, we must embrace it, know its landmarks, own it as part of our being, then lift our awareness above it. This constitutes the raising of our own consciousness, facilitating a cosmic transmutation within us. We ask *Huascar Inca* to open the gates and lead us into the darkness.

We are beings of light and energy who have chosen to incarnate into matter. Unfortunately, few of us emerged from our upbringing with this knowledge. More to the point, few of us have emerged from our upbringing at all. And no one escapes suffering in this life. Most of the mythology that accompanies us promises a reward in the great hereafter. If we don't buy into that, we don't get much support and instead adopt a lifestyle that lives in the moment. So what is it, suffer and be saved or instant gratification? What kind of choices are these? Buddhists speak of endless samsara, endless suffering, and recommend that we adopt an attitude of joyful participation and engagement in the sorrow, for it will not go away. That makes three choices: suffer and be saved, suffer and enjoy it, or seek pleasure while we can and pay for it later, maybe.

The Q'ero, like most indigenous people, believe that we are living in paradise but we do not see it. If we saw it, we would have more respect for it. In the gospel of Thomas, Christ makes reference

The ukhupacha

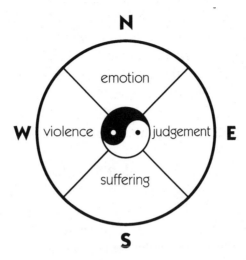

The In-between World

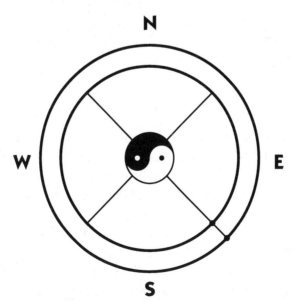

I. The *ukhupacha* is the dark world of interior shadows. We walk in-between the worlds, not yet fully conscious, controlled by the *ukhupacha*, yet our awareness is in this reality.

to the kingdom of God - it is spread upon the earth and men do not see it. Christ knew something that has been misrepresented to us, perhaps for purposes of power and control. How long will the human race live in fear?

If there is a way past suffering, it must be illusive, perhaps masked by something quite repulsive. It is the metaphor of the crucifixion, of course, sacrificing self to The Source, the Great Mystery, but it is far too painful to think about enduring. It is the gateway to the *ukhupacha* and it is guarded by the ominous *Huascar Inca*. To be free of the darkness, we must understand why it exists and recognize it as illusion. Where did the suffering originate and why did we land right in the middle of it?

We need to take a journey of mythic proportions. There is no other way to re-imagine who we are. We need some magic, some fairy dust. To take this journey we must believe that we are called into this life for a reason, that we have intended the entire thing. And we must not get hung up on the mechanics of how it is possible, for the answers lie in portions of our neocortex which we have not begun to utilize consciously. We will draw from many wisdom sources, take what we need to reconstruct our origins, and enter the *ukhupacha* again, fully awake. Let's not forget that *Huascar Inca* has a heart of gold.

THE GAME OF LIFE

First, we must have a clear understanding of the nature of matter for it could provide the greatest limitation to our journey. Matter, classically defined, has weight and takes up space. Historically, it is how we have been taught to conceptualize about our bodies, our brains, our furniture and nature. Einstein impacted our thinking about matter and became a pivotal figure in changing the historical definition. He introduced the idea that energy and matter were interchangeable, the wave/particle theory. He also saw outside of linear time. His limitation was the velocity of light and his belief that particles (matter) could not be accelerated beyond it.

Today, physicists are breaking these barriers, but we are still stopped by them, for most of us do not understand the quantum world.

It is difficult to imagine that there is substance which travels beyond the speed of light at very subtle (high) vibrations. This is difficult for us to believe because we cannot track it with our instrumentation and bring it, in some way, into this physical reality. We, as the observers, and the instruments of measurement get in the way of detection. Yet we know that something subtle animates our world and leaves when death arrives. The shaman is a master of the invisible realms, moving beyond death. It is interesting to note that a number of quantum physicists are now exploring shamanism.

To make our journey, we will have to be shamans, out there cracking cosmic eggs with the certainty that the physicists will rationalize the subtle before too long. Let's loosen our attachment to matter. In fact, let's look at our hands right now and realize that they are frozen light, that they are composed of molecules which are moving at a vibration slow enough for us to see them and feel them. Let's look at the table and realize the same thing about it. Perhaps that is harder to imagine, but it is just as valid. All of life has vibration and motion and some things are more frozen than others, depending on their basic chemistry. Molecules do not stay still but are vibrating constantly at rates consistent with their structure. Yet life is largely beyond detection by instrumentation. And we are multidimensional beings with energetic layers reaching out into the cosmos.

To incarnate is to come into matter, heavy vibration, into positive space/time. And in the process of materialization, we come to lose the memory of how it happened. These are the rules of play for the earth game. The object of the game is to remember who we are and get out of here alive, that is to say consciously. Basically, we seem to keep landing on the squares of the three choices, "suffer-suffer", "suffer-enjoy" and "live it up, life is short". Eventually we hit the terminator square, "you're dead, go back to go and start again". Back at the go square we remember who we are, get our plan together again, and roll the dice. This is reincarnation. Very few individuals have figured out how to win at this game and get out gracefully, much less alive.

The cosmic dice, as you might have guessed, are loaded. By whom? By us, of course. Who else? But that comes after we have decided to play the game. Let's go back before we got the game out of the cupboard in the first place. Better yet, before the game's creator decided what variables to put on the board and how to load the dice. If we see this whole exercise as one of taking responsibility for our lives, we are more than ready to do this work.

Though the analogy of a board game may seem trivial for such serious material, the headiness and inaccessible nature of esoteric knowledge greatly increases our unwillingness to claim responsibility for our lives. It is easy to assign blame when we haven't a clue what we're doing, but everyone can relate to monopoly. We win. We lose. We play the game. However we chose to look at life, the strategy for winning still eludes us. We must cross the boundaries of time and space, imagining ourselves dematerializing, trying to remember what this is about.

First let's allow ourselves to be a particle. Then, let's turn the particle into a wave. We find ourselves cruising along a wave pattern that has no beginning or end. We are partly a photon of light and partly something that isn't even light, something more subtle, spread out through the whole wave. Our heavier vibrations have a feeling of bliss and our more subtle vibrations *are* bliss. We have an awareness, through one of these vibrations, that we are an inseparable part of everything that exists, cosmic consciousness. We are the light and the darkness in one, the Tao.

We feel an urge to coalesce and begin to pull our energies into a ball of very rarefied light/energy, a kind of "self" consciousness. Yet we are not detached from the wave since it flows through our ball of light/energy. We find ourselves sitting in a circle of these light/energy beings. In that circle, we all look alike and we are all riding the great wave of cosmic consciousness.

And then a voice, from everywhere and nowhere, begins to talk to us about a mission, a divine plan. We are being asked to incarnate on the earth. We are told exactly what the score is, the work that needs to be done, and the team that we will work with is this circle of light/energy beings. We have been to earth before and remember the experience, but the voice reminds us again that we will forget everything we know as soon as we get there. It is an anything goes, free-will experience and we are given the option to back out.

From the perspective inherent in riding the wave, it is a great opportunity. Going to earth means adventure, growth and increased vibration. The earth experience is like no other for it contains the vibration of emotion which can be transformed into more light/energy and used to enhance the cosmic consciousness, The Source.

So, of course, we intend yes, and we and our cohorts get our blank earth game boards out and begin making plans. To keep us in touch with the eternal nature of life, it is a circular game. Based on knowledge of the earth experience, it is divided it into four sections for the elements of nature; earth, water, fire and air. These symbolize linear time, an odd feature of the earth experience. Then the circles are divided further into eight directions which symbolize three-dimensional space, the second limiting factor of earth.

Into each of the eight directions, are fused the duality and complimentarity which gives full appreciation and potential to every experience and results in sixty-four possibilities (eight to the second power of the duality) for squares on which to land. Everyone's game board has a different and unique combination but all have a square, somewhere, that says "wake-up". We, and our circle of light/energy beings fine-tune the game board by arranging possible opportunities to meet each other. Since earth is free-will territory, much will depend on the choices we make, so we create a number of opportunities for this to happen. And it looks like great fun, because we have the perspective of the creator. However, on earth, we will forget our part in this game and lose that creator perspective. In fact, we will not remember that it is just a game.

In the excitement of designing the variable aspects of the board, we are already loosing touch with the cosmic consciousness that is directing our purpose for incarnating. Fortunately, it has been built into the game and it is still flowing through us at an unconscious level of awareness.

LOADING THE DICE

The next piece of work is individual, and our circle of light/energy beings retract into greater coalescence. We put ourselves in touch

Chakra	IX-XII	Hologram
VIII Wiracocha		Causal-spirit
VII Crown		Causal-self
VI Brow		Mental-3
V Throat		Mental-2
IV Heart		Mental-1
III Solar Plexus		Astral
II Sacral		Etheric
I Base		Physical

II. Diagram showing each chakra with its number, name, and hologram as referenced throughout the text.

with the unresolved lives from our many earthly incarnations. This is run through a data bank which accesses the board plans of all the souls who are intending to be incarnated upon the earth when we are. We search out ways in which we might resolve the issues we have had with any of these other light/energy beings, and into our dice we load our karmic intention. This intention will bring us into play with them, thereby affording the opportunity for both light/energy beings to dissipate the heavy energy remaining from previous experiences. If successful, this strategy lightens the heavy vibrations and enhances what we can give back to The Source. In our acts of creation, we honor and enhance the creative Source.

This finished, we look into the data bank again, calling up and sorting through the genetic possibilities for parents that will give us the best opportunity to fulfill our purpose. This would, necessarily, be weighed with the culture, gender, race and social environment to fit our plan. We cross reference the genetics against the karmic material already chosen to optimize clearing the heavier energy. The moment of birth is decided to provide us with the energetic patterns of our desired personality.

The dice are getting heavy, but we must throw in the clincher, free will, which puts the entire game into the realm of probability and variable outcome, dependent upon every choice we make. It's a nightmare of complexity by this time, but we are operating within the divine plan and it seems very clear to us. These tasks completed, we are free to relax in the semi-coalesced state until the events pursuant to our final descent into matter are at hand. We and our cohorts ride the wave, board games stored in the cosmic closet, dice in hand, with an ear tuned to the intention of our future parents.

INCARNATION

When the intention to procreate enters the subconscious of our chosen parents, we are ready for action. The descent into matter takes us through twelve perfectly harmonious octaves of decreasing frequency until we arrive at materialization. The beauty of the trip is that each vibration will remain with us, through our twelve chakras, our energy centers, for our entire earthly life.

As we coalesce into matter, we first transit through a set of four cosmic vibrations which will guide us on our return trip into formlessness. The second set of four vibrations contain the blueprint for the higher self. The final four vibrations contain the blueprint of the lower self.

For now, we will look upon these as overlaid holograms which reach out with increasing vibration to the cosmos. With each increase in frequency or octave of vibration, the hologram extends out further than the next lowest frequency hologram. Each is connected to the composite, multi-dimensional human through its related chakra. The four cosmic chakras and their vibrational bodies are either hovering close by us or are at various stages of placement in the cosmos, depending on our awareness of them. To work with them requires extra-planetary expertise, beyond the scope of this book, so we will acknowledge them and connect with them when we are ready. Let us come down through the energetic fields of our multi-dimensional beings one step at a time, from chakra VIII to chakra I, pulling the subtle energies together into heavier and heavier vibrations.

VIII

The eighth chakra hovers about the head. It is the halo depicted above the crown of the head in paintings of Christ and the saints. Its holographic vibration (octave VIII) connects our soul to the divine spirit moving through us and all of life and is our link to the cosmic vibrations. It connects us to the way home as contained in vibrations/chakras IX-XII. It also is our bridge to the collective unconscious. In the Inca tradition, this is called the *Wiracocha*, a term that, at once, refers to our own luminous body and the Source. This chakra is sometimes depicted below the feet for it envelops the entire being and connects us to sky and earth.

VII

The crown chakra and its hologram, an octave lower in vibration, contain the self aspect of the spirit. This is the personality's link to our transpersonal self and the chakra through which the combined, invisible hologram and soul exits at the time of death, if we die consciously. The soul, the eternal aspect of our being, guides us in an unconscious way, until we fully connect with it. This will be discussed later in the text. The soul resides in the higher vibrational aspect of our light/energy as we coalesce.

VI

The brow chakra (third eye) and its holographic body are on the highest vibrational level of the mental plane (M-3, Octave VI) and link the causal plane (soul) with the mind. We speak of the mind's eye associated with this chakra and the more spiritual aspects of learning.

V

A vibration lower, at the fifth holographic body, the intellectual mental plane (M-2) is connected to the throat chakra which guides the intellectual and emotional aspects of the mental body. This completes the second set of four holograms and the vibrations which have an upward draw, *from* the earth *to* the cosmos.

If we are visualizing these holograms penetrating and forming around the fetus in the mother's womb, we need to reverse our thought process. These holograms from the highest vibration to the lowest, are putting themselves in place, at our soul's direction, before conception to stabilize and guide the entire process of pro/co-creation and development. Let's not forget, this is our plan.

IV

So with the second set of four holograms in place, we begin to coalesce the emotional mental plane linked to the heart chakra. There is, with this hologram (M-1), a shift in our awareness as we begin to tune into the pulse of the earth. It is a powerful force, drawing us into matter. In gathering the three layers of the mental plane, we have drawn from past earth experience, collective knowledge and the information gained from pure feeling. These are linked to the causal plane at their higher vibration and to the emotional or astral plane at the lower. So the heart becomes the pivotal point in linking spirit and matter.

III

The astral hologram is an octave slower in vibration than the heart (M-1) and is connected to the solar plexus chakra. It contains the range of emotion we are bringing to this incarnation, gathered from a collective astral field. With the astral hologram, we are entering a frequency range that can sometimes be felt in the physical realm. It is a sensation that we have when we stand within close range of someone who is experiencing strong emotion. It is easy to feel. The solar plexus chakra is the center of emotion and personal power.

II

The second hologram or etheric field contains the energetic blueprint of the physical body and it is coalesced under the guidance of the higher vibrational subtle bodies which call into being the etheric DNA. It is gathered from the ether of those who have left the earth plane, that which is part of nature at large, and that which the parents provide from their own etheric fields. This is the ch'i, and it is everywhere, in food, drink, air and sunlight and in the etheric field of every living thing. Many people can feel, even see, the ch'i and instruments have recently measured it.

The etheric body is connected to the sacral chakra which rules relationship and sexual energy. This hologram provides the energetic motivation for pro-creation, emotional sensitivity, and sensory stimulation.

I

Guided by the etheric blueprint and supported by the octaves of vibration which reach to the cosmic spheres, a sperm penetrates an egg and the physical hologram begins to shape itself. The vibrational frequency has entered the realm of matter, frozen light, and a baby human being comes into the earthly realms. The physical body is the lowest vibration of our multi-dimensional self and is connected to the base chakra. This chakra contains our willingness to live, to be materialized in the physical form. It is the center where we ground ourselves to mother earth.

We must remember that karma is energy and doesn't need physical manifestation to surface. It can take form in any of these holograms, at any time. Karmic debts are often paid in the womb and life outside the womb may not be part of the game plan. The familial genetics are limited to the physical/etheric planes. Personality imprinting, energy transiting through the zodiac at our chosen time of birth, penetrates all layers of the hologram throughout the incarnation. The soul hovers near the human form in the higher vibrational planes of the energetic hologram but generally makes no attempt to consciously connect until the form is capable of holding its light/energy.

BIRTH

In touch with the moment of birth as a destiny with which we cannot tamper, we instigate it automatically. What ensues is trauma of the highest order, and we cannot take it back. The board game goes in one direction only, and we find ourselves on the start square, dice in hand, screaming, bloody, and stark naked in the light. While we are an object of great interest to those around us and react to them instinctively, we are experiencing the loss of soul memory as our journey into matter escapes us. Along with the game plan, we have lost the purpose and all of the power and knowledge we gathered into the hologram during our descent. It is a disaster of unimagined proportions and we spend as much time as possible sleeping, trying to remember who we are.

The limbic brain has kicked in and we behave in the instinctive unconscious manner of any other baby, including animal babies. In fact, we are more helpless than an animal baby because our growing neocortex is down-playing the importance of the limbic brain. If we are lucky at rolling the dice, people take delight in stimulating us with sound, touch and light so that we become more grounded on the earth. They also give us time alone to stay somewhat connected to our energetic bodies. If we are unlucky, they overstimulate us or totally ignore us.

Already we are wishing there were more squares on the board that said "balance", but no one can understand what we want, and by the time they can, the game itself will be a dim recollection. Throwing the dice will eventually become a repetitive motion, something from the limbic brain.

The way we access our multidimensional self is through a process of awakening that begins in the physical body. Imagine then the impact on the higher vibrational bodies, gathered together with power and knowledge, when they are sequestered within the body of a helpless infant. We are standing in the middle of a maze and the lights go out. That's about it. We start rolling those dice.

FAMILY LIFE

Have we ever met someone who comes from a "functional" family? The world is in dysfunction, so why would we expect parents to be any different than everyone around them. Patterns of abuse have been established in families and carried through the generations with remarkable fidelity. These cycles are hard to break. Identification of abuse is the first step, breaking the cycle is the second, and repairing the damage in our subtle bodies is the third. Just achieving the first two steps in our own lives means our children will be rolling the dice with new probabilities. Energy is shifting now. Couples are waiting until their thirties to have children and many are attending to their healing work first. We can't really know the potential of a child's life until we get in touch with our own. We can't really love our children until we love ourselves.

Repairing the damage to the subtle body is hard work, the work being put down in this book. It is a process of self-discovery and healing that results in empowerment. Empowerment is taking responsibility for our own life, and that includes owning up to the fact that we picked our parents. Instead of feeling victimized by our child-

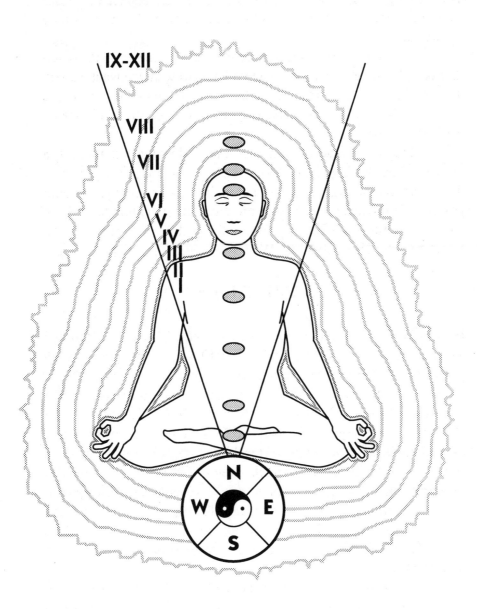

IX-XII

VIII

VII

VI
V
IV
III

N

W E

S

III. The path of coalescence into matter which is the soul's journey during incarnation. Roman numerals refer to the chakras and holograms.

hoods, we learn to see the great lessons, the gifts, that came with parents and siblings. And we break the cycles with our own children. This is part of raising consciousness.

But, we have lost the game plan and are traveling in the in-between world, our lives enslaved to the *ukhupacha*. We are completely disempowered. Family life is rich in karma, both the kind we planned and, unfortunately, the new karma we are all creating. That's how the data bank got so full in the first place. Before we get to a point of realizing what is going on, we have increased our workload considerably. It's that probability factor with the dice.

We need to know that there are karmic cycles of inheritance as well as genetic and that patterns of abuse running through family history can be either. The neediness that leads to co-dependence and addiction has an energetic link with the child who wasn't nurtured in all necessary ways. Energetic links to abandonment in its many forms lead to enormous fear issues throughout life. Children who are silenced may never be heard as adults. The child who must withdraw from violence lacks the grounded personality necessary to connect with life.

We must also look to the family history for diet and lifestyle imprinting, social skills or lack thereof, and the harmful effects of television which imprint and control both a need for visual stimulation and distorted human values. Educational motivation, judgment style and role playing can also be traced back to the family of origin as well as any ingrained religious beliefs.

Yet we have picked our families to provide us with the genetics, intelligence, opportunities, and conditioning to follow the path of soul potential. It may not seem that way at the time, but some of us thrive on struggle. The important piece to keep in mind is that we planned it this way, we picked the family, and we really aren't "related" to them at all. Our "real" family, the circle of light/energy beings with whom we planned the game, are out there floundering around just like we are.

THE SOCIAL NUCLEUS

When we first reach outside the family, we encounter individuals of similar background, usually relatives and playmates right around us. Families gravitate to cities and neighborhoods where similar karma is being acted out. We expand our awareness and at the same time take in more individual diversity in the personality overlays of these people. In the process of maturation, we react to people with our unique unfolding composite personality. The pressure of the social nucleus will favor development of certain aspects of our persona depending on its nature. If we are constantly bullied, we will either lay down and take it, run away and cry, fight back, or go tell on the bully. And it has nothing to do with physical strength. This is our own personality imprinted with notions of behavior drawn from the family and social nucleus. Do we succumb to the lure of peer pressure or have we a sense of self that allows us to be independent of it?

All imprinting occurs in the early socialization process. We may come in to this life with karmic debts to pay, but how we pay them reflects the imprinting. We may bring cycles of abuse or victimization from previous incarnations, but how they are acted out in this life reflects the imprinting. The same is true with the personality aspects. It is important to realize the complex nature of the *ukhupacha* as well as the nature of our entrenchment in it.

One aspect of socialization that merits further discussion is religion. Whether you follow one or not, the social imprinting is pervasive and largely negative. Religion supports suffering and is, along with government, the most employed means of controlling personal freedom. Religion imprisons us in the *ukhupacha*, feeding us suffering, violence, emotion and judgment. Rules and regulations do not support consciousness. Dogma establishes limitations to human potential.

Why do we believe what we don't truly understand? Because knowing exists in the light and we are traveling at the edge of darkness. When we are traveling at the edge of darkness we are told to "have faith" because we are not capable of having wisdom. Who has the wisdom? Our leaders do not. It is a well established game of deception in which the faithful participate in furthering the illusion. Knowledge is accessed from the mental plane and we are locked into the lower vibrational realms.

Religion is a crutch for the spiritually disabled, a way to rationalize the world of suffering, the *ukhupacha*, into which we are born. It is a way to remain in denial about who we are. Many of us born into the catholic religion have taken leave of the opinionated, aloof, and unyielding attitude of the patriarchy. Gender-bias denies the earth mother and she knows it. The hierarchical structure denies "enlightenment" to the common man and creates a climate of shame and blame which further immobilizes us on the journey of spirit. Yet we are grateful for this gift, for we were drawn to its ritual which awakened a need in us that would one day lead us to the path. The entire experience of religion has enriched us beyond measure and it was most assuredly part of many of our game plans. However, as a people, we are ready to move beyond it.

ENVIRONMENT AND CULTURE

Another consideration of our journey into matter was race, nationality, and precise location, if required. There are karmic debts being acted upon by nations and different advantages to nationality depending on our game plan and goals. It was known that the United States would become the focal point for an intense search for the sacred at this time. Our plan may have involved that search. The present times offer great opportunity for soul growth and we all knew that when we designed our game boards. There is a polarity emerging in the United States that will propel us into action soon. From this action will emerge a way of life more deeply connected to the planet.

Nationality and the culture are not always the same, especially in the United States right now. We are the melting pot of all nations, with greater diversity than has ever existed on earth. Many of our origins are so diverse that we are indigenous to nowhere. It is time to push past our race and roots on earth and remember our celestial origins, but until all of our hearts are open to that, the race we are born into does make a difference and we will have picked what suited our plan. Race may be the very thing we chose to challenge us, to awaken others to the soul that knows no color. Often we abused others in previous incarnations and will reincarnate as the victim to set the records straight or vice-versa.

The cultural imprinting is still very strong on earth and creates biases which are supported by all the other imprinting from our upbringing. We are drawn to the locations and situations we need to do our work if, and when, we get past the point of repeatedly asking anyone who will listen, including our gods, "why me?". It can get very dark in the *ukhupacha*. One important point to remember is that light emerges from the darkness. From the perspective of the soul, it does not matter with which side we chose to align ourselves. What matters is that our choice is the choice of our soul and not of an unconscious human being.

ENDLESS SAMSARA

The *ukhupacha* is a medicine wheel we need to explore. The road signs are the four directions and we always start the medicine wheel in the South. In the *ukhupacha*, this means suffering, endless samsara to the Tibetans. We are good at suffering, experts in fact, from all that imprinting we endured while growing up. Perhaps we crave martyrdom because it gives us someone to blame for our misery. We don't have to be responsible for it. We have our hair shirts in the closet and our bed of nails hidden under the couch, ready at a moment's notice. There is an unexplainable comfort in pain that defies reason. Once we get to rolling those dice, we don't know how to stop. That is called being unconscious and it is the hallmark of the *ukhupacha*.

Our responses are conditioned by our imprinting and these cycles of self-abuse are hard to recognize until they are outrageously out of control. That usually means disease has set in at some level of awareness. Unless we are traumatized in an accident or are born with a genetic anomaly, we come by our diseases through a chaotic etheric body blueprint. The physical body is given to chaos, obeying the laws of thermodynamics. The etheric body, conversely, tends towards order, and the two, in optimal health, operate in a dynamic tension. Chaos usually originates in the emotional body, the astral plane being the most common hologram to become spontaneously chaotic. We hold our negative emotions inside so well that we lose the ability to feel. We can even turn love into something emotional. We take on the negative vibrations of other people's emotional dramas.

Where do those withheld emotions go? They are in our emotional hologram and they start working away on the etheric hologram with which it interfaces. Disorganization or stress in the etheric blueprint disrupts the smooth flow of ch'i and balanced energetics. These disharmonies will, before long, cause disease in the physical body. Though not as often, we can begin this process in the mental body by fixating on something obsessively, mental stress, and the unguided use of mind-altering drugs. And it is not uncommon for someone to have experienced a loss in the causal holograms (soul loss) from traumatic abuse as a child.

Our energy bodies begin to look like the earth's atmosphere, full of space age garbage, satellite selves and negative energy. We don't know how to clean that up either and adopt the same attitude with it - that we can't really see it so it doesn't much matter. For the most part, we are sound asleep and don't feel it coming until it hits the physical body, and then we can be harboring an enormous tumor without really being aware of it.

The medical establishment has no more enlightenment than we do, they just have more power and instrumentation. We rarely exercise our options, are ill-informed, willing to put our lives in the hands of people we barely know. Where have we practiced this kind of faith before? We are driven by a bone-deep fear of death that is born of our ignorance. It is rarely discussed in our culture. Resistance to enlightenment is also common to the *ukhupacha*.

All suffering is self-destructive, but addiction, which plugs into the endless cycle of the *ukhupacha*, takes our imprinting to new heights. We love habits, good, bad, or indifferent. When we are in habit, we don't have to think, we don't have to be conscious. We can be unconscious, in the *ukhupacha* again, on automatic pilot. That is what makes it so easy to be in denial about addictions. And we can move from one addiction to the other with ease. If something like alcoholism surfaces, and we are made to deal with it by our conscious mind, we will feed the creatures of the *ukhupacha* with cigarettes and coffee. One way or another, we will plug into mindlessness.

As a nation, the United States runs on addiction. It is considered normal behavior unless your addiction steps outside the law. We start early with visual stimulation. Beginning with television, it moves to Nintendo, computer games, video games, movies and the epitome of mindlessness, music videos. The subliminal messages in all these forms of stimulation keeps us under tight control. We are presented with images of the ideal man or woman and instigate an array of eating disorders, fitness addictions and clothing obsessions. This is so prevalent we consider it a way of life. It is our life. We are completely motivated by it and it becomes a life goal in and of itself.

We can be addicted to all kinds of recreational drugs, alcohol, food, cigarettes, anything with chemicals that alter our moods. We forget how humans behave without stimulation, sedation, or gratification. It is all conditioning, yet some of us are so creative we take things to totally new levels, even risking our lives for a thrill. We must not forget our addictions to money, possessions, pleasure of all sorts and especially sex.

What does addiction mean? It means we do not know how to love ourselves or appreciate our self worth. If our love and nurturing needs were not met as children and we were not given role models of self esteem, we will be searching all our lives to fill that gap. As a people, we are remarkably gifted but often insecure. There were all kinds of role models of self-absorption but not self-love. We find all manner of ways to make ourselves feel loved and appreciated, and these become our addictions. We can move around and change them but no matter what they are, they are all feeding the same neediness. We really don't know what love "feels" like.

Addictions feed the creatures of the *ukhupacha* through the physical body as does most of our unconscious suffering. It is related through the holograms to the base chakra, and our willingness to live, as well as to the sacral chakra, and our need to indulge the senses. Sometimes we find ourselves in deep despair, depression, or chronic pain and think it would be better to be dead. In fact, it would be better if we quit being dead and started being alive. A deep connection to the earth, through that base and sacral chakra, is the best medicine available. We will talk about the earth connection and effective ways of breaking addictive patterns in the *kaypacha* medicine walk in Part II.

Don't forget that the physical body is part of the hologram and that all of our suffering is held in it somewhere. It ripples out through all the subtle bodies in the form of emotion and memories as well. As we continue to journey through the *ukhupacha*, the clutter in our energy fields gets worse and worse and we can really begin to feel heavy from the weight. Because we are unconscious, we have no idea what is happening in the multi-dimensional subtle bodies. We just feel rotten. We can, and do, blame an infinite number of things and people for that which is clearly our own creation.

2

WEST:
VIOLENCE

When the god, Rual, at Pachakamak's command, sent the cosmic transmutation by way of *Inti*, the sun, the *Naupamachu* crawled through the cracks and crevices of the rocks to live, aligned with the forces of violence, in the *ukhupacha*. The violence, already present, was made to hide from the light in the shadows of the earth. This is the nature of the duality, light and dark, yang and yin. They are mutually dependent, can transform into one another, contain one another, yet are distinct. This is the meaning of the Tao symbol. We are not going to make the darkness disappear, for it will not. We need to look at ways to restructure its expression.

For most of us, the darkest of all human behavior is violence, yet we let it go on around us all the time. Instead of changing the reality, we try to hide from it, build walls around us to insulate ourselves. It will come to meet us though, for there is no escaping the *ukhupacha* when you are walking between the worlds. We live in a violent world. The creatures of the *ukhupacha* feed on violence like no other human activity and thereby perpetuate an endless cycle to fill their needs. For the most part we are helpless to find ways of extracting it from our lives to change the reality in which we live. Even if we move away from the scenes of violence we take our personal violence with us, and everyone has it. We need to take a good look at where it originates before we can begin our quest to transmute it.

HUMAN HISTORY

Human history is violent. It's a wonder we managed to employ the small fraction of the neocortex now available to us. It likely assists us with strategy and control. The history books read like one continual battle, with a few interludes of isolated human growth. Barbaric behavior gradually became more organized but the patterns remained the same; invasion, conquest, looting of wealth, and blending of culture. Boundaries moved with the gold. As the world was divvied up into smaller nations life got complicated and most peasants had no idea who was ruling them. It didn't much matter for they were slaves to their lives anyway. Slavery and suppression, acts of control, are forms of violence as well. About the only thing that changes over the span of recorded history is the sophistication of the weapons and the speed with which people can be wiped out. We have invested a lot of human and natural resources in war. Those of us who couldn't stay focused or awake in history class were doing this medicine wheel work at an early age.

War is an established way of life then, driven by greed and a thirst for power. And we cannot think for a minute that there will ever be a lofty way to justify it. It is the game of sleeping people. Let's look at the history of America, a brief one in the annals of time. The colonists landed on the East coast, a few seekers of religious freedom. They were followed by many others seeking freedom, including a fair number of released criminals, the rejects and opportunists from Europe. The drama started right away when the colonists got going on a war with Britain. Then they involved the French, enabling Europe to conduct a war in North America. In time they were pushing the Native people off the land, had them involved in the fighting or just wiped them out when they got in the way. Tribe after tribe, nation after nation of Indian people were annihilated as our bloodline ancestors pushed their way over the Eastern half of the country. Finished with the Europeans, finally independent, they continued the Indian killing on the frontier and eventually started killing each other in the Civil War. A country fighting over slavery, meeting violence with violence. They pushed further and further West coming into conflict with the Spanish in the Southwest, and finally arrived on the West coast, triumphant. Nearly every Indian had been wiped from the land and those who hadn't been were confined to reservations on land felt to have no value. Later, surprised to find resources of value there, these pioneers took back what they'd given and confined the Native people further. This process appears to be ongoing.

Like slavery, this was justified because Indians weren't really human. Why would they want to be? Humans were obviously savages. This isn't to say that Indian tribes were not warlike, for their societies had broken down to some extent before our arrival. But the Indian people held a respect for the earth, the environment, and all creatures. By the time the indigenous people were conquered, our ancestors were already engaged in the assault and plundering of the earth herself. We know all of this to be true, but it is not what we are taught in our history classes or what our government acknowledges. This denial sustains negativity and will forever inhibit the healing which would accompany forgiveness.

Little wars, big wars, world wars. We have kept ourselves busy this century. Lately we have come to realize that no one wants to fight with us anymore so we talk little countries into inviting us in to keep their neighbors under control. We subsidize the wars of little nations when it is to our advantage and are quite adept at subversion and sabotage behind the scenes. It is becoming hard to tell the difference between the drug cartels, the mob and our government agencies. We can rest our bombers now though, for our current war is in our own cities and bombing them is somehow inappropriate. Over time, mankind has been motivated to fight for honor (ego), social injustice (what is war if not injustice?), God and religious freedom, and territory. Now it is all economic. Money is our new god and it will be until we stop worshipping it.

Fighting for God is a fascinating concept. The Crusades, the Inquisition, the Spanish conquest of South and Central America, and much of the history of incessant fighting in the Middle East were all, purportedly, about God. God does not seem like a good excuse for exploitation. But, when we look at the Old Testament, we find it filled with violence. Maybe this God gets a lot of satisfaction from fighting. He banished Eve from of the Garden of Eden, turned people into stone, sent his only son to get killed by the barbarians on earth, and is waiting to judge us when we die. This is not a benign God. Maybe He started all of this fighting in the first place. Perhaps our image of God could use some transformation.

CONDITIONING

As a population, we remain sound asleep in the *ukhupacha*, mindlessly rolling our loaded dice, hoping we will not be drawn into the violence. The bad news is, it lives within us, it follows us everywhere like a stalking cat. The jaguar is a fitting archetype for the West direction for she stalks us with our fears and is never seen. At the same time, she is the one who forces us to meet our fears and frees us from them. Right now, we are stalked by violence and we are trapped in the fear. The most interesting thing about our society is that we balance a thirst for violence with an overwhelming fear of it. It keeps us on the edge, filled with adrenaline, waiting for the next thrill.

Our newscasts devote their prime time to violence, misfortune, and scandal. The heartwarming stuff is left until after the third commercial break, unless it is Christmas. Newspapers operate under the same principle with disasters, scandals and murders taking top priority. We must find this interesting or we would not devote so much time and space to it. Interesting? We are riveted to the television. We are addicted to the news and are therefore addicted to the violence. Television stations hype their newscasters in local popularity and image contests to capture your addiction. Step number one in mindfulness is to tune out.

Moving beyond the news, the television brings us all manner of violence in movies, dramas, police shows, emergency medicine re-enactment, and so forth. Guns are everywhere, going off left and right, and sexual violence is graphic. This has come to television from movies and with this shift to the home, where several televisions can be on at once, it has reached the eyes of young viewers whose parents do not monitor what they watch. Often television is used as a baby sitter. Even classical children's stories have violent themes. We must look at them carefully. If there are control situations, competition with winners and losers, physical contact which isn't lovingly portrayed even if it is funny, and demeaning depictions of the male or female role, it is violence. When the bad witch meets her death, everyone cheers - except the bad witch.

Children think that killing is a fact of life. It used to scare them, but now it is part of their picture of life. When you haven't been around all that long on the planet, you don't have the adult depth of fear for pain and death. Children are less attached. When murder is depicted in cartoons and children's shows, what is to stop them from using the weapons they find in their parent's drawers? What is to stop them from entering the war that is being fought on our city streets when they don't even value their own lives? Children are more impressionable than their parents. The media has locked into their subconscious as soon as they can sit in front of the television.

That is the blatant portion of the media and if we stop to contemplate any of it we will necessarily conclude that it is all about money and power. Money is tangible power in our society, so it is really all about power. This kind of power is into control. To be controlled by violence/fear, is to be kept in that place where, like sheep to the slaughter, we mindlessly do another's bidding. Remember the Nazi state, the Inquisition, the conquest, the crusades? It has been working well for a long time. We are giving our power away with this behavior. It is service to the *ukhupacha*.

Fine tuning the control is the more subtle side of the media. If we can watch a movie or television drama and get involved in it (that's the idea) we have also lost our sense of reality and self. We live lives of fantasy by transference to the actors on the screen. In this way, we can lead exciting lives and still be mindless. This is totally disempowering. Who are we? Lifestyles, images, sexual behavior, food, and over the counter medications are all dictated by media through programming and advertisements. Listen to the words of commercials. Maybe we feel we don't pay attention so it doesn't impact on us, but when we find ourselves at the pain relief counter, the imprinting is there. The belief that we need pain relief is an imprint. There are subliminal messages flashed on the screen that do not even enter the in-between world but go right for the unconscious mind. We need to begin paying attention to the media and find healthy ways to entertain ourselves and our children.

The children move from television to Nintendo. Later on this gets more complicated with video games and computers. We need the communication and data storage capacity of computers. What we don't need is the visual stimulation. Watch the addiction pattern of visual stimulation in the children who participate in these activities. They cannot sit quietly and listen to a story or a teacher. Their attention span is difficult to extend. They are external, quick, and intelligent, all the attributes that are rewarded in our society. It is possible to operate in this way without feelings. We secret them away and sit around with cheery smiles on our faces and time bombs waiting to go off inside.

COMPETITION

Where do are bombs go off? We can see them exploding on the football field, the ice arena, city streets, our own back yards and bedrooms. Where did we get this need to compete, to demolish each other? We have a warrior component that needs to be engaged in battle. Siblings invade each other's space at a young age and establish roles of weakling and bully. The weakling will go outside the house, or wait for a new sibling, to take the bully role. What are they doing? Vying for the parents affection? That must be how it starts and so it is wrapped up in the complicated role playing of parents. A parent with an opened heart has room for all of humanity in it, but the patterns of our lives build walls around our hearts.

Millions have been made transferring this childhood violence from physical contact to the game board. In this way, as children we are encouraged to compete over adult issues like property, money, even countries. From there, we take it to the playing field. Sports are a good way to work out that warrior energy. Children get to yell and scream, run like crazy, experience some risk to their physical boundaries in a setting where they can do something about it, and have fun. Unfortunately, adults enter the scene and organized sports pit children against each other, emphasize winning as the only reasonable outcome, and fun doesn't much matter. These are war games and the adults are the strategists. They are gearing the kids up for success. A lot of parents unconsciously instill this need to win and be first into their children at a young age, getting them ready to enter the corporate world.

From sports competition between schools which become rivalries, we move to towns, cities and nations that hold animosity over the outcome of sporting events. We are right back in the Roman amphitheater throwing each other to the lions. And there we are perched on the edges of our seats at the stadium or in front the television, perhaps at a sports bar, beer in hand, living the life of a hero without having to make any effort. We can be sedentary while they go out and kill each other. We adore them, pay them millions, and when they fail us, we destroy their lives. And we don't see this as very strange behavior.

All competition is a measure of success because, in our society, the winner takes all. We live in a hierarchy and it permeates every aspect of our life; the home, our peer relationships, methods of schooling, our places of employment, and houses of worship. At the top of the heap are the powerful and it is the object of life to get there. But there is room for only one person at the top of each heap, and so enters the competition. We have forgotten how to live and work in community and council, in circles of unity.

FAMILY VIOLENCE

In addition to the sibling competitiveness for the parents' attention, the children bear witness to the disharmonies of the adult world. Even if parents act on their differences when the children aren't around, the energy of violence is there. Most marriages are karmic, but we rarely have that insight when we are in the throes of love. Partnerships of all kinds are the richest source of soul growth. If we approached them in that way, consciously, we could load up the dice even more, and take on a considerable portion of the data bank in one life.

Violence in the home is often the expression of withheld anger from any number of pressure sources. We are trained not to express our anger if it means we will lose our job, our friends, our partner, money or our credibility. It doesn't matter what we believe about it. We are outcome-oriented and sacrifice the expression of our feelings for what we think is a controlled outcome. And there is the key word, *control*. How often is violence triggered by alcohol which loosens the reins on our control? We lash out at our partner or children, verbally or physically, because our boss has us backed into the corner. If we lose control with the boss and let our anger show, we fear we will be out of a job and won't be able to support the family which we turn around and abuse instead. It's an interesting pattern that brings all manner of emotion and role playing into the home. For some reason we feel that our partners and children are there to take on our punishment.

And where did punishment come from? Punishment is retribution, violence leveled against someone for wrong doing. It is usually preceded by all manner of threats and accusations. Our creative style with punishment is usually brought from our own childhood imprinting, experiences of our peers, and the media, of course. It can be physical, sexual, emotional, mental and spiritual. We have a kind of abuse for every subtle body, it seems. Often, growing up, one parent was the intimidator, the arm of authority, and the other parent held out the arms we fell into. Our punishment was another source of conflict for our family. The origin of intimidation is low self-esteem. Sometimes it is the voice of a child who was never heard but, more often, it is an outlet for the grown-up bully. How we react to the judgment levied against us is a reflection of our personality development, the progress we have made with the cosmic aspects present at our birth. If we live in a family fraught with violence, control dramas, ignorance, or self-absorption, it is difficult to bring these aspects to any kind of wholesome maturation. We are at a great disadvantage, more so if we had been overly enthusiastic when we loaded our dice and not so lucky throwing them.

LAW AND ORDER

Our investment in retribution has created an unwieldy judicial system which, in turn, has spawned a litigation-crazed society. Like it or not, we need to take that family scenario out on the streets. We have established a system of law enforcement to control violence for us, another way in which we have given our power away. It is self-perpetuating and very rigid. It is a system that doesn't work, but we are clearly trapped in it. Like everything in the *ukhupacha*, the key to the lock on the gates to freedom is lost in the dark and we wander in the maze. From the organized to the petty, crime appalls us. It fills us with fear, so we make more laws to combat it. The laws clog the judicial system and are incomprehensible to most of us because the judicial system is the creation of the aloof. The do's and don'ts are dutifully passed on to the public by the media and government agencies.

Out on the streets, intimidation reigns. The criminal is an intimidator who works by instilling fear into the victim. A product of the violence of our society, the criminal is getting needs met in a way that, unfortunately, seems to work. Crime, so often accompanied by hopelessness, is an expression of anger at society, at individuals, at one's self. In portions of our society, the criminal is the hero, the one who is taking on the system for the underdogs.

The other half of the drama involves law enforcement, the police. If you are not an intimidator when you join the force, they will teach you how to be one in the academy. It is the tactic used to approach the criminal, meeting anger with anger, fear with fear. Like adults who intimidate their children or partners to maintain control of family behavior, the police use intimidation to maintain law and order. When we encounter a squad car at an intersection, we are consciously or subconsciously checking to see if we are doing something wrong. This is intimidation-based fear, part of our conditioning. We are automatically the criminal. When the police stop us for speeding, their posturing and language are often those used to approach an armed robber. They are under a lot of pressure. The judicial system says something else, something about being innocent until proven guilty. But, on the streets, we are all suspects. It is the nature of this fear-based system.

So, determined to be in *control*, intimidator meets intimidator and the result is more violence, which, in turn, creates more fear. What do we do, make another law? It is a vicious cycle, reaching a dangerous crescendo with a new element to worry about. We have young criminals now who are so disenchanted with life they would risk life itself for money, tangible power. The drug war has spawned gangs engaged in their own reckless control dramas and children barely out of diapers are involved in the game. A person approached by a group of young people on our city streets is paralyzed with fear. These are child intimidators, very likely harboring imbalanced hormones, pent-up anger, and possibly weapons. Who knows what they will do? Just like cold, hard cash, this is power and control, something that has obviously been missing from their lives. It is sad, and we are kidding ourselves if we think we can stop it with punishment, more laws or brutality. These children do not see a place for themselves in our society. There are no rites of passage to bring them from childhood to adulthood and they have likely been raised by parents who haven't completed that transition, coming into personal power themselves.

We will learn, in the *kaypacha* medicine walk, to extract the violence from our own lives. This impacts society in a positive way and opens new possibilities, more flexible systems, to us.

SEXUAL VIOLENCE

The West direction is the home of the warrior who directs energy from the sacral chakra. Imbalances in the sacral energy are directed towards relationships, particularly those which are sexual. Winning is as important to us in the bedroom as it is on the playing field. In fact there is often not a lot of difference. Sex is often about conquest.

It's the imprinting again, and we need to take a look at our role models because it is resulting in a genderless performance anxiety epidemic.

Hormones are interesting molecules. They can help us regulate metabolism, experience bliss, or kill someone, depending on their chemistry and concentration. Sexually, we are regulated by hormones as well. Women have estrogen, progesterone and a little bit of testosterone. Men have a lot of testosterone and some estrogen. Progesterone and testosterone are similar molecules. Any woman who has gone on high dose progesterone therapy knows what it can do to her. It is the hormone of PMS. It makes us moody, aggressive, and, in large doses, potential murderers. Men normally have higher levels of these chemicals than women who experience them periodically. Men are naturally more aggressive, bigger of build and demonstrative. Of course, they are the ones we would send off to war, onto the football field, or into the police force. They're natural warriors.

Warriors have been around forever and sex has been a part of war. They seem to go hand in hand. Why? It's all sacral chakra energy. There was a time when warriors were knights, very noble men, and they were willing to die for the woman they were promised to or loved. That's a lot like war when you think about it. It's also a shame for it has fostered the expectation in women that there are men out there who are going to solve all their problems and die for them if necessary. Everyone loses. This era of our history is called the romantic period and it was, admittedly, a step up from women being regarded as the spoils of war. Women have been raised to be caretakers, to be wanted and needed, regardless of the cost. The cost is freedom, of course, for we give our will away with our bodies. There are plenty of warrior women now who think they are in control of the situation but the fact remains that we have done absolutely everything we can to figure out the opposite sex and still come up empty-handed.

Men and women have different expectations in a relationship. We do not understand each other's motivations and don't know how to talk about it. Let's think about it energetically, for we direct our energies differently and that interplays with the physical body in interesting ways. Think of the eight chakras and the *kintui*, will, wisdom, and love. We will develop this theme further later on, but with what we now know of the chakra energy, place the *kintui* in the energy fields. The three lower chakras, base, sacral and solar plexus, are all about will, manifesting materiality, whether it be a new business, a new baby or money. These are the chakras connected with the earth/matter energy. The heart is the love energy and, like it or not, ours are not open. The higher chakras are about wisdom, the intellect, thinking, speaking, and visioning. We have a way, in our world, of bypassing the heart and going right to our heads. It is very imbalanced, but a way to get rational thought out there without compassion.

Sex, for the male, is all about will. In the bedroom, he can operate fully from the lower chakras and disengage the mind piece entirely. This is what procreation is all about. A bit too much solar plexus energy will turn this into a control situation but, by and large, it is all about pleasure, driven by testosterone, the warrior hormone. Women, on the other hand are given to love. The nurturing mother energy longs for an open heart and we try to pull down that heart energy. We pull down our heads instead, the rational thought, because our hearts are not open. Our mind really gets in the way with expectations, random thoughts and energy that is flying around way outside the realm of matter. Since many of us have closed throat chakras as well, we can't even project the energy to talk about it. In this work, we will develop ways for all of us to balance these energies and open the heart, for sex can be a holographic experience.

Love doesn't have anything to do with sex right now. Love and compassion spring from an open heart, an unselfish being, and they have no strings attached. Unselfish does not necessarily mean that we go out and give our lives for another person. It means that we, in our own lives, are not engaged in self-service, are not self-absorbed, and have found a Higher Purpose to serve. Until then, we have sex and karma. However, love and sex hold the potential of bliss when we are in the right place energetically, so it is something we can look forward to on this journey.

Criminal sexuality reflects a gross imbalance in the sacral chakra taken into the realm of the intimidation cycle. Sexual offenders prey on victims, so a big part of avoiding assault is finding personal power, learning not to be the victim. Sex offenders seem to be able to sniff these victims out and perhaps, as victims, we do give off some kind of chemical that attracts them. They are stalkers, like the jaguar, playing a violent game with their prey. Fearing we might be a victim often invites it to us. The most common sex offenders are the friends or partners who won't listen to, or respect, our boundaries. They can also be someone in authority who misuses their power; a boss, a teacher, a parent, a relative, a baby-sitter, an older neighbor or a sibling. As long as we live in fear, the cycle of violence continues.

VIOLENCE WITHIN

It is easy to see, with all of the violence around, how we could unconsciously engage the path of self-destruction. This can be nurtured by the suffering and addiction present in the South direction of the *ukhupacha* but it exists separate from it. In the *ukhupacha*, we begin dying as soon as we are born. If we live our entire lives unconsciously, we never really wake up at all, so you could say we are the living dead. The human race has spent much of its existence roaming around the *ukhupacha* caught in the drama being acted out here. We bring karma with us, but always the opportunity to land on the wake-up square. With respect to karma, we carry the violence of the human race as well as of our own previous existences. At some level, we know that the wars of nations are enactments of group karma and often you can see the karma coming through human behavior; master returns as slave, cavalryman experiences life as an Indian, abuser becomes victim. We are engaging the human experience, but we are trapped within it and therefore regard it as oppression leveled against us. Healing the violence in the world begins, like everything else, at home. It is the work of the *kaypacha*, but to lay the groundwork for that level of work we need to take a good look at ourselves.

We abuse ourselves at every subtle body level and, because we do, there is a lot of space garbage flying around our holograms. What is it all about? Since we don't know much about balance, we find ourselves in two places with self-abuse. Either we are very hard on ourselves, extreme disciplinarians into deprivation, or we do whatever pleases us. Perhaps we are combinations but, with respect to each subtle body, we are one or the other. Those balance squares are few and far between.

There are many ways to abuse the physical body. If, as children, we are inclined to motion and activity, we will probably pursue something athletic. We may make a life-long commitment to exercise and keep fit. No matter how hard we try, at some point, the cart breaks down and we start getting adult injuries. The injuries we had as children were easy to heal, but these take more time, and we lose our edge. The harder we push, the more we break down. What's going on here, just old age setting in? At forty? Maybe. Every injury, every trauma, to the physical body leaves an imprint on all the subtle bodies. Let's look at an example.

When that big right guard creamed us on the football field at nineteen, a lot more happened than the torn hamstring. There was a lot of tissue damage that eventually healed and we went out to play again. In the course of getting "fixed", no one attended to our etheric body which held onto the memory of the disorganization. The ch'i eventually found a way around the scar tissue, but the etheric blueprint no longer held the image of the original tissue.

At the astral level, we stored the emotional experience of the confrontation, the fear and the anger. The anger was most likely directed at both the left guard and ourselves for being so stupid in our strategy. We may be angry with our coach who sent us into a set-up. Coaches aren't given enough telepathic training. If we were beginning to see some light, we might have been angry that we were engaged in a brutal contact sport, but more likely, we went right out and played again and again. The fear and anger imprint on the astral plane will rise to greet us in similar situations, especially when they involve that hamstring.

On the mental plane there exists the exact strategy that led us into trouble, the memory of every foot fall, hip sway, glance, team support or lack of it, cheering fans, uniform colors, green grass, the smell of the air, sweat, dirt, and the sound of the impact. However, the most vivid memory will be that of the face of the left guard and especially his eyes. We will never forget them. There are three levels to the mental plane remember, the emotional, intellectual and spiritual, and the sum of this experience will be stored there as memory. We will reinforce it by reliving the experience over and over trying to learn from it, but that just deepens the imprint and doesn't change it.

The eyes are important because they are the link to the spiritual plane and through this mental memory we will engage the karma. The experience has either negated previous karma or created new karma. If previous karma has been met, we will be left with the impact on the other subtle fields which have been used, so to speak, to facilitate the negation of karma. We may suffer our entire life from the injury in that respect. If we have made new karma, it will be held in the spiritual plane until we die, ready for storage in the big data bank. Because the karma remains in the spiritual plane, it gives us the opportunity, from the *kaypacha*, to negate the karma in this lifetime. How will we access it? Through the hamstring.

Someday, when a massage therapist gets into the tissue at the site of injury, the face of the right guard will appear in our mind's eye. We will be able to begin the process of healing, of removing the suffering and violence, held in our multidimensional body.

Now, let's look at a different picture. Perhaps we are not an aggressively self-destructive person, but more placid and easy going. If the aggressive type appears to be feeding the ego, the placid type is more likely feeding emotion. They are both self-service. And let's look at feeding, at obesity in particular. How do we become obsessed with food? It could be karmic, from past-life starvation. It could be mental, eating everything in sight because our parents imprinted images of starving babies in Africa or the clean-plate club in our mental plane. It is often emotional, as we try to meet our childhood needs with adult compensations. Our frustration blocks self-love and appreciation. It can be etheric body-related, imbalances in energy that foster compulsive eating, like ch'i deficiency in the digestive system. And it can even be physical, such as a hormonal disorder resulting from a genetic imbalance. Like all manifested self-abuse, there are a lot of levels of entry into our holograms.

Let's say that our food obsession is coming from the emotional hologram, the result of insufficient emotional nurturing from our parents. Of course, when this starts and as long as it remains in the *ukhupacha*, we have no perspective about the lack of self-love. We likely don't even associate it with lack of nurturing. We are getting our needs met the simplest way we can, eating, because we have a placid nature. If we were more aggressive, concerned about image and the possibility of getting some needs met by partnering, we would be more inclined to the bulimic eating disorders. The placid of us are content to keep our nourishment stashes and use them to build insulating walls around ourselves. The emotional hologram holds the original imprint, which might be something like this:

Both our parents worked, and we came home from school to an empty house to take care of ourselves. We were told we could watch television for an hour, have a snack and then get going on our homework. We were not allowed to go out to play with the neighbor children or even by ourselves because our parents did not trust the neighbors, the neighborhood, or our ability to be responsible. We would turn on the tube and plod off to the kitchen to get our snack.

We may have had a feeling of independence, being in charge of the house, but the overwhelming feeling was one of abandonment. We have set up this nurturing system to feed our abandonment. At the time, we had no choice since we did not have a mature level of discernment. When we are adults, the contents of the cupboard can get completely out of balance and the cycle can go on all night, even all day and night depending on our lifestyle. In this scenario, the television knob is the trigger. We're like robots from that point on.

Reaching out into the mental body, there will be memories imprinted from this experience that trigger the neediness. Any form of abandonment will set us off. Old television shows or memories from them will plug it in. We retain the parents' fears and suspicions of the neighborhood and thoughts about safety will take us to the cupboard. We tend not to socialize with the neighbors and have a lot of locks on the doors. We really don't trust anyone and our mind can play tricks on us if this becomes obsessive. We easily enter the fantasy world of television programming, especially the soaps. Believing everything we hear, this becomes our reality.

As the mental body reaches out to touch the spiritual, the karma is imprinted. Abandonment may have been a past-life issue.

We may have abandoned these very parents who have done the same to us. This life experience will serve to negate that karma, but depending on where we take the current experience, we may be racking up more than we negate. In addition to the karmic experience there needs to be some resolution from within, some growth. If it is current life karma we will take it out to the data bank with us unless we wake up and process the abandonment issues.

At the etheric level, this obsessive dysfunction affects the ch'i. We are using all of our ch'i to keep the obsession going, processing the food and storing the fat. Since we have an imprinted emotional aversion to the outdoors, we are not getting enough sunlight, fresh air or activity, the common ways to rebuild our ch'i besides food and drink. As the ch'i becomes depleted we lose more energy until we are chronically fatigued. By this time, our weight may be a limiting factor, requiring too much energy for us to move.

The physical body is out of control. Our food intake is heavily carbohydrate and fat since these are the foods that taste the best and we are trying to feel good. We compromise all of our digestive enzymes, the heart and lungs have to work too hard, and plaque, from the fats, is everywhere. It lines our arteries, heart valves and the gut. If we are not getting enough protein, we will start eating our own muscle tissue to get it. Muscle cells are protein rich. If we eat meat, we are eating muscles of other creatures. In this scenario, we eat our own. This is what malnutrition is all about and many obese and elderly people in our country suffer from it because they do not eat enough protein. We don't have to be born in Africa to starve to death, we can do it anywhere in the *ukhupacha*.

These are two extreme examples of self-abuse. Without much trouble we can think of many more originating in all of the subtle fields. Sometimes it is not really obvious to us. Maybe someone will recognize it in us and ask us why we are so hard on ourselves, why we push ourselves so much. We need to think of and define our own inner abuse, for it is an essential step in accessing the holograms during our healing process. Correcting the violence in the world begins by correcting the violence within, arriving at self-love.

ORIGINS AND SOLUTIONS

We have looked at violence in a lot of different ways but really haven't found its origin. Yes, it is in the nature of the *ukhupacha*. But what creates the *ukhupacha*? *Inti*, the sun, split the world into light and dark, and the darkness is within. But darkness, even in ignorance, does not have to be violent. We must assume that the violence came to the earth through the *Naupamachu* when they aligned themselves with the violent forces of the cosmos. There are many myths of creation in which kind and loving spirits became more and more indulgent over time until they were trapped in the human form, doomed into this life of karma and endless samsara. These are interesting stories and may or may not be true in actuality. What they do symbolize is that process of incarnation, the coalescence into matter which is the path we all must take onto the earth. The soul's journey into darkness.

The banishment from Eden is the loss of the soul consciousness and entrapment in the *ukhupacha*. The process of awakening and enlightenment is the rediscovery, without physical death, of the soul life. What our myths about the coalescence have given us are the seeds of violence. For we have needed to blame someone, like Eve, for the loss of consciousness that was likely part of the great plan to utilize the earth for soul growth. In the process of attaching blame, which means it isn't our fault and we don't have to be responsible, we have sown the seeds of hostility. We are unconsciously moving around this medicine wheel of the *ukhupacha*, incorporating violence into our well-established patterns of suffering and denial.

When we look more closely at this hostility, we see that we direct it towards ourselves and each other, but that a big piece of it is directed towards the earth. If we have been banished from Eden (our soul life), we are in exile on the earth (trapped in matter). Taking the bully approach, if we beat up enough on the earth, maybe it will disappear. That may be exactly what is going to happen as the violence becomes more pervasive. If we wake up and realize that a veil of our own design keeps us from consciousness, we will see that Eden is all around us, held in the infinite splendor of nature. If we take responsibility for our own lives we will, necessarily, have to take responsibility for the stewardship of the planet. To lift the consciousness of mankind, we will first have to lift our own by healing our lives of suffering and violence. Then we will be able to do the same for our mother, the earth.

Violence is about disrespect. A violent act is invasive, moving within the energetic space of another individual. It is an act of disrespect on the part of the perpetrator and is felt as loss of self definition by the victim. Imagine the feelings of the earth mother as we bomb her, scrape her skin, dig within her flesh, extract her precious fluids and matrix, and destroy her atmosphere and energetic balance. We imagine the grief she holds within and all of our violence which she has to bear as well. Now, let's exercise an intention to neutralize this disharmony by invoking the spirit of White Buffalo Calf Woman, the pure embodiment of The Source who gifted the teachings of the sacred pipe to the Indian people of the Northern prairies. We see her coming towards us, a woman of natural beauty, walking barefoot upon the earth, sun at her back, in tune with the earth's heartbeat, eyes shining with the sunlight. Those who embody spirit know their mother and father, earth and sun, and walk with reverence between them, each footfall a caress. Can we invoke this in our own lives? We ask her to infuse our lives with awareness, to assist us in releasing our violence, and to help us acquire a love for all things.

In the prophecies of all indigenous people, the times we are living through have been foretold. In the visions of the elders, the four races come together, at first violently, then in harmony, to birth the dawn of a new age, a new reality. We are on the verge of another cosmic intervention and transmutation, and there will be no corner of the earth that is not touched by it. We are being called to lift our vibration, *now*.

3

NORTH:
EMOTION

Earth is a jewel. Perched on the edge of a galaxy rotating around her sun, she participates in a cosmic drama. Earth is on the verge of coming into her full destiny, and, like her children, she has been engaged in her own process. She has learned from the humans. She has sacrificed herself to lovingly support them. Her mission has been one of providing a unique environment for incarnation, a stage for the drama of human life. Earth is the home of emotion and, in that respect, she is unique in the cosmos. Souls come to earth to engage the range of emotion that is part and parcel of the human experience. And emotion is multi-dimensional, being present in all aspects of earthly potential, from the *ukhupacha* to the *hanaqpacha*. The differences in dimensions of emotion lie in their purity. Existing on its own, there is no such thing as an impure emotion. Impurity is a reflection of the human element, the lack of clarity which accompanies loss of consciousness. The deeper we are entrapped in the *ukhupacha*, the more negative the emotion.

So the earthly experience has, for the most part, been one of engaging the drama; working out our karma, making more karma, living, dying, and coming again. The greater portion of the total human experience on earth has been in the *ukhupacha* and of a negative nature. Earth has held much of this energy because it has been generated here and we take only the karmic piece with us when we go. The great astral field of humanity is unquestionably negative. This sustains the endless cycles of the *ukhupacha*, and on and on we go. As we move forward with this work, we will seek to purify our emotions. Pure emotion can link us back to those four chakras (IX-XII) which are ordinarily out of our reach. It is our cosmic connection, so to speak, our way back home and the epitome of the earth experience potential. But before we can begin to understand what a pure emotion is, let alone *feels* like, we need to define the depth of our misunderstanding about them. And so we dive, once more, into the *ukhupacha*, this time from the North. We will find, in the *kaypacha* and *hanaqpacha*, that the work of understanding and clearing emotion begins with the base chakra and physical hologram, and reaches up to the brow chakra and out to the mental-3 hologram. We will journey through both worlds from the bottom to the top of the spine. This work is part of all spiritual traditions and what we will discuss is a synthesis of these that has been helpful in doing the work of this medicine wheel.

JEALOUSY/BASE CHAKRA

What is jealousy all about? Jealousy is fear of losing that which we have or think that we have. It can be a person, an object or an idea. Closely linked to jealousy and the base chakra is envy. Envy is about wanting something we don't have or something that someone else has or that we think they have. It is about coveting thy neighbor's anything. Right now, we live in a society that is into "stuff". We have manifested everything imaginable and it is out of style as soon as we buy it. We quit outgrowing our clothes and start outgrowing our computers or our partners. Everything looks better to us than what we have, but we don't want to lose what we have either. Jealousy and envy can be expensive negative emotions when you live in a perishable, consumer society.

Envy spawns a few more unsavory activities, like stealing, maybe even killing, to get what we want. It can lead to really obsessive behavior and a lifestyle that keeps us deeply in debt. It is fostered by easy credit and punished with high interest rates. It is interesting that we have built the retribution right into the system. That hints to us that there is shame associated with envy as well. The shame comes down to us with the covet piece, from those ten commandments. We attempt to ease the pain of our shame by buying more.

Jealousy and envy create animosity and hatred for they seek to compare, to measure, and in this way can feed a sense of competition as well. If there is something we want and no way we can afford it, steal it, or otherwise manifest it, we "put down" the person who owns it or the item itself to convince ourselves that we are too good for it. We get into a little name-calling, lying to ourselves, and judgment too. Sometimes we even launch campaigns to destroy the character of the individual whose life we covet. At some level, we must know we are kidding ourselves, for we are dying inside from the negativity. On the surface we can see that it has something to do with not getting our needs met and making sure that we do. But it results in a lack of self-confidence, self-love, and an inability to be happy.

The drive behind jealousy is fear. The jealousy we associate with someone showing an interest in our partner is rooted in fear, fear that we will lose them. This speaks again to the lack of self esteem. It also shows us that we are using our partner to fill our basic needs, and that is called dependency. And it isn't just partners. We see how difficult is to let our children explore their social world when we want the best for them and do not want to let go. The children form peer groups to protect themselves against fear of loss, rejection. Why does our attachment to other people bring forth jealousy? Because it is just that, attachment. We are attached to our "stuff", our partners, our kids, our jobs, our Swiss army knives, you name it. This is the origin of "our" and "mine".

This fear of loss is a key to understanding jealousy and attachment. In the Chinese medical model, fear is the emotion of the kidneys and the adrenal glands. The adrenal glands produce, among other hormones, adrenaline, the molecule of fight or flight. This is the molecule that races into our bloodstream in response to fear. It is the molecule that pollutes our body if we live in constant stress. It can save us, or bring us down. The kidneys and adrenal glands are related, in the esoteric tradition, to the base chakra and, therefore, the physical body hologram. It is interesting that we speak of being frozen in fear, and the physical body is, as we have discussed, light frozen in space and time. Fear has a very dense vibration.

So, the base chakra and physical hologram will hold envy, jealousy and attachment, fear of loss. The physical body is matter - material. Everything we think we need to hold onto in life is matter. We even call the social disease of envy and jealousy *mater*ialism. The base chakra is our root, the place where we can and should attach to mother earth. The base chakra governs our will to live, to be on the earth, what we call grounding. Those of us who are, in a sense, buried deep in the *ukhupacha*, are very much into materialism and seem to be preparing to stay forever. We have difficulties passing over at the time of death and cling steadfastly, through every kind of suffering, to this world. If, on the other hand, we are not grounded, we can feel paranoid at times for fear that we do not belong here. This leads to fear and intolerance of just about anything, and often, we would like to leave. There is a balance to be met and maintained in the base chakra, and, in our *kaypacha* medicine walk, we will learn to ground ourselves and practice non-attachment at the same time.

DESIRE/SACRAL CHAKRA

Desire is delicious. Sensory indulgence and the paths of pleasure it opens to us are fed by desire. We were given our senses to find our way in this world, to find our way beyond this world. As a whole, we are pretty self-indulgent and hold a lot of energy in the sacral chakra, home of desire, because of it. You can see this in the way advertising reaches out to capture our spending, hitting all our desire buttons. Desire is about feeling good, but the way our society indulges is purely from the outside. We feed our senses from the material world. Let's take a closer look at the senses and how we take care of our needs with each.

Sight: Our sense of sight gives us the beauty of the world and the pleasure we take in observing it. The eyes can drink from our surroundings. Potentially, they can be the windows of the soul, but that is something which emanates outward from an inner beauty, and we are generally engaged in inward feeding, desire. We like nice things around us. They please the eye and many of us are offended by things that do not fit our expectation of visual beauty. We make our ugly industrial-type messes in the cities and retreat to the suburbs to live. This is illusion, visual trickery.

Visual stimulation is rooted in the sacral chakra and it takes us back to the video games, movies, sexually oriented magazines and videos. We use our vision to activate the nervous system in any number of creative ways. It is the visual center that is targeted with image-making. How we look is of paramount importance to some of us. There is a look to the successful business man or woman, the eternally youthful world of the fashion conscious, the "old" and "new" wealth, the artist and so on. There is also the look of the homeless and the starving, but society tends to downplay these looks unless they want to make us feel sorry for them and give money to "fix" them up. Then we are presented the most pathetic of pictures. This, however well intentioned, is a visual appeal to the emotional center.

How we look, imagine ourselves to look, or want to look, are all sight-related desires. What we see in the mirror is what we believe ourselves to be. We limit our vision to the lower, material centers with this behavior. We change our natural appearance with make-up, all manner of hair manipulation including transplanted body hair, body shapers, implanted artificial tissue, and clothing that creates an illusion. We seem to be unsatisfied with ourselves, not sure of who we are.

Hearing: How does hearing feed our pleasure center? Ask the music industry. Ask the fans who attend concerts. Ask the kids with the boom boxes. Ask the young people with the car stereos whose music intrudes into your home, even into the dense vibration of your physical body. Music, sound, can be our link to the higher spheres, to the angelic realms, or it can anchor us in the sacral chakra.

Of course the boom boxes, rock concerts, car stereos, and headphones have resulted in an alarming level of hearing loss. Some of it is temporary, the aftermath of one great concert, but the steady stimulation with loud music is truly deafening. And it is often invasive. Those driving around town with the suped-up car stereos blasting are like mobile concerts. It takes an intense self-absorption to assume that the whole world shares your taste in music. We do need to pay attention (how could we not?), for these are young people who have, no doubt, had a lot of trouble being heard. However, it doesn't respect boundaries and this violence clearly falls into the sacral chakra/West direction of the *ukhupacha*. Music choice is chakra-related too, depending on where you feel like gathering the stimulation. Rock, rap, Latino, jazz and blues primarily feed the lower centers while classical music appeals mostly to the higher centers. New Age music is about opening the heart.

Some of us need noise around us all the time, radios, television, stereos or incessant talking. Maybe we are lonely or afraid of being alone and this is a comfort to us. Maybe it keeps us from facing our feelings or thoughts or tough issues. Sound can be very diverting. We live with white noise no matter where we are. If we live in the city, it can get downright gray with traffic, neighbors, and industry. But even if we live in the country, the white noise from our appliances is still with us, and air traffic is everywhere. All of this sound stimulation will keep us from hearing our inner voice, the intuitive center that lies hidden within. Again, we are pulling our stimulation from the outside and will look, later, at how to open it from within.

Taste: This one is easy to relate to indulgence. As a people, we find a lot of sensory satisfaction with eating and flavoring. And it isn't a simple world anymore, either. Just picking an ice cream flavor, a coffee flavor or candy bar can be a mind-boggling experience and an insurmountable task for the indecisive. And food is everywhere. The groceries have imported food from all over the world including fruits and vegetables normally out of season and all manner of prepared food. The number of restaurants far exceed the needs of the population and often cater to specific tastes and desires. Being an instant gratification society, clearly a sacral chakra orientation, we have even developed drive-up fast food. Think of it. We don't even have to take our foot off the accelerator to get a burger. We can drive down the street eating it, perhaps talking on the car phone at the same time.

If we are lucky and over forty, we may remember our grandma's old fashioned kitchen with the cook stove heating the room and bread rising, getting ready for the oven. The soup pot stayed on the back of the stove and everything got thrown into it. We sat down to tune into each other while breaking the bread. And it all tasted pretty good. This is the meaning of the word savor, not just the taste but the moment. Where does our food come from now? It could be three thousand miles away. It could be completely fabricated. We are not sustaining a healthy vibration when we don't take care with our eating, food preparation, and the space and time in which we eat. This is called mindfulness. Mostly we will find it in monasteries. It is also called paying attention, if only for thirty minutes. It puts us in a different place with food.

But we aren't mindful. We reach for the chocolate, the cookies, the coffeepot, perhaps even the caviar, and we rarely think about what we are doing. We run out for a sandwich and wash it down with a soda. We don't read the labels because a part of us doesn't want to know. We are feeding the sacral center, not listening to what the body needs. But it all tastes *so* good.

The Chinese five element medical model relates the five flavors to the organs and meridians. Imbalances in the energetic system (ch'i) lead to cravings in the flavor department. When these are coupled with the emotion related to the five systems, some interesting observations arise. The pungent flavors, hot and spicy, of the lung system, when overdone, invade the liver system and feed anger, the liver emotion. The raging liver will invade the spleen and result in sweet cravings. The spleen will also draw from the heart's bitter flavor and the result is chocolate. Round and round we go, never stopping long enough to get in balance. These imbalances can be the result of many factors in our lives, but the amazing thing is that we can cause them and sustain them with food.

It is noteworthy also that we meld sight and taste together when we offer our opinions about who does and doesn't have "good taste". The inner voice, with taste, lies in the sensitivity to know what the body needs, not what the emotions desire.

Smell: What are people supposed to smell like? If we do not mask our own odor with deodorant, after shave or perfume, we smell our body odor. We find ourselves so offensive, we have to put odor protection in our shower soap as well as directly under our arms. Our body odor is one of the ways we excrete wastes from our system. If we are a toxic dump station, that is what we will smell like. If we eat a steady diet of meat, like a jaguar, we may smell like a jungle cat. Most of us have so much environmental and dietary toxicity in the liver that we require detoxification therapy, perhaps long-term, to dislodge and excrete the toxins. We may experience interesting changes in body odor as we transit through detoxification. When we can eat and drink mindfully in a good environment with no stress, we will know what humans smell like. Until then, we'd better just cover it up.

Masking odor comes in as many flavors as ice cream to attract any number of things to us. Generally the odors are gender-specific or at least favored by men or women. One interesting thing happening in our society now is a profound loss of the sense of smell. We are bombarded by so much of it, in cleaning solutions, air filters, environmental waste in the atmosphere, room deodorants and the personal battery of scents, that our sensors have been in overdrive, out to lunch. The work we will do in the *kaypacha* seems to open this sense back up again and the amount of scent needed or desired is greatly reduce. We develop a greater sensitivity to the scent of others as well.

Aromatherapy, the use of scent in healing, is based on the energetic power of volatile plants. It works on the vibrational level and is very effective in mood stabilization and clearing the etheric and astral field. Here, scent is used therapeutically, but it will not be very effective if we are living at the sensory overload level.

Touch: Pleasure and touch are easy to relate. We all need to be touched and to touch. If we are not, we suffer from sensory deprivation and withdraw from society. Touch is also about feeling. Though all the senses are nervous system organs, this is the sense we most clearly associate with the nervous system response. We can feel good in a hurry with touch and our greatest overindulgence with touch is sexual pleasure. This, more than anything, separates sex from love since the vibrations are totally different for the nervous system. We find ourselves using sex as a pressure release for stress, as a way to fight the blues, and as a way to manipulate the opposite sex. These are all indulgences. Sacral chakra energy gives to well-balanced sexual contact the emotional sensitivity of the duality, and every other chakra makes a contribution. In desire, it is purely a nervous system stimulant. And it feels great, for a moment. But instant gratification is not concerned with forever.

Touch is the nurturing stroke of a parent and the feeling of safety and security that a child needs. Look at the animals and the amount of touch in their lives. It is absolutely profound when the intent is pure. It can be devastating, violent, when it is not. Touch can unlock the mysteries hidden within our tissue and massage therapy is a fast-growing profession because so many of us are ready to face the work of healing our woundedness.

Drugs: Because all of the nervous system and senses are involved in the drug experience we look at drugs alone. There are all kinds of drugs available to us, legally and illegally. Some of them wire us up and some of them cool us down. There is a drug for every occasion, every pleasure and every pocketbook. We all know the harm of hard drugs but try to minimize the damage from alcohol and marijuana. Prescription drugs and over the counter drugs are legitimized by the medical profession so they are morally approved. It's all the same from the energetic point of view. Our relationship with drugs is about intent. If we take them to mask reality, avoid our healing process, or to provide pleasure, we are operating from our emotional center.

Our bodies, little miracles that they are, will provide us with every drug we need, when we need it. The endorphin release of the runner's high is our own morphine. Once on to this, running can and does become an obsession for some. To be in bliss because we have snorted cocaine is quite different from being in bliss because we have cleared and opened our energetic fields and accessed the crown chakra. We will explore these possibilities in our *hanaqpacha* medicine walk.

Extra-sensory sense: There is a new indulgence developing from the current engagement in the spiritual quest, the so-called New Age Movement. It is a higher chakra pleasure and it involves seeking validation for ourselves as healers, miracle workers, masters of the extrasensory and spiritual advisors. It can involve fantastic stories, visions and dreams, that keep us anchored outside this reality. It clearly offers a stimulation to the nervous system and emotional center of the seeker. In fact, it can be very emotional with compelling charisma, and large numbers of people can be taken in by it. It can be well-intended or the activity of a charlatan, but if it is glamour-based and emotionally compelling, it is spiritual manipulation. Miracles are shifts in perception, energetic transformations. Miracles can't be performed. Magic is performed. Miracles must come from within, from pure intention, though they can be assisted by a master of energy through the fully opened heart. Christ was such a master. Validation must come from within also, from touching our own souls and opening our hearts to give unconditional love.

The sensory stimulations of desire are the cornerstones of addiction and co-dependence. Perhaps we can see, now, how we can substitute addictions and still be feeding the same pattern of desire. And we have an unprecedented number of addictions from which to choose. How does this relate to the sacral chakra/etheric hologram connection of desire? It is the nervous system. The etheric body interacts and directs the physical body through nadis (end points) which interact with the nervous system. The nervous system regulates hormonal release and, in this way, the etheric body keeps the physical body humming along. It also sends energy through the sacral center to the reproductive organs.

We can see where over-stimulation of the nervous system not only dulls the senses, but backs into the etheric field and affects the ch'i. Sacral chakra energy gets hit first, and we find ourselves seeking more pleasure. Round and round we go. Those of us who are living life from the sacral chakra will be overly sensitive, very emotional and easily fall into addictive behavior. There is a tendency to stir up and feed off of melodrama. Conversely, those of us who are pretty disconnected here will have a hard time understanding how we feel and we will avoid emotionally demanding relationships. We will seek to balance the sacral chakra in our *kaypacha* medicine walk by cultivating mindfulness.

ANGER/SOLAR PLEXUS CHAKRA

The sacral chakra may be connected with our sensitive emotional self, but the emotional field or astral body is linked to the solar plexus chakra. This is the collecting place of our emotions and the center of our personal power. Since we, in our world, equate power with control, it can get quite messy in this area. The most damaging emotion to the solar plexus is anger which, in the traditional Chinese medical model, manifests in the liver.

If, in our lives, we have always had a healthy way of expressing our anger, we tend to have a balanced liver system. Of course, the only healthy way to express anger is to confront people with our feelings after we have examined our reactions and taken responsibility for our part of the conflict. If we are angry with ourselves, we must come to peace with our own issues then acknowledge and release the anger. Ninety-nine percent of the time, a child is not permitted to express anger towards the parents. Oftentimes, the child can't express anger towards the siblings who push their buttons either, so healthy expression is a bit of a myth. And don't forget the bullies that we didn't dare stand up to. One way to look at withheld anger is by comparing the liver to our little bomb factory. More and more bombs are made over our lifetimes in this pattern. There are a few different scenarios to choose from when we think about cause and effect.

In our first scenario, someone bombs the bomb factory and it explodes in one incredible disaster. All the bombs in the inventory go at once. This might manifest a retaliation that harms the person who has bombed the factory, or someone close to them. Or, the factory owner might self-destruct in the bombing. Either way, the damage to the neighborhood is extensive and many are involved in the drama. This is a pattern of violence. It is the mass murderer, the angry employee who guns down his co-workers and kills himself, the instigator of domestic violence, even the volatile, overworked secretary who, in a modified version of "berserk" says her piece and walks off the job. The key to this scenario is that, until the bomb hit, no one knew there were bombs inside the factory except the owner.

In our second scenario, a little gunfire comes in the window of the factory and sets off a small explosion. A spark from that explosion hits another bomb and it explodes. A chain reaction is instigated. This can go on for a long time or be relatively short, but the shrapnel keeps flying around the inside of the factory and out the windows for an indefinite amount of time. This kind of scenario, often out of control before it is discovered, causes harm to the factory owner and any innocent bystanders who happen to be in front of a window when the shrapnel flies out. Here is the rocky marriage with few moments of peace, the small time investor whose losses on Wall Street becomes the source of open hostility towards everyone in his life. It doesn't really matter who fires the shots that start it. Everyone knows this person is angry. No one knows how to stop it.

In our third scenario, the owner fails to upgrade the old wiring in the factory and a smoldering situation results. This doesn't manifest as a fire until it is too late and the whole place is destroyed. The owner is completely responsible through ignorance and neglect, yet he will be suspicious that this is the work of someone else. Here is the person who was conditioned to withhold anger all of his life. It manifests occasionally with a very cynical or snide remark, but generally it is internalized. Look for the digestive upsets, eye problems and perpetual frown of the imbalanced liver. All the nasty anger is smoldering inside causing increasingly serious symptoms. The big fire may turn out to be liver cancer, stomach cancer or a heart attack. It isn't a surprise to people who know him, but it is to the factory owner. Even though the electricity was beginning to short out, and the assembly line was stopping now and then, he seemed to be able to ignore it, lost in his chronic complaining. No one likes to be around this person so he has a hard time keeping employees and doesn't really have any friends. He has no clue about how he really "feels".

Our fourth scenario is, by far, the most insidious. Here, the factory owner tries to buy out another bomb factory, to monopolize the industry. The other owner refuses all advances. Rather than retaliate, our factory owner decides on sabotage. He sends his own employees in to work for the other company and they begin to undermine the workplace. He influences the other company's creditors and bankers to begin questioning the stability of the company. He has a little group of supporters who buy stock in the company in small blocks, knowing that they will be selling it to him when he is ready to drop his bomb. This guy is a control freak who doesn't like to be turned down. He takes his anger out in manipulative gestures designed to bring the opponent to their knees. He hooks up to our solar plexus chakra and he sucks us dry. He knows how to pull our strings, is an expert at emotional blackmail. He is sneaky, intelligent and ruthless.

This last scenario bears close attention because it is not so obvious. This master manipulator is such a smooth talker, so good at his con game, that we are always surprised when the bomb is dropped. He can even get us to believe he didn't really mean it and do the whole thing all over again. We internalize some major trust issues with a few of these encounters. We all know what it feels like to be manipulated and controlled, but are we all conscious of the ways in which we do this ourselves? Do we gossip about the people we can't control, try to buy friends with money, smooth talk, or favors, or take advantage of people's weaknesses? Do we give with strings attached?

What makes us angry? People who don't do what we want them to do or don't live according to our standards make us angry. We get mad when we don't get what we want or aren't appreciated. People who invade our space and personal boundaries, even our lane on the freeway, infuriate us. Then there are the people who speak for us, make our decisions for us, those who refuse to help us, steal from us, beat us up and leave us for dead. Anything having to do with money can set us off. We get worked up over prejudices, injustices, the suffering of the world, environmental disasters, personal disasters, even a rip in our pants or a bad hair cut.

This is all related to anger and frustration which *is* a form of anger. And it has everything to do with personal power. We watched our parents engage it, our siblings and neighbors, then we got in the act ourselves. If only we had some control over our lives. No one can control life. It is far too great a responsibility. This is hard to accept and will be our greatest wall of resistance until we surrender to the flow of something greater than ourselves. We are blind in the *ukhupacha* and the solar plexus is the last bastion of resistance. We can have little or no energy in the solar plexus and become victims of this abuse and control. In contrast to the outwardly angry, controlling individual, we shut down as a form of protection and trust no one. This is actually a form of anger too.

Why are we so angry? Aren't we really angry at God, at Eve, and at the earth for turning the lights out, for that loss of consciousness? We don't know who we are or what we are doing here. We have no idea where we are going. This is abandonment, pure and simple. We want to direct the drama of our life, but we just can't pull ourselves off the stage. We will learn to do this as we walk the *kaypacha* medicine wheel. We will gradually step out of the drama and begin directing our lives. We will see that directing is not the same as controlling.

GREED/HEART CHAKRA

Let's make sure we know the difference between greed and jealousy for they both have to do with "stuff". Remember that the jealous person is afraid of losing their "stuff". The greedy person has the "stuff" but cannot get enough of it. No one else can have as much "stuff" as he does. The greedy person and the jealous person set each other up for major drama. We don't have to be wealthy to be greedy either. It doesn't have to be gold. It can be junk. It can be a beer bottle collection or gold bouillon. Greed doesn't know class distinctions. Let's face it, most of us don't want the beer bottle collection as much as the gold, but the collector would have just as much trouble parting with his treasure as the gold collector. It's all the same.

So, it is a combination of selfish acquisition and stingy possessiveness. In greed, we collect our "stuff" and make sure everyone else knows how much we have. We are very public with it. It does no good whatever to be privately greedy for the whole point is to impress people and draw attention to oneself. It is a kind of nourishment. Sometimes we use underhanded, manipulative methods to acquire what we want but it doesn't seem to bother us. Anything goes.

Greedy people also expect everyone else to take care of them, adore them, and this brings up a slightly different way to look at greed - self-absorption. To be stuck in self-absorption is to be deep in the *ukhupacha*. Our life, our problems, our opinions and desires are so important to us that others simply exist to listen to us and serve us. And we never shut up. We have no time in our lives for others, especially if they are in need. It is an ungenerous heart that cannot listen to another with compassion. It is the dead-end of self-service, adorning the exterior of the temple with gold but closing the doors to the poor. Greed is everything we draw to ourselves to make us feel secure and important. It is how we imagine we are loving ourselves and it may give us a really satisfied feeling inside.

The heart that is not opened can only love conditionally, with strings attached. There is always something to be gained, something to be added to the trophy collection. Generosity as a business investment is not generosity. Love for diamond bracelets is not love. Knowledge held within is not knowledge, and support for special treatment is not support. All of these are conditional. It is hard to imagine unconditional love. It is like a golden temple whose doors are open to one and all every day, all day and night. It doesn't make distinctions and it holds no possessions. It gives generously with no expectation of return. It meets everyone, even its owner, where they are, with no judgment. It's rare.

For as long as men have known of it, gold has been the most enticing and coveted of earth's treasures. Why? Because it shines? Because it can easily be made into objects of adornment and art? Because it is heavy? It certainly gets the sparks flying in the eyes of the greedy. We can look at the movement of gold around the globe as people were conquered and civilizations ended. Most of the gold from the South and Central American Indian civilizations ended up in Spain. The conquistadors knew that the treasures would bring them great favor with their monarchs so any method was acceptable to acquire it. They were as greedy as those they served. Much of the ancient art was melted and retooled into Christian art, an exact analogy to what they attempted with the lives of the Indian people.

The mystery of gold is the alchemy of fire, the sun, *Inti*. The melting of gold to become form in beautiful art is symbolic of our own journey from matter to spirit. The sun and earth know. Veins of gold run deep in the earth mother like arteries of sunlight. She carries the mystery and vibration of the sun within her and so do we. From the earth, matter, we fashion a temple, our bodies. In the mystery of alchemy we can become the sun, we can purify the temple with unconditional love and invite in our cosmic self. Our hearts turn to gold and gold runs in our arteries and veins and the doors to our temple are always open. Could this be the temple of the Holy Spirit, or Vilcabamba, the fabled lost city of gold?

PRIDE/THROAT CHAKRA

Pride is the manifestation of our egos. We take pride in that which identifies us, that which validates us in the eyes of our fellow humans. There are a lot of different faces to pride and many ways in which it can be used. The throat chakra is connected to the mental-intellectual hologram (M-2) so much of this manifests in the cognitive or higher centers, through our rational minds. It is what we <u>imagine</u> ourselves to be, not necessarily who we are. Where the ego manifests itself depends to some extent on what we are doing with our lives at the time.

We may take a lot of pride in our job or in a business which we own or share. Because our jobs bring us money, they are a measure of our success. Success brings more money and prestige. If we work in corporate America, climbing the ladder of success may be the source of our pride. Perhaps it is the fact that we do what we do very well and pride alone is our motivation. Those of us who are barely surviving on what we make or who really hate what we are doing do not find our identity at work. Many of us turn to our accomplishments in sports or as fans for our identity.

Education is a source of pride. We live in a society that equates credibility with titles and degrees. If we seek an intellectual identity this is our ticket. There is a rigid hierarchy in academics which requires enormous self-absorption, intellect and political skill to penetrate. We may be more inclined to teaching where we can seek validation from our students. We give honorary degrees as stamps of approval. In spite of the rigidity of our systems for educating ourselves, there are 'institutions' which offer advanced mail order degree programs in some very loosely defined areas. We provide credibility to the incredible. It is, perhaps, in the spirit of American entrepreneurship.

Many of us find our identity in the success of our partners and our children. We push them to all manner of accomplishment because we are so proud of them. We may see in our children the lives we never had and direct them into areas in which they have no talent or interest. The pushy parents of children engaged in the adult world of acting and modeling often have no consideration of the child's life but are projecting themselves and their agendas through the children. These unfortunate children are thrown to the creatures of the *ukhupacha* early in life.

We can be proud of our lifestyles, our possessions, our charities, our appearance, which club we belong to, our fitness level, where we live, what we drive, even the therapists we see. These are all ways in which we identify ourselves. Therapy brings up a very curious aspect of identity because it is so completely cognitive. Therapists are trained to listen and to help you "hear" yourself. As a healing form, it is completely oriented to the throat chakra and even the attempt to get you to express your feelings is through the mental body. This is cognitive therapy and it anchors us so much to "hearing" our outer voices that we miss the inner wisdom. Identity here is with the analyzed self, the speaker, keeper of knowledge.

Many of us seek our identity in spirituality, belonging to an organization or church and being actively involved in it. We belong to different groups because they help us in our work of self-realization, but the search for the self can become a manifestation of ego if we over-identify with it. The spiritual path is alive with pride and, to some extent, it is the ego's search for power and knowledge that brings us onto the path in the first place. Guruism, the emotional manipulation of devotees on the spiritual path is pretty common and many so-called spiritual teachers are arrogant and self-serving. Sometimes the most important spiritual lessons can only be learned through adversity and we call in the charlatans to help us. It is part of the journey to learn to discriminate and to take the lessons into our own hearts for consideration. Perhaps we have come into this life to explore trust and we will constantly be challenged with it until we have learned what we had intended. We are not always blessed with the clarity of intuition needed to guide us towards path and teacher.

And it isn't just the spiritual teachers who know how to work with our egos. How about the government? Be all that you can be, in today's army? All branches of the armed services use the enticement of identity to recruit. Once inside, of course, it is a rigid hierarchy where "intelligence" and politics reign. Where there is hierarchy, there is ego identification. We see it in academics, government and politics, the judicial system, law enforcement, churches, corporate America, world politics and trade, and culture. Arrogance established slavery and identification of sub-human savages. Class distinction, discrimination of any sort, shaming and blaming, snobbery and aloofness are all rooted in pride.

This brings us to a serious form of discrimination, widely practiced in our culture at this time. Why aren't we more concerned about the testing and labeling of our children? Mandatory school testing imposes conformity on our children rather than allowing self-expression and individual growth. When children are separated from each other on the basis of left brain skill and I.Q., we establish discrimination in the schools, and we give children learning-related labels which haunt and limit them all their lives.

Arrogance can be the manifestation of great insecurity. It is also the stomping ground of kings and queens. Energetically it looks like a heart bypass, where the solar plexus personal power meets the throat chakra ego without touching the heart or soul. And it is all very predictable considering that we have no idea who we are, walking between the worlds. Removing greed from our lives opens our hearts to unconditional love, the great goal of the *kaypacha* medicine walk.

IGNORANCE/BROW CHAKRA

Ignorance is the absence of wisdom. Wisdom is awareness of the game plan, superconsciousness. Everything else is illusion. We can spend our lives acquiring knowledge, and in the process become very attached to what we know. But knowledge is information already present on the earth, something we collect and store. Wisdom comes to us when we are clear enough to put the knowledge aside and let divine inspiration and insight flow through us.

The space garbage in the astral field of this solar plexus world of emotion is awesome. It cranks up all the chakras and clutters the entire compliment of holograms. It is the work of the earth plane, the drama in which we are engaged. And we must be willing to take responsibility for calling it into our lives, engaging it, and losing ourselves in it before we can find the gates out of the *ukhupacha* which *Huascar Inca* guards.

4

EAST:
JUDGMENT

Everything we have experienced in the *ukhupacha* thus far, suffering, violence, and emotion, leads us into the East by providing us with the framework for our opinions. It is our need to judge that stands in the way of the open heart and gift of vision, the East direction of the medicine wheel. Our vision is obscured because we are wearing blinders. We do not have a "world view", but are lost in a microcosmic dilemma of our own making. Let us look first at how judgment originated in Western mythology and thinking. This will give us a basis with which to look at judgment in our own lives and how we as a people have used it as the very foundation of our society. We must first understand the origins of the systems that no longer serve us to know how to transform them.

GOD AS JUDGE

In the Eastern religions, the theme of reincarnation goes hand in hand with the belief that each individual has the Buddha nature within. This pretty much puts us in the driver's seat, having to take full responsibility for our life and actions, lest we fail to bring forth the Buddha. To some of us, the compassionate interpretation of Buddhism implies that if we fail to do our intended work in this life there is always another life in which to work out our karma. Unfortunately, this interpretation will not sustain us through the coming transformation.

In Western religion, God sits on a throne in an inaccessible heavenly kingdom waiting to judge us for our actions when we die. There is no theme of reincarnation and the belief in retribution, crime and punishment prevails. Rather than awaken the Christ within, we are taught to concern ourselves with obeying laws, to give responsibility for our spiritual life to the hierarchy of the church and to watch our step because God is watching. Western religion lacks creativity and the teachings tend to be do's and don'ts rather than self-potentialization. Western religion, like all organized religion, was birthed from the *ukhupacha*, the darkness of loss of consciousness, and the theme of judgment takes our power away. Now we are being asked to find the Christ within, our Buddha nature, as we step into a new reality. We do this with release of judgment and reclamation of our power.

The foundation of Western religion arises from the creation myth found in Genesis. The serpent in the Garden of Eden was considered evil, tempting Eve into sin. Eve, exercising her free will, lost paradise for all of us. We now recognize this as a metaphor for the loss of consciousness and journey of the soul into materiality, but the fact remains that it has molded every aspect of Western civilization and we are trapped within it. Good and evil were born at that moment in Western cosmology, and because we are linear thinkers we must separate everything in life into these two categories. Good and evil spawn what is right and what is wrong, the basis for all of our law. So even if we do not believe in Western religious thinking, these principles are a part of our life.

In the Taoist cosmology, the first thing that came into being was chaos and from that came the Tao, yin and yang. Western religion personified yin and yang as Adam and Eve, and instilled in the myth the patriarchal propaganda that Eve came from Adam's rib. Yin and yang are the duality, male and female, yet they each contain the other, each become or birth the other, each depend on the other for transformation and they co-exist in harmony. This is exactly the cosmology of the Andes, the yin and yang being light and dark, sun and earth, with the entire cosmology being slightly more centered in the magical, elemental, and animistic than the Taoist. The yin-yang symbol and the medicine wheel are circles. Linear thinking does not exist in these cosmologies. In Genesis something new was created every day for seven days with man being the pinnacle of creation. In circular mythology, creation is an ongoing process in which we participate. There is a need for both darkness and light. Evil is not inherent in creation but is a product of our mythology and is supported by the darkness of the *ukhupacha*. In the shamanic and Taoist cosmologies, darkness and shadow are not locked away in a box but are a cherished part of life. This takes care of denial.

Because we are prisoners of linear time, we see our path as a straight line, with forks in the road where choices must be made. We can sit at these forks in the road for our entire life, trying to make the right decision. What is right? What is wrong? God is watching and this decision could take heaven away forever. We could suffer eternal punishment, the fires of hell, or, at the very least, banishment. We become paralyzed. How could we have any vision in this disempowered state?

A circular path has no beginning or end and supports a flow of life that is natural. To walk the path we must give up control, and for outcome-oriented people, this can be the wall where we crash and burn. Linear time results in history which imposes core belief systems and dysfunctional patterns of behavior in nations and bloodlines. Linear thinking supports cause and effect which lock us into these belief systems. At the core of this thinking, man is seen as the center of the universe, the pinnacle of creation. In this position, man is superior to nature. Within the microcosmic world of the individual ego, it is easy to take this one step further, seeing ourselves as being superior to fellow humans. In judgment we compare ourselves with others. We draw lines on the playing field and walls around our hearts.

And we establish goals, small ones like test results or big ones like heaven. Life is a challenge rather than a gift.

We can, and will, rewrite this creation myth. We can, and will, step out of linear time and thought. We can, and will, reclaim paradise. We can, and will, accept the darkness, not as evil, but as that which is transforming into light. However, before we can bring the medicine wheel into our lives, we need to recognize the depth to which the myth of God as judge has permeated our existence, for it has taken away our power.

BIG BROTHER AS JUDGE

Back in the days of the Old Testament, when Genesis came into being, religion <u>was</u> government. The laws generated to govern the people came right out of the laws of God. Retribution for indiscretions has varied with the times, but crime, judgment and punishment are part of our everyday life. Through our belief system, we have given the power to discern light from dark to higher authorities, the church, government, teachers, parents, and even our partners. Judgment feeds the hierarchical system established in our mythology, trapping us in a never ending cycle of control. Who makes the laws now that God is no longer sending stone tablets? We elect people along party lines, good and evil, to make them for us. We assume that perfect strangers will hold our intention for us and we go about our business until our business gets snagged in the laws we sent them out to make. How could they do this to us when we trusted their judgment? And entering the arena of litigation quickly defines what kind of power we have. How big is our bank account? How many strings are we capable of pulling?

Let's be honest. Down through the ages, we have interpreted the laws of God to suit our needs. This seems to be one of the few aspects of our way of life that maintains some flexibility. Let's take, for instance, thou shalt not steal. Stealing is taking something that doesn't belong to you. It shouldn't matter why it doesn't belong to you or what manner of injustice put you in the place of need and greed. It just asks us to have respectable boundaries. This law of God has no place in war, so conquering countries, corporate manipulators, embezzlers, pass interceptors, looters, bullies and petty thieves put a lot of creative thought into justifying their actions. Robin Hood is the archetype for justifiable stealing. Champion of the poor, he reverses the typical drama and steals from the wealthy, from the hierarchy. How is he any different from those he robs? His boundaries are just as superficial.

We could go through all of the ten commandments demonstrating how we have manipulated the laws of God to suit our needs - true entrepreneurship. Killing is justified in war. How? We have created a new set of gods (we were warned not to do this in the original set of laws) and have given our power to them. These systems of government, judgment, and punishment will not fall until the hierarchy falls. The hierarchy will not fall until we step outside of judgment and take back our personal power, aligning ourselves with a cosmology that will not backfire on us.

In truth, we will need, eventually, to shatter our belief systems entirely but, for now, it is enough to understand how illusory they really are. We have created the illusion of God-given laws to build a civilization. A belief system has manifest as a social identity and because God is illusory those at the top of the hierarchical ladder can easily step into His shoes. These are the false gods to whom we give our power, our free will. These are the doctors who decide what is right for our bodies, the priests who decide what is right for our souls, and the elected officials who decide what is right for our society. It is important to understand that it has been our choice to give our power away.

We need to look at the origins of our thinking, for the alchemy of mixing lofty and linear Hellenistic ideals with largely barbaric behavior patterns has contributed richly to our dilemma. It makes for great drama, a perfect hotbed of emotion and turmoil. The creatures of the *ukhupacha* are eating it up as we spread it around the globe with our economic packages. How have we, as individuals, come to embrace judgment with such passion? We haven't left it to the church and government, but have brought it into every aspect of our lives. We have established it as our cultural philosophy. The purpose of a philosophy is to create a foundation for living, and ours is based on judgment. The way in which the Greeks secured the place of rational, logical thought was simply by teaching it - in schools. Schools of thought blossomed into broader institutions of learning based on the school of thought. Educational institutions took on the authoritarian hierarchy of church and government. Western philosophy became institutionalized.

What do we do in school? First, we learn to count. This is a linear system. It's a way of knowing more from less, of ordering by value. We learn to write and speak our language so we can put our experience into something concrete and linear. Then we learn to read so we can put the concrete of others into our own thought. We are allowed to imagine within the confines of the system. Discipline is everywhere. Hierarchy is everywhere. We are asked to conform and those who cannot are labeled with learning disorder acronyms. No one teaches us to feel or express what we feel. No one knows how. Next we pick up history which is our linear time line. It is also told from the perspective of our societal belief systems, establishing further right/wrong delineation. The way we tell our history promotes discrimination, elitism, and criticism - judgment. Then we move to social sciences which imprint behavioral patterns. The combined result of history and social science is the creation of an approved structure in which the individual may express ego. This is propaganda of the highest order. We are deluding ourselves if we imagine that we live in a free society.

Finally, in our schooling we study the physical sciences, linear thinking at its best. Much is made of the separation of religion and science at the time of Descartes. Without the religious myth to provide boundaries, linear thought became a new god and the investigation and conquest of the natural world was underway. Science is the epitome of judgment. It loves to compare. We categorize species, name every aspect of everything, pick it apart and see how it works, and find the smallest parts. It requires rational thought and very little imagination. In school we are asked to memorize everything that has come before us in science, its history. This provides us with yet another hierarchical belief system. The periodic table orders all of the elements by their weight and the order found in each element's electron rings and subatomic particles. We may not feel attuned to this if we are not scientists, but every time we use a can-opener, the energy of this rigid system enters our subtle field. Is there anything around us that is not the product of science? How much of the natural world do we invite into our lives? At this time in our history, we are as far removed from nature as man has ever been. We are completely locked into these belief systems by our dependent relationship with manifested matter. Science teaches us to believe only what we can perceive with our limited senses. It is as rigid a belief system as religion.

As we progress through the schools, we are not only immersed in linear thought, we are trained to formulate opinions. This is what we believe thinking to be. So we are taught to make choices based on the good/evil model and to compare everything as the basis for choice. As we formulate our belief system, the comparative imprinting forces us to gather that in which we believe around us as reinforcement and to give negative energy to anything that doesn't "fit". This is how we learn to discriminate and identify ourselves with our beliefs. This is how we construct our ego. Our role models for this process are our parents and elders and, to a large extent, our teachers. Certainly, as we enter the arena of high school and more so in higher education, the teachers become the principal influence. Teachers we admire are drawn to reinforce the belief system already in place. The teachers who rattle our cages either cause us to adjust our belief systems or become more deeply ingrained in them.

Teachers, in the conventional school setting, are passing down knowledge in a stratified system. Most of them entered their teaching programs in post-secondary settings with good intent. Like well-intended medical students, they are forced to comply with the existing systems to be employed. Achievement in our school systems is based on testing, cattle herding, and very little individuation. The knowledge is passing through an individual who is not free from opinion, who is "in ego". In this system, the teacher is passing his/her belief system on along with the knowledge held in the cultural belief system. We become an interesting amalgam of our teacher's and society's beliefs, integrated into our individual personalities. We are taught to criticize, to compare, and to formulate a life for ourselves based on models of success already in place. We may join fraternal organizations, street gangs or girl scouts and further delineate a core belief system with our peers. We learn the power of group and find our way as leaders or followers. We seek out others who agree with our opinions to further validate ourselves. This is how we become "empowered".

The school experience prepares us, with models of success, to enter the world of work. We see before us a mountain to climb, the ladder of success. The degree to which we are concretized in our belief system and the appearance of role models will determine how we visualize success. Some of our mountains will be very tall, others of us will climb ant hills. Some of us will climb many mountains while others will be content with one. The point is, we all climb because we are taught to keep wanting more, to keep moving forward and up. We manifest counting, comparing, and linear thinking in every breath we take. Power becomes attainment of status, control over others in the microcosm of our climb.

As parents we turn right around and imprint our belief systems, the interesting amalgam of everyone who imprinted us, onto our children. An endless cycle is kept in motion. This begins before they are born. Our children's lives are imagined for them and any deviation from the plan is considered rebellion. There are long lists of do's and don'ts, punishment systems, and generational ideas of success. Children learn to lie and sneak in attempts at individuation, but eventually come under the umbrella of hierarchy through peer relationships, advancement through school levels, and increased responsibility. This isn't to say that they all discriminate good/evil in the same way, for some find support for rebellious behavior in counter-culture belief systems which adhere to their own hierarchical model. Either way, it is the imprinting of survival skills. As we learn to take our power back, we will find ways to empower our children within the framework of their personalities and natural intelligence.

YOU BE THE JUDGE

We are birthed from the womb of our family/school experience into the competitive world of work as passionately opinionated, completely powerless young adults. The result is an astounding degree of self-absorption. We have built our ego, our identity, from the suffering, violence, emotion and judgment of the *ukhupacha* and the energy needed to feed and sustain our identity clouds our vision and further entraps us in the darkness. Free from the controlling grip of parents and teachers we, as young adults, enter a time of self-exploration which becomes a discipline in and of itself. Slaves to self-service, we gather the *ukhupacha* around us, feel the pressure of society at every level and enter the self-sustaining cycle of suffering, violence, emotion and judgment. We are on auto-pilot, powerless prisoners of our core beliefs. We derive our power from judgment and decision making, exercising our free-will while we are, in reality, digging our hole deeper and deeper, moving further and further from the light. The flip side of judgment is judgment against us. It is painful, hurts the ego and moves us right back into the South of the *ukhupacha* with suffering, then violence with our reaction, emotional justification and judgment against our accuser. Throw the dice, throw the dice.

If we are extremely critical people, we allow little room in our lives for diversity for it does not sustain our idea of "self". We become more intolerant as we grow older, more solidly entrenched. How many times a day do we say "I think..."? This is how we sustain our identity- with opinion and thought. We are caught in the pattern of weighing value, or making choices. What we will learn to do is replace judgment with discernment which has its foundation in soul wisdom.

HIGH LEVEL SPACE GARBAGE

Our level of space garbage from judgment is astounding. It extends outward through all the mental planes as it helps us to formulate our egos. Directly related to the M-1 or emotional mental plane, it blocks the energy of the heart chakra and keeps us from experiencing unconditional love. The disempowerment that comes with this imprinting masks our true self. Our true self is our power. As long as we continue to give our power away, we obscure the gates out of the *ukhupacha* and remain in the in-between world of unconscious living.

It is a difficult task to dissolve the black and white, the evil and good, and learn to perceive in feelings rather than thoughts. We must learn to value our entrapment as a gift, the raw material of our journey to the light. Those who pass judgment upon us are our greatest gifts for they become the mirrors of the "self". They reflect back to us our own behavior and patterns of judgment. It is through the mirroring that we come to see this reality as illusion and our belief systems as the blinders we have been wearing. The ego, who we think we are, reveals its transparency. The true self, or soul being, emerges as our indestructible link to The Source. Our work in the *kaypacha* will open us to the discovery of our true self.

SUMMONING *HUASCAR INCA*

Perhaps, at this point in our journey, some of us are wondering at the harshness of this exploration of the *ukhupacha*. It may seem like a judgment against our society, a purely cynical look at life. On the other hand, some of us may feel we have only touched the tip of the iceberg, that it has been a very shallow look at the dark side of our world. Deep in all of our hearts, we know what is wrong with our world and we all want very much to transform it. We have been living in an illusion. We are all part of this illusion. We created it. And it isn't good or evil, right or wrong. It is the gift of our own making, the raw material with which to do the work of raising our consciousness. It is all there, right in place, waiting for us to land on the wake-up square. *Huascar Inca* stands ready to assist us with our work. The energy for the cosmic transmutation has entered every one of us. We are here to shatter the mirrors, to destroy the core beliefs, to shake up the world and walk into the light. We acknowledge the *ukhupacha* for what it is and with the greatest intent move beyond it. It's time to finally pick up those dice and get lucky.

PART II

THE *KAYPACHA*

To instill in the Rhunakuna, the first people, a desire for consciousness, the god Rual created Inkari from a ray of the sun, Inti. Inkari, child of the sun, was filled with munay, loving power, and was accompanied on his earthly journey by the rainbow, and the light of his father, the sun. Inkari was the first Inca and established the noble lineage of Incas, the children of the sun. He was guided by the sacred flight of the condor on his journey which began in the harsh mountainous region of Q'ero. This environment, austere, cold, and challenging, represented the masculine of his nature, the warrior spirit. In this place, Rual gifted him the Rhunakuna, his supreme creation, with whom he could found a great civilization. Inkari was given the llamas and alpacas by the ukhupacha to assure his well being and comfort while on the earth.

In the land of Q'ero, Inkari founded the first social nucleus. He began to spread the knowledge of the sun as a great teacher. He first taught the concept of sharing, ayni. With ayni, the Rhunakuna learned to gift to the Pachamama, the apus and each other, before taking for themselves. In sharing the coca leaves, a staple of the people, Inkari taught them of the kintui, the three powers of man; will, wisdom, and love. In this ritual, he held three coca leaves up to the sky, and blowing on the leaves three times, sent the power of kintui to its destination. Inkari established rites of passage, initiation ceremonies to assure that a lineage of shamans would remain to anchor consciousness. He then took his leave of the Q'ero and began a journey into the feminine, walking to Lake Titicaca to embrace waka, the feminine light ray.

Inkari, in his impatience to found an empire, had not yet taken a partner to compliment him in the earthly life. It was the nature of his journey to come into the land of Q'ero as the masculine warrior and embrace the feminine within himself at Lake Titicaca. He was led by the white deer and the snow lion into the symbolic North. His earthly incarnation tied down infinity and prolonged time, creating the kaypacha, this reality, the second order. The way of return became long and well obscured. Inkari learned the magic of harmony *from the medicine women of Uros at Lake Titicaca. The feminine creativity became the foundation of the Inca destiny. He taught the mastay, or magical ordering of the coca leaves with munay, loving spirit. This ritual gave the priests and priestesses a way of bringing the people to balance between heaven and earth. He eliminated the practice of sacrificial offerings and led the people into a new consciousness, self-consciousness. He established government and expanded the social nucleus to an extended village. Inkari demonstrated impeccability and revealed the fiery nature of the heart. In exploring mystery in opposites he was able to fully embrace waka, his feminine self.*

Inkari left the people of Uros, sailing across the waters of Lake Titicaca, to continue on his journey, the flight of the condor. He was to establish the Inca empire and sought the fertile valley where he might plant the seeds of the spiritual. He was led to a mountaintop overlooking Cusco where he planted a golden staff of lineage after offering the kintui and performing mastay. At this same time, following the call of her soul, Qoyari, the rising star, she whose destiny was to be light, prepared herself to come together with her soulmate Inkari. She was sent by Inti to Inkari, the lord of the golden rainbow, that together they might reflect the universal balance, the duality in all things. She found a place in the center of his heart and, in Cusco, they established the fourth kingdom, the empire of the Incas.

Together, they reflected equality, sweetness, mutual respect and brotherhood, ayni. She taught the people to hide the occult mysteries into their weaving designs and to spin the duality into the thread. Hers were the gifts of wisdom. Inkari gave them the art of agriculture and the potato. His were the gifts of will. But in all things the men and women participated together, in complicity, and love was the gift of their co-creative effort. They built cities of precise and beautiful structures all reflecting the universal balance. They settled differences with neighboring tribes by creating one language, and peace reigned in the empire. Inti smiled down upon them in happiness and the apus, the mountain spirits, were very content.

5

SOUTH:
WOUNDED HEALER

Inkari, being a ray of the sun, came into this world with full awareness of the *ukhupacha* and did not experience the suffering of the earth plane. He came to enlighten the people and establish a higher level of consciousness. We can think of this as moving into the conscious mind from the unconscious and becoming aware of self. This gifting of consciousness symbolizes the arrival of the neocortex, or thinking brain, in man's evolutionary path. In our conscious realms, we have learned to tap only a small fraction of the neocortex, but in doing so have moved from the instinctual limbic brain mode of existence, that of the *Rhunakuna*, to add the pre-meditated world of thought. Inkari did not experience suffering because he was not fully human, but a god-man. He shone like the sun to lead the way out of the *ukhupacha*. He helped the people befriend *Huascar Inca* who

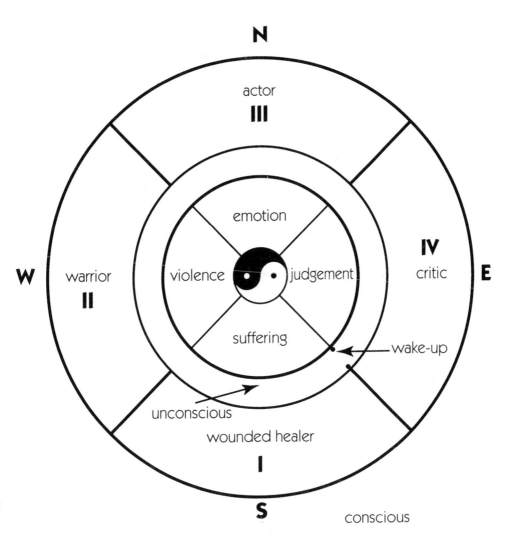

IV. The *kaypacha*, the world of this reality which exists in linear time, overlaid on the *ukhupacha*. After we wake up, we begin the journey from South to East, the journey towards fully conscious living. Roman numerals refer to the chakra and hologram where the work is taking place.

could then open the gates to the *kaypacha* - "come with me into the garden", *Huascar* beckons.

When he manipulated time, Inkari created the *kaypacha*, or this reality in which we could explore consciousness and grow in wisdom. It wasn't meant to be forever and the time of its closure draws near. We are nearing the end of linear "time", or history, and many of us are being drawn into an energy of completion, of purification. We have spent many lifetimes in this reality though trapped between the worlds, and we must loosen the grip with which the *ukhupacha* holds us. We must come into a peaceful place with the shadow world and move past the suffering, violence, emotion and judgment into higher consciousness. It seems an awesome task, but it is precisely what we came to do. We are here to lift the vibration of life on earth into a new reality, one which exists outside linear time and space, and speaks more fully to our multi-dimensional selves.

Because we are still prisoners of linear time and thought, we take comfort in a path, something defined, and begin our journey in the South of the *kaypacha* medicine wheel. It is in this place that we ask *Huascar Inca* to open the doors to the *ukhupacha* for us that we might begin to cut our ties to it, string by string. We must clear ourselves of suffering, extract it from our lives, and take responsibility for everything that has happened to us. We can carry no pain with us into the next level of consciousness, so we must release it here and now. *Sachamama*, the great serpent, is coiled within the earth waiting for us to connect with her. She is the great healer, guardian of knowledge, and archetype of the base or root chakra where our journey begins. The *kaypacha* medicine wheel takes us through a cleansing process that clears the first four chakras and their subtle fields and culminates in the opening of the heart. The first three directions and chakras clear the fields of *llankay*, or the will. With the clearing of the heart we come into *munay*, loving power, and completion of two parts of the *kintui*. In the *hanaqpacha*, we will work with the power of *yachay*, the wisdom, giving potential for the completion of *kintui*, the highest attributes of man.

THE WOUNDED HEALER

Where are we in the maze when the lights go on? We can be lost in meditation before the *Pachamama* stone at Machu Picchu or throwing our garbage in the compost heap. It really doesn't matter. What matters is that we finally got lucky rolling the dice in our game, and landed on the wake-up square. Often we are at the darkest of hours in our lives, at the depths of the *ukhupacha*. As unsavory as it sounds, this can work to our advantage. The clearest and simplest way to walk through the South direction is to have reached a point where we have seen through some of the illusions of this reality and have little to lose in releasing them. Perhaps we force ourselves to the darkest point because we know, on some unconscious level, that it holds the key to opening the gates and befriending *Huascar Inca*. From this point we begin to see light.

This journey into the darkness gives us the opportunity to shatter the physical form. From this shattered state, it can be reassembled with light. Let's imagine the body in a cosmic explosion, organs, bones, cells, and DNA flying all about. This is what happens when light penetrates the darkness, and it is what needs to happen to open us to the path. And our darknesses are many. We may be seriously ill, in chronic pain, every last drop of energy sucked from us by life. We may be in the deepest unrelenting grief, severely depressed, experiencing catastrophic loss, caught in the most abusive addictions, or living with constant fear. There are many dark places, but common to all is the feeling of hopelessness, despair. How we even have the presence of mind or strength for that final throw of the dice is a wonder. But, there it is, the wake-up call. It comes in many forms; a book, a word spoken by a friend, a vision, dream, experience in a healing, or a class that we decide to take to which someone drags us. Whatever it is, it breaks us out of our pattern, and the shattering experience begins. It is the greatest gift we will ever be given.

We may even get a little sicker, feel more severe pain, but it doesn't matter because once the light hits, we are already feeling the warrior energy of the West and begin to fight our way back. This is the path of the wounded healer, a journey as individual as each of us.

The South direction is the home of the healers and our journey through the process of our healing, of releasing ourselves from suffering, is like climbing out of a pit that is too deep for us to manage alone. We need helpful people to throw us ropes and tools with which to carve out our footholds. Sometimes we need to rest a bit at a natural plateau, but if we stay there too long, our feet get stuck in the mud and it is hard to get going again. The one thing common to all South direction work is that it seems like it will never end.

This path of the wounded healer challenges us with major lifestyle changes. It is a process of taking responsibility for our bodies and investing in wellness. Unfortunately, it rarely starts in the office of a Western medical practitioner where suppression of symptoms, masking of opportunity, prevails. The depth of the darkness may occur there however, for we often don't know where else to turn. Maybe we are referred to a psychotherapist or psychologist with whom we begin a cognitive exploration of our past. This is a start and it is usually covered by insurance. Cognitive therapy teaches us to verbalize and think through our suffering and the events of our lives. It pulls things out of the mental holograms for discussion. Because it is discussion, it centers around the throat chakra holding the healing within the mental body as well. The lower vibrational holograms don't have access to this healing. If our emotions still seem to be out of control, we may end up on anti-depressant medication for an extended time, perhaps forever. This masks the *ukhupacha* and we make little or no progress in our climb from the pit.

What is wrong with this picture? Many people spend a long time in psychotherapy without full resolution of their suffering. Treating emotions from the mental plane is a good business but it does not remove suffering from our lives. It has its time and place and would be instantly effective if we were ready to clear the mental body. But, when we begin this journey, we want the mental body to work for us as we clear from the physical body outward through the subtle fields. Western medicine doesn't accept the subtle bodies so our belief systems trap us once again. Cognitive therapy could be a beautiful adjunct to clearing the lower vibrational fields, but acceptance of the subtle fields will need to happen first.

This path of the wounded healer has definition and order. We must begin with the physical body and the base chakra. Let's look at the healing process one step at a time and keep in mind that if we have begun our process at other vibrational levels it's okay. Those levels will be right there at the surface when we do our physical healing. No time is ever wasted in the work and there are no mistakes. Let's keep in mind that the South direction *kaypacha* work is that of clearing the physical hologram and base chakra, but there are many ways to support it from the other subtle bodies.

HOLOGRAPHIC HEALING

Physical hologram/base chakra

It makes no sense to begin anywhere else for we hold our pain and suffering in the vibration of our tissue. And it makes no sense to take our physical bodies to the doctors unless we must have surgery because the options are medication or psychotherapy. Neither the doctor nor the therapist will touch us in a therapeutic way. They are not allowed. If we qualify for some physical therapy, we receive the minimal number of sessions with no alternative intervention by the therapist.

What we want to do is get ourselves to a bodyworker. We may need to try a number of bodyworkers before we find the right one for our work. What we want is someone with impeccable boundaries who will respect our process and hold it in confidence. Someone with a rooted spiritual background is an added advantage since we will most likely need to process some of our work on the table. To get in touch with our suffering, it needs to be palpated, brought to the surface and released from the physical out through all the subtle bodies - definition. Our bodyworker may be a spiritually aware chiropractor, a massage therapist, rolfer, oriental bodyworker or healing touch therapist. We may need to go from one to the other, finding the right person or combination of persons. Often we are led to these practitioners by our friends, family or intuition.

It is common for the weight of our lives to have thrown our physical bodies out of alignment. If we are holding grief, our chests are caved in to protect the heart. If we are holding fear, we have low back pain and knee pain from the weight and coldness of the fear. If we are holding anger, we have painful digestive problems and constraint in the liver and diaphragm region. Our bones hold the information for our spiritual lives and need to be properly aligned before we can enter the higher centers. At some time in this process, we will most likely seek out a chiropractor. Our muscles, interstitium, and organs hold our suffering and they need to be released by loving, well-trained hands. Homeopathy and herbs act at the heavy vibrational levels and can help clear the physical and etheric fields also, healing their interface. The healing work on the physical body is ongoing, as we move out into the subtle bodies. bringing the healing forth in the physical.

Etheric body/sacral chakra

In the process of releasing pain and tension from the physical body, we bring the situations and events related to them to the surface in the more subtle fields. Conversely, emotional work can bring forth pain in the physical that can then be released. Eventually we will need to completely release the energetic or ch'i aspect of the physical pain by bringing the meridians and whole etheric body into healthy balance. Acupuncture therapy is primarily attuned to the etheric body but can release dynamically into the emotional body at the same time that it supports the process of change in the physical. We must support our physical body work with the etheric for these two vibrational fields are deeply intertwined. Craniosacral therapy is another modality that interfaces these two vibrations with primary emphasis on balancing the fluid of the nervous system which is the instrument of this interface. Acupressure and shiatsu also treat both the physical an etheric bodies.

The etheric body can be depleted of ch'i, have ch'i in excess, ch'i can stagnate in places of vibrational fallout, be constrained in organs holding emotion, or fly out holes in the etheric body where blocks occur. Just about anything can happen. The ch'i must return to the smooth flow and abundance of a baby to maintain optimal health and immunity. We will address practices to support this when we move into the West of the *kaypacha*, the clearing of the etheric field. With respect to the South direction work and release of suffering, the etheric body holds the blueprint of the physical body, and all suffering is reflected in imbalanced ch'i.

Astral hologram/solar plexus chakra

As we release the pain and suffering of our lives from the tissue, emotion will come up around the remembrances of injuries, abuse, illness and so forth. The "experience" of the emotion will help to heal the physical body by clearing the emotional hologram of the feeling. The feeling is supporting the suffering held in the physical and the experience of emotion will help to release it. It may or may not happen on the bodyworker's or acupunturist's table. Oftentimes the emotion surfaces spontaneously after a therapy session, while we are speaking about it, or even in dreams. Flower essences can be used to assist this process and those of the mental and spiritual holograms. It is important to acknowledge the feeling, to allow ourselves to *feel* it rather than to think about it. The astral body is cleared by the feeling not the thought of the feeling which is coming from the mental plane. It is a very personal experience.

Mental-1 hologram/heart chakra

With this subtle body, we enter the mental plane and world of cognitive healing. This does not necessarily mean that we need to see a psychotherapist, for most of us do not, but it indicates the need to arouse the mind to release its hold on suffering. The mental-1 hologram is the emotional mind and what we must call to mind are the remembrances of the feeling around the suffering. Now we can think about the feelings, process them with a friend or therapist, perhaps the bodyworker, and let them go, supporting the healing process at the physical level.

Mental-2 hologram/throat chakra

At this vibrational level, the suffering exists as rational thought forms. The amount of thought and verbalization we give to our suffering is awesome, and this field can be very cluttered with pain-related debris. We need to release the rationalization of pain and suffering in order to completely let go of it. We hold onto these memories like they were our long-lost loved ones. We regurgitate the situations over and over trying to make sense of them. In doing this, we keep them alive, well-fed and close by - co-dependent creatures of the *ukhupacha*. We need to create a method of acknowledgment and release to clear this field. Telling our stories is a good way to bring things to the surface. Usually when we tell about our lives what we tell at a given time has everything to do with the suffering we are trying to release. Telling our story to a stranger is most helpful, with the intention of listening to ourselves to capture the piece we need to release. Combining this with the bodywork prevents the suffering from getting stuck in the mental field.

Psychotherapy works well at this level if we are drawn to one-on-one discussion. Sometimes we are able to discuss this with a friend. However, if we value the friendship we may not want to use our friend as a dumpster, especially if we have a lot of garbage. Sometimes we need to speak our truth to the persons involved in our suffering to release what we are holding of them from our mental plane and throat chakra. This can give immediate release to the muscles of the neck and jaw and free the voice. Seeking out group support for this process can be very healing. In a community of people with similar histories, one can find an acceptance that is a powerful cleansing in itself.

Mental-3 hologram/brow chakra

At the mental-3 vibrational level, the cognitive work is more spiritual. The pain and suffering of our lives has everything to do with our belief systems. Beliefs are so pervasive they inhibit the soul life and seem to have a grip on us right down to our DNA. Unfortunately there aren't many spiritual advisors or teachers who aren't entrenched in their own belief system, who can't break free of their identity. So this work is often done on our own, later in our spiritual journey. We will meet it again in the *hanaqpacha*, at which time a little more clutter from the mental-3 hologram can be released.

That brings up a very important point. The work of the South direction, the clearing of the physical field is obviously complicated and difficult. It is also ongoing and we do not have to wait for complete healing before we begin further spiritual work. But the intent must remain to remove the suffering and each step we take facilitates more release. So we must not let ourselves have unreasonable expectations, but be steady and patient, like *Sachamama*, the ally of the wounded healer.

Spiritual self hologram/crown chakra

Physical healing may be blocked in two ways by the causal body. Events in our life may have been so traumatizing, such as childhood sexual abuse, that the causal self was fragmented and pieces were lost or stolen. This can also be viewed as the perpetrator invading our causal body and exercising control over us from that hologram. For these issues to be resolved and the pain and suffering related to them released from the physical body, we seek the assistance of the shaman. This is the work of soul retrieval, and to assist us with this healing, the shaman enters the dimensions of the causal planes to retrieve our soul pieces or to extract the soul pieces of others. The shamans in indigenous cultures are the high priest/esses, and as we will see, they have healed their own lives and cleared their vibrational fields from the physical to the causal. It is not an easy journey and their paths are very narrow. If they were not that clear, they would risk losing their own life and do nothing for those they help. Our culture does not validate this form of healing nor produce the shamans to facilitate it, so this healing often comes in dreams supported by combined therapy.

The second type of healing from the causal plane is the karmic. When we can find no reason for our suffering or we identify patterns of behavior in our lives that have no roots in our history or genetics, we are tapping into the karmic pain. We are paying our old debts at the same time we are challenged by potential karmic situations throughout our lives, just as we had planned when we loaded our dice. Much of the physical healing from the holograms as described above is karmic in nature. At the causal level we are discovering that lifelong self-abuse patterns are carryovers from previous lives. The souls from those lives don't have to show up in this life to help us resolve this either. We need to recognize the pattern and release the hold that the former lives have on us and our physical body. These are powerful healings and can be spontaneous remembrances or those retrieved through regression therapy. We must also be aware of the healers that work with us from other dimensions and the gifted bodyworkers who are able to balance the energy in the subtle fields to assist the physical realignment. Often there is a harmonious cooperation between these dimensions and we must consider ourselves fortunate if we are able to call in these healers.

Here in the South direction, it doesn't matter what kind of life we have chosen. We can be a longshoreman recovering from alcohol abuse or a stockbroker with peptic ulcers. In the holographic model, our differences can be defined not by social conditioning but by the depth and breadth of the garbage cluttering our fields. Our pain, our history, is locked in our tissue and our addictions not only mask the pain, they nourish it. It all has to go. We can't allow ourselves to be overwhelmed by the process either. We are tapping into the warrior energy which is pulling us to the West and we will need it, for this process isn't much fun.

After we identify and work with our major issues, the little ones start coming up. Will it ever end? Let's take a moment to look at the way the dice are falling. It's different now. They feel much lighter. We are calling in the right people to help us with our work. Sure, there have been a few of them who have no boundaries and questionable ethics but they have their place as the mirrors which help us identify pieces of ourselves. Recognizing them in this way prevents our interactions with them from adding to our South direction work with negativity. Everyone who comes into our life can and must be seen as a gift, for we have called them in. A big part of the work of releasing our suffering is acceptance, that piece which is about taking responsibility.

ADDICTION

We explored addiction in the *ukhupacha* as the way in which we mindlessly seek to nourish that which was never nurtured. We try to make ourselves feel good and it becomes a need, a driving force in our lives. It gets control of us. Many of our addictions serve us as anesthetics, to numb the pain and suffering of the *ukhupacha*. However, they do not make it disappear and if we unplug from the addiction, the pain is right there. Breaking the patterns of addiction requires that we do the life-changing work of the South direction *kaypacha*. We will meet with a lot of self-resistance and, oftentimes, complete denial. Control dramas can be integral to our pattern of addiction, manifestations of a deep-seated anger and resentment. Issues around co-dependency and caretaking surface and require further life-style adjustments if we are really to attend to our behavior.

Common to most recovery processes are the substitute addictions. We nourish ourselves with cigarettes and coffee instead of drugs. We take in sugar to feed our alcohol cravings. Perhaps we turn from drugs to sex, another form of pleasure-seeking and anesthesia, the momentary high. We fill the void. We are still addicted. It is the pattern of addiction that must be broken. If we join an alcohol support group to quit drinking, we must guard against co-dependency with the group. This is substitute addiction. There has to be a way out of the pattern. At this point, if addiction has been a big part of our lives, we will be taking our issues around co-dependency and denial into the West for further healing. In the South, it is important to break harmful patterns with the body, to begin the process of healing tissue and instituting some cleansing rituals for this process. Usually our chiropractor or natural healer will help us through this cleansing with treatment and natural supplements.

This is a good time to mention the use of psychotropic drugs. Many justify the use of drugs such as LSD as mind-expanding tools to help us see past the illusion of this world. Mostly we get lost in fantasy and forget what we're supposed to be doing here. We are seekers of vision. There is no denying that fact. It is what leads us into those experiences. But if we explore that reality before we have cleansed our holographic field it can be horrifying and the creatures of the *ukhupacha* will haunt us forever. We can permanently damage the protective membranes that sit, like spider webs, between the chakras as they come up the spine. The good news is: If we follow the medicine wheel into the higher realms, we will have visions from the *hanaqpacha* without the use of drugs. They will be clear, under our own control, and will be used to guide our journey here on earth. To seek them by artificial methods before their natural occurrence is to risk the possibility of ever having them. And the bad news is: This level of clearing does not happen without the painful releasing work of the *kaypacha* medicine wheel. We did not appear on mountain tops in Q'ero, like Inkari, free of suffering and pain, drama and ego. We came to play the game.

PLATEAUS

No one said this work would be easy, but eventually, we reach a point where we begin to feel a little better and need to take a rest. It is good to bask in a sunbeam for a moment as it transits by the little ledge we have carved out of the wall of our pit. Remember how easily our feet get stuck in the mud, though? We must be careful not to slam the gates of the *ukhupacha* shut, to sit in smug denial that we have further work to do. *Huascar Inca* has a kind heart but we don't want to test his limits. As long as we have the gates open, we need to keep shoveling the garbage out.

If we have begun this journey at a place of very low self-esteem and self-pity, we might at this time be feeling our self worth. And it feels good, long overdue. The ego expands and begins to explore aspects of itself which are surfacing for the first times in our lives as suffering and suppression are lifted. We may even think we have all the answers. We are lacking the perspective to know we have just begun a long journey. The exploration of ego leads to needed introspection which can trap us in self-absorption. It isn't uncommon to arrive in the West feeling self-righteous, fully informed, self-assured, co-dependent and in complete denial. Physically we are feeling pretty good, but we have brought forth a whole new level of work. This is all very beneficial because we will need the ego to assist us in our journey around the wheel. The nourishing of our little lost child selves, retrieved from the debris of our South direction work, is essential. These pieces need to blossom and grow, catching up with the rest of our personality. To have moved from self-pity to self-righteousness is an astounding achievement and it sets the stage for the warrior work of the West.

SUFFERING AS HISTORY

As our bodies heal and our holograms clear the physically related garbage, the past begins to fade. We tend to lose touch with the South of the *ukhupacha*, but we need to keep the doors open. South direction work comes up constantly in the human experience and our new awareness can assist instantaneous processing. Until we really sharpen our skills at recognition and responsibility-taking, we will struggle a bit with "new" history. But, in time, we will become very adept at releasing ourselves from painful situations. We will become masters of the *kaypacha* South direction and turn to helping those who are still struggling with pain and suffering. The impulse to do this comes from our souls which are responding to the way we have lifted our consciousness. It is an obligatory piece of the South direction work to assist those trying to get out of their own black pits.

South direction work is about responsibility. If we were just to remove ourselves from the drama of life without clearing our past, without releasing our suffering, we would be living in denial. If we go back and look at the core beliefs around our suffering, we come to rest on the banishment from the garden of Eden. In this South direction work, we take our first step in reclaiming paradise with the realization that our own ignorance, entrapment in materiality, has caused our suffering. We are responsible, not Eve, not God, but us. Bringing it into the realm of our own soul's process means we can do something about it as well. The process of walking the *kaypacha* medicine wheel breaks down the structure of our belief systems, like thinning the veil that denies us the garden. Empowering those on the path behind us thins it even more by further raising consciousness. Suffering becomes much easier to release as light is shed on the *ukhupacha*.

The entrapment in materiality is another piece of this South work. The base chakra holds the negative emotions of jealousy and fear. These emotions support suffering and pain, and in the process of healing the past, they will begin to dissipate. Most likely, we will need to do some active work around them also. The base or root chakra holds that connection to the earth, to manifested material. If we fear death we will be so attached at the root by our fears that we will be paralyzed in life. So what do we do? Our grounding is necessary, but it must not be based on fear. As we extract the fear from our lives, we will need to practice wholesome grounding to the earth. The earth is our mother, providing all that we need to survive, and we need to exercise this with appreciation. Regularly spending time in nature will not only help us to heal ourselves, it will connect us in a beneficial way to the mother. The vibrations in nature are those of the physical/etheric planes and much harmony and balance can be invited in from the natural world.

Perhaps the most beneficial thing that we can do for ourselves throughout this process of healing is to engage in ritual and ceremony. Oftentimes we do all we can to heal the past, but still feel there is no closure. The shamans believe that we can change our history, our past and our future if we can work outside of time. We learn to do this in ritual. We can reach a point of releasing ourselves from our lives completely but as long as debris around issues remains in our hologram this will be denied us. Ritual allows closure, a subtle shift in perception, a unique stabilization. How do we do it? Meditative acts of forgiveness are important. Again, we are taking responsibility. Acts of purification involving fire are helpful. Offering the pieces of others that we harbor in painful memories to the fire will allow those pieces to return to them. This is soul return. Since it often brings us back pieces of ourselves that they have harbored, it is a form of soul retrieval which we can do for ourselves. If we can take the fire into our chakras and luminous bodies, we will raise our vibration and shake loose more garbage.

Another helpful ritual is journaling, to release the history from the conscious mind. At some point, summations of the painful memories can be written, burned and buried in a ritual, asking the earth mother to take the pain from us. Digging a little hole and shouting into it can be enough. We should be sure to involve the earth mother in our ritual because of her connection to the South. The most important part of any ritual is that we use it to take responsibility and release ourselves from it and that we not engage in blaming others for our suffering and attempt to symbolically do away with them. This suggests black magic and *Huascar Inca* will take delight in slamming the gates in our faces.

If we can arrange it, being in a sweatlodge is a very cleansing ritual for both body and spirit. We need to be careful of the intent of the sweatlodge and leader. The lodge should be for healing, not for the warrior, and the lodge itself should be regarded as the earth mother's belly. It is a tremendous re-birth in this way and a deeply grounding experience. All of the elements are present: earth, rock, fire, water and mist. The experience of sweating can provide a transition point in the physical healing process. Care must be taken to avoid situations where boundaries are not well-established and spiritual intent not apparent, for we must put ourselves in extreme vulnerability for this experience. If we have a heart condition or have experienced heat exhaustion in our lives, we will want to consult our physician before participating in a sweatlodge. The cautions are similar to those of sauna use except that you are usually not free to leave when the ceremony is in progress.

SHIFTING PERCEPTION

With our healing work comes the need to make some major lifestyle changes. Apart from the physical abuse and addictions we may have been involved in, which obviously must cease to facilitate healing, there are other levels of perception that must shift. Because the physical hologram is a heavy vibration, the changes are not subtle. Depending on the nature of our illness, we need to work with our physicians and therapists around the possibility of freeing ourselves from dependence on non-essential prescription drugs, or at least reducing dosage. If they are just not willing to help us we will have to search out someone who will. There are many tuned-in doctors and therapists now and this is not an impossible task.

If we are dependent upon replacement hormones for glands that cannot be induced to function by natural healing or have been removed, we must reconstruct the energy around taking drugs, from dependency to a gift of holism. This can be accomplished with intent. It should be noted that a balanced holographic body will sail smoothly through menopause without the need for chemical hormone replacement. If we have difficulty with this rite of passage, we can and should seek out the alternative healing professionals that can help us balance our subtle bodies. There is an element of work in menopause for all the directions of the *kaypacha* medicine walk. Acknowledging the flowering of the spiritual self with this passage is as important as good nutrition.

What we put into our bodies is a primary concern for facilitation of the South work. Drugs, stimulants and chemicals of all sorts including food preservatives, first and second-hand smoke, alcohol and dietary imbalances must give way to healthy food. Moderation in coffee, tea, sugar and fat, perhaps even protein intake, must be made to balance the diet. Our health practitioners may recommend vitamin and mineral supplements to assist us with this passage but eventually, our bodies will learn to select and eat the natural foods that supply all of our needs. We may need to take the time to learn how our body works and processes food to appreciate it and care for it. One perceptual shift that we need to make at this point is to respect and cherish the physical body. We want to make sure that this "self respect" is not egotistical but spiritual, a necessary part of our growth. We have begun a process of bringing spirit into the human form. We must be very clear with our intent, to provide a temple worthy of the spirit. We must do our housekeeping on all levels.

Exercise is very important. Long walks in nature and exercise systems that promote grounding, such as tai chi ch'uan and yoga, are excellent forms of movement that support the South work. Daily stretching and engaging the body in this movement will assist the etheric body in moving ch'i and blueprinting the physical body in an organized way. Remember, our etheric hologram is the organizer while the physical is the chaotic complement. As we exercise, we move nutrients to the tissue and remove wastes. It allows us to efficiently digest our food, to make the most of the air we breath, and to feel good through mild glandular stimulation. Oxygenation of the tissue is the key to regenerative processes.

Another element that we want to begin shifting is our engagement in the drama of the world. At this point in our healing process, we might need a certain amount of it to keep us from complete self-absorption, but, in time, we will begin to tune out. In this way, we begin to construct a new reality around us that supports health and balance. Unplugging the television and radio and stopping the paper may seem extreme until we have grown accustom to the changes it facilitates. Not only do we find ourselves with time to read, think, exercise and walk in nature, we realize that some portion of our being, our hologram, is no longer being assaulted with negativity. And we need to take the plugs out of the sockets to remove the energy from our space.

All of these changes in lifestyle require that we engage the will and have the support of those around us. It is more challenging to shift our perception with families who do not fully understand, or partners who do not share or support our spiritual path. As we walk this path, we want to be sure that we respect the boundaries of those around us, our family and friends. In time, they will come to appreciate what we are doing, tolerate it, or move away from us.

THE SERPENT AROUSED

A meditation practice should be initiated at this stage of healing but we want to make sure that it is grounded. Spending time in our higher centers will be of no benefit to our South work if we cannot stay connected to the earth. Earth is the element of the South, so while we are engaged in this work, our meditations should be designed to connect us to the earth energy. We can open the base chakra and send a dagger of light, an anchor, to the center of the earth. In this way we stay grounded as we begin to invite the earth energy into our bodies. We are awakening the sleeping serpent, *Sachamama*, from her fiery home in the earth's center. She holds the knowledge, a vibration, that is the key to cleansing our subtle bodies. This is called the kundalini. It is the energy of the earth mother and a gift of warmth brought to us by *Sachamama*.

As we clear each chakra and holographic field in our journey around the *kaypacha* and *hanaqpacha* medicine wheels, we invite this energy up the spine and out into each hologram one at a time. What we are inviting is a holographic kundalini rather than an energy limited to the spine as kundalini is usually portrayed. We penetrate the spider web membranes between each chakra slowly with steady work and good intent. When psychotropic drugs are used, the membranes burn out, and we can permanently disable our nervous systems by the power of the kundalini coming into us at once. We must be very careful as we seek out help with our spiritual path that no teacher ever forces kundalini up our spine. If a teacher offers to demonstrate this on our body it is the signal that our time with the person is complete. This is ego manifesting itself. We accept it as a gift of further light upon the path and should take our leave, membranes intact. Each individual's energy awakens as the soul has intended.

When the physical hologram clears, we will feel a vibrational shift. Since the frequency of the physical body is heavy, rather crude, we may be startled by some serious shaking or vibration. Usually it is momentary and happens only once as the nervous system integrates the kundalini. This is the first stage of awakening, actually feeling the physical body vibration, and it is not only warm and exciting, it is very encouraging and spurs us on towards the West. This is what it means to raise awareness, to raise consciousness. We are already penetrating the membranes a little further up the spine, but would have difficulty perceiving the vibrations at this point. If we go back to that image of the shattered body with organs, bones, cells and DNA exploding all over the place, this point is the coming back together of the pieces, cleansed, renewed and slightly luminous. Following the DNA on an esoteric level, broken DNA has been repaired and

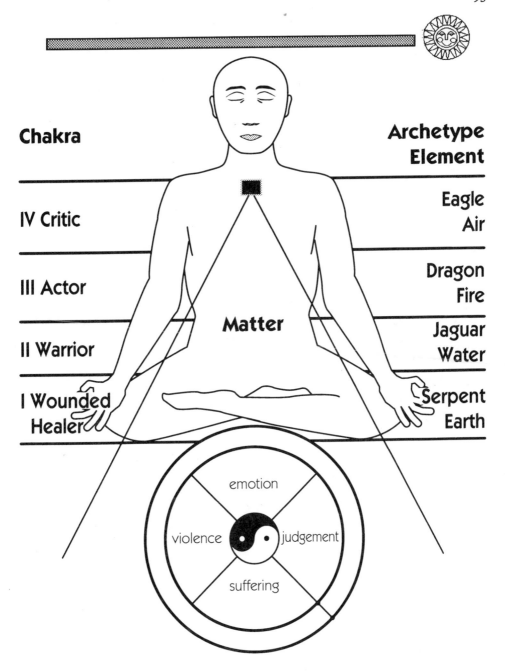

Chakra

IV Critic

III Actor

Matter

II Warrior

I Wounded
Healer

**Archetype
Element**

Eagle
Air

Dragon
Fire

Jaguar
Water

Serpent
Earth

emotion

violence

judgement

suffering

V. The *kaypacha* medicine walk clears the first four chakras and holograms which are associated with the material world. This path of disengagement from the ukhupacha allows us to make a conscious connection with the soul, at which point we can begin to bring spirit into human form.

strengthened on one side of the ladder, and awaits our work in the West to fully reform as a spiritual template.

At the same time that this base chakra work asks us to be grounded children of the earth, it is provoking us to look at materiality, the fear and jealousy issues. What we want to begin cultivating is non-attachment, the purified emotion of the base chakra. It is good to look around us and evaluate our connection not only to our 'stuff' but to those around us. Are we clinging to our children, partners, parents and friends in unhealthy ways? The only healthy relationship is unconditional, without expectations, dependency or obligations. As we walk the *kaypacha* medicine wheel, we will learn to let go completely. At this stage, we begin the work of non-attachment by releasing those connected to our pain and suffering. As we move around the wheel we become lighter and lighter, creating more room in our luminous fields for our souls. To remain grounded in a state of non-attachment is the first step in facilitating the embodiment of spirit. We have built a firm but non-grasping foundation for our temple.

6

WEST:
WARRIOR

From a ray of sunlight, Inkari manifest on a mountaintop in Q'ero, entering the West direction as the spiritual warrior. Our journey into the West is a little different. In fact, there isn't any clearly defined line of demarcation to let us know we are there. The energy shifts are subtle at first. We arrive in a variety of ways but we have one thing in common, baggage. We are still processing the suffering and will be for some time, but we have found ways to go about it that are working for us. We may come into the West afraid and insecure about letting go of dependencies and attachments, or we may have come such a long way with our healing work that we think it is finished, that we have arrived. Guess again. If we have really put the intent into doing this work, what we will most likely be feeling is resistance. We can be smug about it, or insecure, but the resistance is there. The West direction is about letting go and changing our whole attitude about life. How could we possibly have to change one more thing? Look what we have been through in the South? We can get pretty indignant about our arrival in the West.

The West is about moving the ch'i energy in our body and unblocking all those places in the holograms where we are stuck. These all appear in the etheric body as blocked or stagnating ch'i. This work sets in motion an energy of letting go that will follow us around the medicine wheel as far as we choose to walk it. From the West direction on, we can stop or loiter along the path but we cannot return to the unconscious life of the *ukhupacha*. This is the place where we really engage our consciousness in the quest for balance and wellness. The West work is between us and the Source, with or without the guidance of a teacher.

MEETING THE SHADOW

The first time we ask *Huascar Inca* to open the gate to the *ukhupacha* from the West, we experience the fright of our lives and slam the gate shut. The monsters chase us any time we turn the conscious brain off; daydreams, sleep dreams, meditations. Like stalking jaguars they will not leave us alone. Dark and sinister, perverse and violent, the monsters keep us running in fear. Fear of what? Fear that we might have to admit that the monsters are us, that we have portions of ourselves that are violent and dark? These are our shadows, ready to teach us about death and transformation, ready to push us to the limits with acceptance and surrender, ready to rattle our cages, forcing us to be free of them.

Why do we persist in kidding ourselves about being perfect? How much denial can we hold in our holograms? We have to shake it loose and admit that we have a shadow side. The only way to avoid the West direction work is to die, literally. The way to do the West direction work is also to die figuratively. People who have near death experiences report a thorough life review just after death. They are taken through the events of their lives backwards, an accounting that requires them to take full responsibility for every moment they were alive. They must meet and embrace the shadow side, and when these people return to this life they no longer engage in violence towards themselves or others. Unless we can arrange such an experience, we have to do the work in this reality. If we can extract our violent pieces and come into love and light, our life review won't blind or disorient us when we do die. Waiting until then to meet the shadow is not the best idea for those shadow pieces grow bigger and uglier the longer we keep them locked away in the *ukhupacha*. When we are finished in the West, they have been transformed into those funny creatures who used to scare us when the lights were out.

One really good way to begin looking at the shadow is to ask *Huascar Inca* to open a peep hole in the gate so we can observe the monsters at play without them knowing it. In meditations or a series of journalings, we can take ourselves backwards through our lives the same way it would happen when we die. We have to agree to look at everything and say "yes, that was me", "I did that", and "I thought that". If we share this with ourselves, there is no one to judge us but us. Taking responsibility for our lives puts the blame where we can do something about it - in our own laps. Eventually, we will realize that there is no need for judgment and no value in blame.

From the meditations or journalings, we extract the violent and sinister pieces, separate them out and have a look at them. We look for patterns repeated in our lives, pieces that look like the behavior of our parents or siblings, events and acts that clearly relate to the imprinting of childhood. When we get them out like this and take an honest look at them, the shadow pieces begin to make sense and we engage a kind of befriending. We can make them work for us if we can transform them spiritually. Of course it hurts, but we shake loose a little fear of the dark this way. And we know how to release the pain and suffering around it because we are becoming masters of the South direction.

Another great exercise which will carry us into the North work is directing. There is a little voice that keeps prompting us all the time. Sometimes we hear it saying, "do you really want to do this?", when we are about to plunge into something mindless. We have other voices that argue with each other, but we want to get to know the voice with the common sense, the one that seems wise to us. We all have this voice so we might as well put it to work. We will make it the director of life's drama and begin empowering it in the West so it will be ready to help us with the really heavy drama in the North. We can be the director, we can be an actor, or we can be both. All we have to do is wake up the director and begin observing ourselves in our daily lives. In the beginning, it may go something like this:

Sue, a friend from work, comes towards us in the lunchroom and asks to share the table with us. As we eat, she begins to tell us what a disaster her marriage is. We have heard it many times but continue to listen. Several times Sue pauses to take a breath and we try to change the subject to our new aerobics class. Sue doesn't even hear us and begins talking right through our sentence. When she finally is finished she packs up her stuff, says "nice talking to you" and walks off. Now we are realizing that our shoulders are three inches higher than when we sat down, our food is rolling around violently in our stomachs, and we have a headache and want to go home. Then our director taps us on those shoulders and says "wow, she really got you that time. Feel like a dumpster?"

When Sue sees us again, it starts all over, but at one of those breaths she takes, we snap at her to shut up. She ignores us, of course, and talks right through it, perhaps a little surprised. At the end, our director says "meeting violence with violence?"

As Sue launches into her drama the next time, we ask her to go away and when she doesn't, we do. Our directors asks us "what are you doing, running from the mirror?" Now what does that mean? We go back to our office and think it over. We think about the friends we tell our troubles to and have to admit that we see a whole lot of Sue in ourselves. We even call one of them up to ask her if she feels like a dumpster when we do that.

The next morning, we go to see Sue in her office. We take her some flowers and tell her that we care about her, are very empathetic, but are unwilling to listen to any more of her hardships unless she is going to do something to change her life.

We have learned that we have some ability to redirect energy in interactions and that we have mirrors of our own shadows in everyone we encounter. These are the great gifts of the West. By catching ourselves in the middle of our dramas, we begin to direct the energy of the interaction. By heightening our awareness to direct from the beginning, we come into our power while we learn about acceptance of our own shadow. If we don't figure out a way to step aside, we will continue to grovel around in the muck and never understand the *ukhupacha*. It is an exercise just to listen to some of the things we say; catty, mean, threatening, arrogant, cynical, seductive, nasty, self-centered, malicious, complaining, and on and on. Do we know this person? Who created this monster? Where were we going with this? Broadway? From our perspective, the peephole, we have to laugh about it. So what happens if we open the gate?

We have a little expertise now and these monsters aren't scaring us nearly as much as they were. The one thing we can be sure of is that they don't want to change, they're having too much fun scaring us, blocking our path. That means we have to change our perception of them so that they don't have control over us again. Since the West is about transformation, we might just as well transform them into great gifts which drive us to the point where we have to change our lives. We can't ask Sue to change if we are not willing to do it ourselves.

HEALING OUR LIVES

There is only one fear - the unknown. We are afraid of death and afraid of life. Both are mysteries to us. We are afraid of being alone or abandoned at the same time we fear entrapment, loss of freedom. Most of our violence relates to fear. When we don't understand, we lash out defensively. This is basic survival mode behavior, that linear thinking again, cause and effect. It is unconscious. In true wisdom, death and life are no different, the yin and yang of a continuously changing landscape. The fear of the unknown paralyzes us and prevents us from making changes in our lives that would allow us to really live. It is a catch-22 set-up. We are insecure. As a result, we end up fabricating lives from illusions. Some lives are very impressive fortresses while others are huts of sticks or straw like those of the three little pigs. And as long as the lights are on and the wind doesn't blow too hard, everything is okay. In this scenario, most of our energy is expended trying to control the weather. The minute the wind blows, we're a mess.

Controlling the unknown is quite challenging. Instead of chopping down the trees to build walls around us, we have to get out there and be the trees; blow in the wind, bask in the sun, be cleansed in the rain and sink our roots in the earth. Trees are not insecure, fearful or rigid. They are completely open to every possibility and they never stop growing and changing. To trust the flow of energy in life and our ability to find our natural place in it requires a warrior's courage. To find that kind of courage within ourselves, we become the wind and start blowing our own walls down. Why wait for someone else to do it?

First, we have to look carefully at our addictive patterns and learn to break the energy that sustains them. Some of us have addictive lifestyles and have quite a bit of fun ahead of us. We are an addicted society so there is no end of material to work with in the West. It's good to know we are not alone. Identification of the habits we have been able to break is a good place to start. We will need to consult with our director again and ask for some assistance. We step out of our lives and watch what we are doing with things like food, coffee, sugar, alcohol, drugs, cigarettes, sex, media, exercise. Have the director log in all fetishes, obsessions, and patterns that depend on each other. We call in the energy to be totally honest with ourselves for all we have to lose is fear and insecurity, the unknown.

For example, we reach for a bonbon every time we have a certain feeling in our chest. What's that all about? Sounds like self-pity, a very indulgent pastime. Maybe we thought we were loving ourselves or healing a grief that we can't get rid of. First we identify the feeling around our need at the same time we break the pattern. There are a lot of options with the bonbons. We could be conscious of our pattern at the grocery store and at least think about it before we put several boxes in our cart. We could keep them in the freezer, giving ourselves a fifteen minute thaw-out time to consider what we're doing. We could move the bonbon to a separate box which we take to work to share with others. Maybe we would be best off digging a hole in the yard and burying it, *ayni* for the *Pachamama*. This is a game of outfoxing our addicted selves, of getting the upper hand. Once we have established a random pattern of sabotage, the bonbons aren't half as important as what we are engaged in. This is a new sport. What is happening is consciousness. Control is the *ukhupacha*. We want consciousness.

We are looking to surrender this need to unconsciously make ourselves feel loved. We want, eventually, to love ourselves and know who we are. This is the best way to start. We can't overlook any addictions. While we are in this state of elevated consciousness, it should be fairly easy to avoid substituting addictions. The more we play the game, the more flexible we become, and unlike the alcoholic who needs to control the desire to drink, we can take it or leave it without dependence. This is real, hard-won freedom. We are getting loosened up for higher levels of surrender by getting past these control issues.

With increased flexibility in our lives, we can begin to look at how we get our needs met with other people. This is an addiction too, a way to nourish ourselves. When we are insecure, not sure who we are, we wear masks. It's part of the illusion. We need a lot of validation to keep whatever mask we are wearing in place. We are willing to compromise ourselves to get this validation too, at work, at home, at the club, in bed. Perhaps we have allowed ourselves to become completely dependent upon someone else - entrapment, possibly very abusive. The flip side of the dependent relationship is the partner who likes the authority, likes to be dominant. Step number one in any case is to take responsibility for it. We don't do these things unless we want to, so what did we need? If we choose to run away from these addictive situations without taking responsibility, without healing our lives, we will repeat the same pattern until we die.

How do the wild animals take care of themselves without becoming co-dependent? Their parents teach them to be independent and resourceful, to be little warriors in charge of their own survival. If we've never felt like a little warrior, it is time to wake up the sleeping giant.

OUR WARRIOR SELF

Warriors are doers, and the West direction is the action aspect of the medicine wheel. We will feel a lot of resistance if we haven't broken free of our unconscious addictive patterns and we will just get stuck in the West. It may be that discovering our warrior is exactly what we need to do to break our patterns. Conversely, we may always have been or wanted to be the warrior and will get stuck here because we love it in the West. It feels very powerful to us. We don't have to lose our warrior self. We just have to transform it, using the West direction energy of change, into a spiritual warrior. Our warrior manifests the violence of the *ukhupacha* and the West work is to identify it and extract it. Extracting our personal violence will help defuse the violence around us and contribute greatly to higher consciousness. How do we manifest violence? How can we identify it? We ask *Huascar Inca* to open the doors to the *ukhupacha* and we get our director ready to help us.

There are a lot of ways for warriors to play the game of life. We may be an outwardly aggressive control freak, egotistically self-assured, a stern disciplinarian, a bully intimidator, a passive aggressive controller, a master-manipulator, a tooth and nail fighter, a malicious gossip, or a mild mannered volcano awaiting eruption. How do we fight? How do we win? What is the nature of our militancy? How does this weave into the patterns we are trying to break? Sometimes we scare ourselves and those around us with our violence. We often hurt people getting what we want. Having what we want is power. Getting it is being powerful. This is the warrior mode.

Now we ask *Huascar Inca* to open the gates again so that our director can observe our behavior and tell us who we are. We need to see ourselves in action trying to get what we want. Then we need to go back to the bomb factory and get the director to watch what happens to us when our bombs go off. Next, we will have to look around the *ukhupacha* to figure out how we came by our hostility. And it may be a combination of social imprinting, family patterns, karma, or the personal patterns of our life resulting from this combination. Astrologically, we may be inclined to our pattern. The important piece is that we acknowledge who we are, as scary as it may be, and begin to heal ourselves.

As long as we maintain the notion that we need to control our lives and the lives of those around us, we will not be able to extract these violent pieces. What will happen if we let go of the control? That's exactly what we fear. We will not be able to survive. Those who "love" us will abandon us. We won't have any fun. We will be harmed in any number of ways. Yet we are deeply angry that we have no clue about who we are, are not truly free, and can't take care of ourselves. This is our trap. Becoming conscious of our behavior around violence and how we get our wants and needs met is a great step towards healing our lives. We know how to heal the painful pieces from the South direction and this will help to dissipate the anger knotted within us. The West work is that of changing the behavior that supports it. Again, we ask the director to help wake us up every time we are involved in confrontation or control dramas. Once we really know who we are, we can begin to withdraw from the patterns. We will find this to be extremely empowering.

We will feel a natural expansion of the ego as we gain power and knowledge over our lives. It is a healthy expansion, leading us forward into our future work, so we can assure our friends and family that it is just our warrior-self learning about self-empowerment. Sometimes it is very difficult for those who are close to us to support these changes when co-dependency and shared addiction are issues. In some cases where opposition becomes actively aggressive, we may need to, at least temporarily, remove ourselves from the situation. Often when we must break a pattern of caretaking, it is very upsetting to those who have come to depend upon us. These changes must be made with compassion and unconditional love. We must take responsibility for setting the patterns up and supporting them. If our intent is to do the work of the West, make the changes in our lives that will, eventually, put us in touch with our souls, we will be given all kinds of energetic support for this work. We can only be on our own journey here on earth, and must release the lives of those we caretake or otherwise control or depend upon, to give them their own journey. Putting some ritual closing on the behavior pieces is also important, and those we learned to use in the South work very well in the West too. Surrounding them with the intent and energy of surrender is very important.

Our whole concept of competition and winning will have to change. What are we trying to prove? That we are stronger, faster, more skilled, smarter than someone else? That we can knock someone's head off in an instant? This is the imprinting again, doing a masterful job of masking who we really are. Winning, remember, is getting out of here alive. It doesn't have anything to do with anyone else. It has to do with finding those four chakras out in the cosmos, the road home.

When we raise our awareness and step out of the competition, so will our children, because they are only trying to be like us. Often we are forcing them to be like us, aggressively. We are asking for angry, ugly scenes of separation when they are old enough to leave home, perhaps before. We can play games without needing to win, just for fun, and teach our children to do the same. We will find or help to establish schools that do not pressure them to compete, that don't drill in the linear thinking but develop both sides of their brains. We will allow them to discover who they are and what they want to make of their lives so they won't be afraid to be on their own and won't build traps that inhibit soul growth. This is wild animal childrearing.

We will stop supporting military aggression and violence projected on the media of any kind, the television, movies and newspaper. When we buy out of these control dramas, tune out, they lose their power over us. Before we quit watching competitive sports on television, let's listen to the sports casters hype the competition, danger, and violence, then let's take some peppermint tea to calm our tummies and tune out forever. We will naturally move into more inspired reading material and notice that we have a lot more tolerance for other people's dramas and a peacefulness about us that they seek out. A steady glow will begin to shine from our eyes. We will find it much easier to challenge ourselves to overcome our little fears, like falling, the dark, public speaking and so forth.

CULTIVATING MINDFULNESS

We are engaging the sacral chakra in the West direction work. The West element is water which represents the flow of surrender that is the hallmark of the West direction. Emotionally, the work of the West is around desire, the indulgence of the senses. This is a big component of that addictive behavior we've been working on. Those addictive patterns will tip us off to the senses that are out of balance. Sometimes recognition is enough for healing but we are often challenged to bring things into balance without substituting another form of indulgence in that sense or a totally different sense. Again, our best strategy is to keep changing things to heighten our awareness. Much of our warrior work has to do with boundaries, ours and others. All violence disrespects boundaries. Coming into that place of peacefulness means that we respect the boundaries of others and establish appropriate boundaries for ourselves. This is part of empowerment.

There are some obvious gender differences in the warrior work since men are naturally more drawn to it. The challenge in the West, for most men, is to step out of the competition, to give up the control and turn the quest inward. For women, it is more often necessary to discover the warrior, to seek the power of independence. Either way, the work is very difficult, but rewarding. Sue walked right in and dumped her stuff on us because there were no boundaries. In the end, we established boundaries with compassion and unconditional love. We can't have boundaries that inhibit our flexibility, but in the beginning, if we have been boundary-less, we will need to be firm about them. Conversely, we may have six foot walls around us that no one can penetrate. Balanced boundaries are soft, transparent, yet effective. People know they are there but are not threatened by them. We will need to stretch and modify our belief systems later in this work, so we want to have that flexibility from this point on.

The sacral chakra and West direction are all about jaguar energy as well. Not just the stalking of the shadow self, but the smooth sensuality of the jungle cat. We've got to get comfortable with our sexuality because insecurities, control dramas, and addictive behavior in our sexuality will keep us in the West forever. Boundaries are paramount in the sexual arena. Even with long-established relationships, we often don't speak to our own needs or to imbalances that are obvious to us. Much of our work around sexuality requires us to go back into our childhood imprinting and pattern dissection work from our past to define our imbalances. If we are trying to get basic needs met, to be wanted, loved, we will want to do some work with self-love. This pattern often establishes a caretaker, co-dependent relationship with our lover. The transformational work goes hand-in-hand with the medicine wheel work of self-realization. If our imbalances are purely indulgent, pleasure-seeking, we will have to address what is behind our need for so much pleasure. This is warrior energy that is not being properly channeled and, left unattended, will lead to severe energetic loss and the debilitation of premature aging.

The shame we may associate with sex is part of the religious imprinting on our society. Some esoteric practices have used celibacy, even in partnership, to turn sexual energy inward for attainment of enlightenment. The religious hierarchy, aloof and self-absorbed, imprinted shameful imagery around sex to support themselves as enlightened beings and keep everyone else in tow. Sex can be part of the spiritual union which we will find in the East and sexual energy can be usefully channeled into higher consciousness, but it is far more important to find the balance than to let the pendulum swing one way or the other. Let's remember, this isn't about right and wrong, but darkness becoming light, and light becoming darkness, evolution. We seek balance and conscious choice in all things.

All of this introspective work causes us to pay attention to what we are doing in our lives. This is mindfulness. Mindfulness is the fulfilled emotion of the sacral chakra, the opposite of desire. It builds on the non-attachment growing in the base chakra from the physical body work. At this level of the work, we are engaging the etheric body, and all of the changes we are making in our lives are allowing the ch'i to find a smooth flow, free of obstruction. As we clear the blocks in our thinking and behavior and smooth out the ch'i, our etheric hologram begins to clear. Of course, we are still dealing with the suffering of the South, but it is beginning to diminish. It is an ongoing process that gradually brings the pendulum into balance.

The West work is dramatic and causes immediate and long-lasting changes. All the great transformational events of our lives were West work. It is just that most of them were made unconsciously. Now we are facilitating our own transformation and future journeys into the West are nowhere near as scary as the first conscious one. We meet the death of these old selves by engaging consciousness. If we choose to follow this path into the *hanaqpacha*, we will meet the death of our ego in the West and shatter our belief systems. We will learn to love this energy.

It's important to make the changes in our lives with self-respect. We may be eager to be out of the violent environment of our job but would cause ourselves and family undue hardship by quitting immediately. Understanding that we need to change the scenery is the place to start. Putting clear intent into the change is the next step. While we are waiting for the energy of this intent to bring us the next job in the environment of our choosing, we can spend the time reaping the harvest of the gifts around us. We let our director have a field day. The situation provides unlimited opportunities for healing the relationships with co-workers and bosses. This is tremendous soul growth. Before we leave, we release our part of the anger and aggression that has led to dysfunction in the workplace, establishing a harmony that remains after our departure. We may even decide to stay, since the environment has been transformed. Either way, consciousness has been raised.

At this point, mindfulness will start becoming a part of our lifestyle. We will begin paying a lot of attention to how we spend our spare time, who we are with, how we take care of our bodies and how we eat. We begin making conscious choices about all of these, taking into account the path we are trying to walk. The clearing of blocks in the etheric field is facilitated by energetic and dietary changes which reflect the West work. An aerobic form of exercise is essential to support our work from this point on. Something like low impact aerobics, race walking, swimming, rebounding or bicycling are examples. It is best if we can be outdoors with these exercises since we can be taking in the base chakra earth energies at the same time. Aerobic exercise moves ch'i and the oxygenation of the tissue provides regenerative power and boosts immunity. A healthy heart muscle will keep pumping oxygen and nutrients to our tissue for years to come. If we are restricted by our doctor, we should ask for ways to do something aerobic. Keeping this at the low impact level prevents compression of tissue which counteracts increased vibration.

Another part of this West work is breathing, something we can all can do. We will want to get some instructions on ch'i kung, pranayama, or kundalini breathing from a good teacher or a book that will help us develop a practice on our own. With the breathwork, we master our own ch'i and will eventually be able to direct it towards areas of our body that need healing. After we have reached higher levels of training, we can use this energy to assist others in their self-healing by directing ch'i into their bodies. The ch'i kung doctors in China are masters of the ch'i.

In this mastery of ch'i, we are in the process of raising our vibration, our consciousness, to the etheric body. Our dietary requirements are going to shift as well. We will want to eliminate the heavier foods, like red meats, from our diet. We will find that they make us feel heavy and imbalanced. This is a natural part of the process and goes hand in hand with the releasing of violence. Unless we hunt animals because we have no other source of protein, killing and eating animals from the wild puts us in a compromised place with this work. It is the equivalent of ingesting a plate of violence and fear. For most hunters, hunting is sport, competition and challenge. It's the hunter and the hunted, the deer, or bear, or rabbit. This is the drive of the warrior and all that energy goes right into the meat. We eat the fear that the animal feels and the hopelessness of the hunted. Investigation of the food industry and the practices employed in the raising of the country's meat supply would make most of us violently ill. This may be the point in our work where all commercially raised meat is eliminated from our diet. The Source moves through all things and all things feel. When we eat food raised and prepared in unconscious ways, we are nourishing ourselves from the *ukhupacha*.

It is also a good time to get a naturopath or chiropractor to test us for food allergies with applied kinesiology. Often the discomfort and pain we feel has a simple etiology - we are poisoning ourselves.

There are many food intolerances and they can make us feel awful. For instance, we are made to believe that we need milk after we have been weaned because we have a large dairy industry. Many of us have an intolerance to dairy products because our enzymes are not equipped to digest them. Since we engage our genetics at the direction of the etheric body, to live at odds with that direction suggests the aggressive posturing of the uniformed warrior. Once informed, we have new opportunities to explore balance. All of this teaches us to begin listening to our bodies. From a clear place, eating what our body is craving is a spiritual practice. This is mindfulness in action.

Our meditation practice should have the fluidity of water now. We are beginning to let ourselves go, practicing surrender without losing consciousness. We must stay focused, not fall asleep or wander off daydreaming, yet we must let the mind expand and flow like a river. We allow thoughts to enter and leave with a fluid motion, observation, and release. We are exercising the director. We want to remember to stretch thoroughly before each meditation so the physical body does not cry out and break the flow. If we have not already made a little altar in our living space for meditation, now is the time to do so. It can be elaborate or simple, even portable, providing a focal point for our developing practice. Candles, favorite stones and powerful objects belong on our altar. In time we build a spiritual power there that protects us while we journey inward.

THE SPIRITUAL QUEST

The West direction is such a cage-rattler that it launches us out into the world looking for a teacher. The work has to be introspective, done alone, but guidance is sought from those who have been there before us. Sometimes it's hard to tell if a teacher has really been there before and moved beyond the West or if they liked it so much they decided to make a career out of it. We all know someone who got involved with a spiritual teacher emotionally, even sexually- maybe us. We cannot judge whether this is right or wrong but, instead, assume that this was exactly the way things were planned and some important work needed to be done around it. We call in what we need.

If we need to look at manipulation, we will call in someone to manipulate us. They will lock into our solar plexus or sacral chakra and suck our energy until we wake up.

It is not uncommon for those who call themselves spiritual teachers to lack boundaries. We are the ones who have to establish our boundaries. If the teacher doesn't respect them, he or she is not our teacher. Often we learn the most from abusive people or those who are completely self-absorbed. Truth comes in strange packages because we are teaching ourselves to recognize the truth without becoming attached to the package. We learn to separate the truth from the person delivering it. This allows teacher and student to continue moving forward with their individual spiritual quests. The last thing we want to do is form a co-dependent relationship with a teacher since it creates a growth-inhibiting mixture of addiction and spirituality.

Some of us are able to follow a spiritual path in denial about having any work to do ourselves. This causes us to see the work we are reluctant to do as that which others need to do. If we are judgmental, we will find others to be judgmental and call them on it (judging them). This is projection and it is often targeted at good teachers who are able to mirror our work back to us with uncanny fidelity. So we call forth wisdom and engage the director to fully understand what we are seeking from an individual. Good teachers challenge our beliefs, rattle our cages, and look serene doing it. It's amazing.

There is, in the spiritual quest, an element of devotion that is completely necessary. Devotion to the teacher, the path and the process is imperative. In our culture it is important to support the teacher and the path financially since that is our chosen form of energetic exchange. If we lived in a culture that traded chickens, that would be appropriate payment for teaching, but we live in a culture that shops at the supermarket and teachers get as hungry as we do. We create problems with devotion because we don't know what devotion is. We get it mixed up with kneeling before statues or pictures of gurus in acts of adoration and subservience. Often we are looking for miracles, the quick fix, instant enlightenment. Devotion is dedication, a real commitment to the path. It is that awesome surrender piece that opens all the doors for you. It means hard work and sacrifice in a system that doesn't punish or reward. It tests our limits, gets the ego in an uproar and breaks our warrior spirit. We are once again wanting so badly to believe in ourselves and we become as total strangers. This is good West work!

Good teachers will make us take responsibility for our own process by not caretaking us or being substitute parents. They will not tell us what to do but support our process with love and compassion. They may not even be people we like to be around. They are also in their own process of becoming and don't mind tripping and falling in front of us. They aren't attached to the knowledge coming through them. They seem content, secure, yet they may have few attachments. They are experts at assisting us, at helping us unlock the truth within. Because we don't live in a true wisdom culture, and the prevalence of guruism has been a great setback in our culture's quest for the sacred, good teachers are few and far between.

SPIRITUAL WARRIORS

In his West direction work in Q'ero, Inkari typified the realized man, the spiritual warrior. He came with rituals of mindfulness, of honoring earth and sky. He was a warrior with no war, no enemies and he possessed *munay*, loving power. For every man, the West direction can be the realization of the masculine, the peaceful warrior. It is as far as a man can go as a male. In the North, the warrior must embrace *waka*, the feminine light ray and bring the duality within himself, male and female. This is a very difficult part of the journey but one necessary to open the heart. In the West, women learn to explore their male part and become warriors, some for the first time in their lives. Since it is very empowering, it is easy to get stuck in our male side for many years, living aggressive competitive lives in male-dominated occupations. This whole process may have begun during tomboy years when girls explore the male to be more like brothers, perhaps to win father's attention. In the North, women reclaim their feminine part and come into balance with varying degrees of difficulty. If we have been in our male self for a long time, we may need to get some help with this transition. Releasing blocks in the etheric body will help.

An important piece of the West work is gathering power and knowledge. It is rarely in balance when we arrive in the North, but at least we are trying. Our expanding egos can amuse and/or infuriate our friends and family. We may even feel completely out of control. Everyone around us is asking us what we think we're doing and we have no comforting words for them. We need to remember that the spiritual quest is not a competition either, that there is no real agenda or judgment about progress. The journey is as individual as we are and we need to find compatriots who can support that.

The quest for knowledge is a big part of the shamanic path as it translates into our culture, but the real power of knowledge is knowing who we are. The path is as interesting as it is difficult. What we want to be alerted to is ego. If we get into power with the ego, we will not get very far on this journey, so we spend a lot of time questioning our intent. We spend a lot of time practicing mindfulness, conscious thought. We put clear intent and mindfulness into everything we do, every step we take, every meal we prepare and eat. In this way, we nourish the etheric hologram.

When the sacral chakra and etheric hologram are cleansed, our vibration raises an octave to that of the etheric body. We can feel it. It is what the Chinese call "coming into ch'i". Along with it comes the healing of the entire DNA ladder though some of its structure may still be imbalanced. It is nowhere near as dramatic as our first transition but a noticeable, warm current running through us. In tai chi ch'uan, it is known to take ten years of practice to come into the ch'i. In an instant gratification society, this sounds outrageous. It takes a lot of mindfulness, but it is true. However, because the energy for transformation is so intense on the planet right now, the combined practices of movement and breathwork are allowing us to access the ch'i much sooner. We do have to establish a regular practice which has a sense of timelessness about it. That way, we will not get hung up on how long it takes, falling backwards into more linear competition patterns.

Before we move out of the *kaypacha* West direction, let's look at a historic model of transformation for the warrior. Our culture is very attracted to martial arts at this time. The martial arts can help us explore our warrior nature, and for women this is sometimes a very empowering experience. Unfortunately, most martial arts are taught in the energy of competition, combat and aggression. In other words, we might as well be playing football. The energy of martial arts has shifted globally, not just in the United States. The original purpose has been lost in the Orient as well as in the West.

Martial arts are not about the physical body. They are about the etheric body, the ch'i. The quintessential master, in the old days of China, did not need to employ the body at all to defeat the opposition. It was all energetic without the need for violence or contact. The great masters were working out in the hologram to affect change in the mind of the opponent - no need to fight. Awareness, consciousness, was such that the opponent never entered the master's holographic field since the master could project his energy outward and still maintain boundaries. This is the work of the spiritual warrior. Families in China cultivated techniques based on the observations of the movement of animals and martial forms came into being. These families were in the ruling class with plenty of time on their hands, so much of the day was spent in breathing and meditation practices and incorporation of these into the martial forms. This was a spiritual practice.

These practices were taken into the Buddhist temples and the priests became masters of different animal forms. It was a natural place for these arts to flourish because they were spiritual by nature. These priest, in their own way, were shamans mastering the medicine wheel. Projection of ch'i through weapons or from the body could only be accomplished from a cleared holographic field. They had done their spiritual work. And their engagement in the practice with each other was a kind of sport that allowed the natural energy of the warrior to be expressed in a spiritual way. It allowed them to balance and move past this energy into their duality. This priestly work is a little premature for us since it really demonstrates the warrior with no ego, the *hanaqpacha* warrior. But it is food for thought, to nourish a sense of the possibilities, a sense of the limitless potential within us all.

7

NORTH:
ACTOR

Because the theme of death and transformation is an essential part of our work in the West, arrival in the North of the *kaypacha* can be very much like a birth experience. Kicking and screaming, with renewed energy from lighter dice, we come North looking for wisdom. We are met by the dragon, archetype of the North, who breaths fire in our faces. We look around for *Huascar Inca* and find him leaning against the gates, a big grin on his face. We definitely have a sense that it is too late to change our minds and that the path is getting narrower. The changes we have been making in our lives have led to turmoil within our familial and social nuclei. The way in which we have been clearing the suffering and the violence from our lives has opened our eyes considerably, and there is a lot around us that suddenly seems intolerable.

It is also apparent that we are feeling everything more intensely, that we are caught in raw emotion a lot. We have fleeting thoughts that it was more comfortable to be sound asleep, back in the unconscious lives we had led. But we know we are here for a reason and look around to see what must be done to get the most out of this North direction. What we see is the earthly experience, the great drama of life. It is fascinating, yet it sucks us in and we can feel brutalized by the emotional turmoil. Of course, since we are more open than we had been, we are less shielded from the impact and are affected by it in a more conscious way. We are feeling how this impacts on our bodies and how the creatures of the *ukhupacha* use this emotional turmoil as food. They love stirring up drama because they get more to eat. They must love to eat.

What we notice more than anything is feeling. It isn't like we never felt anything before but it never hit us like this. When we give it some thought, we realize that we weren't really feeling before but were intellectualizing our reactions to people and events. To say "I feel really angry" is not to *feel* really angry. To burn in the solar plexus area is to *feel* really angry. Now we identify the feeling and separate it from the thought. The burn may have been there in the past but it was thought to be the result of the feeling. It is the feeling, expressed in the physical body from the astral hologram through the release of neuropeptides. The mind is easily engaged because the astral and emotional mental (M-1) holograms are an octave apart, but the clearing of the astral hologram cannot be done from M-1. It must be done from the astral plane which triggers the release of the peptides with or without glandular assistance.

Our ability to discern feeling is empowering but overwhelming at first. Until we get a grip on it, we are wiped out by every intense interaction we have and feel as if everyone is trying to take our power from us. This is good, since the solar plexus chakra is being cleared and it is the place of personal power. Here we will find out how to claim that power for ourselves. It is also disconcerting that the past we thought we let go of re-emerges. We can get indignant about it, too. It isn't quite the same though and soon we realize that it isn't about suffering this time, but about feeling. We are asking ourselves to own and release the feelings around the past situations. Since we are pretty good at extracting patterns from our journaling at this point, we can use that exercise as a way to get in touch with our major emotional traps. It isn't like the South direction work where individuals caused us grief or anger, and so forth. The individuals have been released and the emotion remains.

When we look at the patterns, we see how we kept feeding that negative emotion to make it more and more a part of our hologram. If we have suffered a lot of loss and have not been able to let go of our grief, there is a very real constriction and heaviness in the chest where we carry it. Shaking loose the emotion will free the physical body from this constraint. Our bodyworker can help us with this work by releasing the muscles of the chest and the ribs to allow the grief to move and release. Anger patterns can take the solar plexus/ digestive system and crank it into a knot. The anger releases in increments and gradually we restore some softness and relaxed balance to this area. We may have to go on restrictive diets during the anger work to get the physical body to support us.

This task of clearing the emotional hologram is well-supported by group work, bodywork, nutritional, flower essence and herbal therapy, and acupuncture/pressure. Cognitive therapy could be geared to assist in identification of the patterns if the journaling technique is not satisfying. Because men tend to exclusively rationalize feeling, the North work is particularly difficult for them. Experiencing emotion for the first time can be shattering. Since men are better at storing emotion away than women, their physical bodies can be impaired by it. The shattering experience unleashes vast storehouses of feelings and it comes pouring out in an uncontrolled way. What is needed is some strong support which doesn't caretake and a clear understanding that things will come into balance. The inclination to make erratic and instantaneous changes in our lives should be tempered with the wisdom we are gaining. It can be a tumultuous time.

ENGAGING THE DRAMA

Step one. The first thing we must do in our quest to purify the solar plexus chakra and astral hologram is to begin an in-depth study of our "self". We all have dominant aspects of our personality with which we identify, but it is not so simple as all of that. We have many selves with particular traits and little child pieces that call out for nurturing and love. We are a lot more complicated than we think we are. To work in the North, we need to recognize our different selves in action and that is a good way to begin identifying them. These aspects of self have been called subpersonalities.

We begin with the most obvious subpersonalities, those which we send to work, to school, to social events, and those which interact with our families and partners. These are pretty easy to identify because of their familiarity to us. The difficulty here is the exercise of breaking our self up into subpersonalities. Once we get comfortable with it, it's a lot of fun. There are two ways in which this must be approached. First, we observe our "selves" in everyday situations. We probably utilize a number of subpersonalities at work. Sometimes we're called upon to be a warrior and at other times a caretaker, or scholar. It is okay to make associations like these. The associations that don't work well are the adjectives, such as pensive, subversive, sneaking and so forth. These could apply to any number of subpersonalities. As we observe these subpersonalities in action, we will come up with some subpersonalities that make cameo appearances. These are so surprising they require a double-take.

The second way we work with subpersonalities is historically, by going back over our lives looking at the patterns of behavior and finding the historic subpersonalities. Some of these subpersonalities will still be around, others will have become current subpersonalities, and a few will still be stuck back there as wounded children or adolescents. Those which are not as mature as we are will have to be acknowledged, nurtured and brought to our present level of growth. We may need to let our little children play and have fun while they grow up. We must give them what they had not received as children.

After our exhaustive search for subpersonalities, we can sit down with this information and examine it carefully. Many subpersonalities overlap one another and can be combined into one. Little children aside, we should be able to come up with at least four subpersonalities. Women should be able to identify a male subpersonality, though it may not be very active. Men will usually have a more difficult time finding their feminine subpersonality, but it is there and will emerge if we ask it to reveal itself. Our subpersonalities need to be named, so that we can distinguish them from each other. The best way to accomplish this is to invoke the subpersonality and let it name itself. These are our actors, and once we have them identified and named, we can begin to use their talents.

<u>Step two</u>. Now we are ready to engage the drama. We have a feel for our actors and what they are capable of doing for us but we are now going to have to dissect the drama itself to see what is going on. We can think of this as method acting on the stage of real life. Following through on our initial experience of identifying the subpersonalities, we now find one of our subpersonalities in an emotional drama - not surprising. That's what acting is all about. Our goal, to begin with, is just to observe the process and often we are so caught up with it that this is reserved for a retrospective analysis. Eventually, we will know what is going on right in the thick of things and begin observing then.

After we have mastered the observation, our next goal is to notice what we are "feeling" in response to particular emotional dramas. We may know that Spike, our belligerent adolescent subpersonality, reacts with a barrage of nasty words every time she is confronted with responsibility. We are even beginning to feel Spike take "us" over. What we want to grasp now is the way Spike makes us feel. We are hot all over, our face is flushed, and our eyes even feel sore after one of these outburst. We always have indigestion right afterwards and pop an antacid in our mouth without really thinking about it. Look at the amount of data we have collected. Not only do we have a grip on a subpersonality with the potential of a spiritual warrior, we know exactly what anger feels like, how other people react to it, and how we react to it. We may also be realizing that Spike may not be the best choice for these situations and that she definitely needs to grow up.

At first our exercises will be with each of the subpersonalities. What begins as observation can be extended to basic training. Our subpersonalities gain expertise at their drama parts and we are learning who to send in when. We are ready to ask for help.

<u>Step three</u>. At this point, we would like to call in some particular dramas both to exercise our subpersonalities and get used to the

feelings of our emotions. Beginning with the base chakra, we call in the energy of jealousy/fear of loss with our good intent. If we have not yet discovered the power of our intent, it will become clear to us in this phase of our work. It may be helpful to reread chapter III at this time to review emotion in the *ukhupacha*. Before we know it, we are in the thick of these emotions with particular people in our lives. For all of the emotions, we will first engage drama in one-on-one situations. Here we get to grovel in the emotions and understand where it is affecting our body. Of course, at the time we may not have quite this depth of perception. Actually we don't want it, and we get into the jealousy and fear as it gets into us. A second stage of this work will be to call in the emotions as a third party and see how we get drawn into the jealousy and fears of others. It isn't even our experience, and there are the same physical feelings! We're getting a sense of the power of this work.

One by one, we call in the six negative emotions with our intent; jealousy, desire, anger, greed, pride and ignorance. Different subpersonalities will rise to the occasion and we can send in subpersonalities inexperienced with the particular emotion to get some training. Now it is easy to see that certain people in our lives stir up emotion. They are experts at creating and sustaining drama, regular servants of the *ukhupacha*. They were right there for us when we put our intention out, and they will come whenever we need them for our exercises. All of our actors are honing their skills, becoming more versatile, but we are missing one key element, our director.

Step four. A little wrung-out from the emotional work, it is good to see the director waiting in the wings. We have been working with her in the West, so she already has some basic training. We have our repertoire of well-trained actors, our subpersonalities, and the clear intent to call in drama and emotion. We are ready to get to work. We call in desire, and our most dependable desire characters rush onto the stage. There is Cloe, our seductress subpersonality in her close-fitting jersey dress, ready to play her role. She is looking and feeling good and before the director can even get to the director's pit, the scene is over and Cloe's desire has been fed. She comes into consciousness in bed with a perfect stranger. The director is scratching her head. She gets some information from Cloe and a few folks in the audience and begins to analyze what happened during the scene. In the meantime, Julia, our caretaker subpersonality, yanks Cloe out of there and is busy trying to repair damages.

Ready to try the scene again, we call in the intent for desire and Cloe is off and running again, just like a bad habit. Somewhere in the middle of the drama, our director gets control of the situation and Cloe, looking around startled, begins to see what she is doing. She pulls herself out of the drama enough to take directions from the director. Suddenly, she is not out of control but is consciously engaged in desire, aware of what the feeling is doing to her body. She may think she felt a lot better before. Now she sees she has been unconscious, and is suddenly more aware of her actions and feelings. This scene ends differently, with Cloe in command of the situation and actually learning something from it. She shares this with the director and the other subpersonalities. The director is seeing the drama on a much larger scale and is thinking of playing this one out with Julia instead.

Again, we call in desire and everyone arrives on the scene. This time, the director is in control from the beginning and sends Julia into the drama. This doesn't even look like desire with Julia, who ordinarily doesn't engage in anything but caretaking, not falling into Cloe's traps. It's not her scene and it doesn't really affect her physically. Here, the director has found a way to short circuit the drama so that we can learn something from it without getting hurt. Eventually, we learn all we can from desire and are finished with it. With time, we work through all of the emotions in this way and get to a place where we are no longer lost in the drama, and engage it when we choose, consciously. This is empowerment. And it doesn't mean we never feel anything again. It means we are never controlled by it again.

There are several important points to remember while we are engaged in this work. Before we have much practice, it is easy to get lost in the drama, to slip into unconsciousness. We can ask an uninvolved subpersonality to watch out for that and wake us up. If we are doing this work with a friend who is close to us, we can ask that person to tap us on the shoulder when we lose it. Another point to remember is that we called this in with our intent. It is not about condemning those we call in to help us. They are our greatest gifts, even though it is hard to acknowledge this when we are in the thick of things. It is interesting to note who shows up and whether or not they stay in our lives once we have pulled ourselves out of the drama. Usually they quit coming around when they don't get fed and then we know the work is done. There tends to be a lot of friendship fatalities at this stage of the medicine wheel walk.

THE GIFTED DIRECTOR

Since the solar plexus chakra is the emotional center, we must concern ourselves with all emotion while clearing the astral hologram. We have already begun working with jealousy and desire as we have cleared the physical and etheric holograms, but there remains the astral space garbage that comes from our emotional attachment to life's drama. We are already cultivating non-attachment and mindfulness the purified emotion of the first two centers. This is ongoing and we will continue to cultivate the purified emotions as we journey upward and outward through the chakras and holograms. At this stage we need to review the negative emotions from the astral hologram and make the shift from actor to director, calling in the drama to facilitate this shift.

Jealousy. Out in the astral hologram, we harbor a feeling of neediness. This feeling may have arisen from lack of nourishment, lack of boundaries, losses of all kinds or having had to give things away that we treasured as children. As soon as we put our intent out to work with this emotion, we will begin to remember some of these events from our past. It is the past re-emerging as a feeling. At the same time people start showing up in our lives who put us right back in that feeling. The drama is engaged first as the actor, allowing us to get fully in touch with the feeling. Then, as we have been practicing, we gradually pull ourselves out of the drama and become the director.

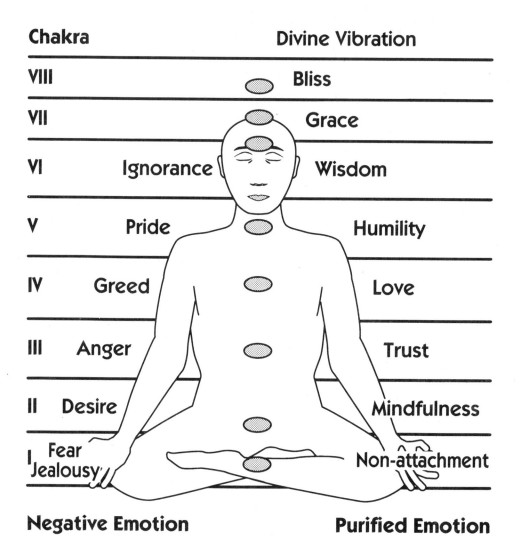

Chakra		Divine Vibration
VIII		Bliss
VII		Grace
VI	Ignorance	Wisdom
V	Pride	Humility
IV	Greed	Love
III	Anger	Trust
II	Desire	Mindfulness
I	Fear Jealousy	Non-attachment

Negative Emotion   **Purified Emotion**

VI. The work of purifying the emotions parallels the clearing of the chakras and holograms. The purified emotions strengthen our soul connection and help us access the higher self.

Now we have some perspective. We can see which subpersonality is involved in the drama and have some ideas about how this subpersonality allows her/himself to get involved in jealousy or fear of loss.

The path to healing here is two-fold. First we acknowledge the neediness of the subpersonality and design ways to nourish this part of our self. We can't expect anyone else to do this for us. It doesn't work that way. This will, eventually, bring the subpersonality up to a balanced and mature place. The second part of the healing is to send in a different subpersonality to facilitate our extraction from the drama. This will allow us to enter negative situations and experience the feeling but not harbor it in the astral hologram. We don't get involved or sucked into the situation. We feel jealousy or fear, acknowledge it and decide it doesn't belong in our energy field. We need the expertise and expanded view of the director to facilitate this. What we are doing in this experience is cultivating non-attachment. Healing the neediness puts us in a place of balance with what our needs are.

We will repeat this exercise until jealousy and fear come and go in an instant, barely entering our consciousness. This takes some practice. The desired result is rootedness in the earthly experience without being attached to it. The jealousy and fear of loss cause us to live in a state of stress which overworks the adrenal glands. Many of us live with higher than normal steady-state levels of adrenaline and cannot get our muscles into a relaxed state, even while sleeping. This work of non-attachment will help us relax our physical hologram and begin healing the body of the effects of stress.

Desire. The work with desire, which proceeds in the same manner, is about healing our senses and bringing them into a place of balance. It is about feeling good naturally, without the stimulation we have become addicted to. We have done a lot of work around addiction in the West and should be ready to begin removing the emotional aspects from the astral hologram at this point. Hopefully, we have made some major lifestyle changes and are less influenced by the media and advertising, movies and television dramas. As we use our actors and directors to decipher our involvement in desire by calling the work in, we will be able to identify the subpersonalities that need healing and how to do it. It is good that we have done a fair amount of groundwork with this chakra because it is the hotbed of emotion and drama. As a society, we are spoon-fed sensory stimulation and these patterns are difficult to break.

As we call the work in with our intent, we will need to take one sense at a time and really look at where we are with it. Let's take sight for our example. Which subpersonality has been dressing us, buying our clothes? Is this out of control or balanced? How much visual stimulation do we invite around us and which subpersonality is responsible for that. A balanced sight sense is exemplified Zen. Our lifestyle is simple, our dwelling reflects a clarity and simplicity with artful placement of beautiful objects. We are not trying to make statements. Our dress is simple, of natural fiber, easily to care for and not excessive. It compliments our body without calling attention. We become more a part of nature, a reflection of balance. By calling in alternative subpersonalities with this sense, we can begin to curb excess and see ourselves more as spirits. Eventually, while doing this work, we will have less of a need for adornment and variety. People around us will never notice what we wear but will bask in the energy of an opened heart.

So we work with each sense in this way, practicing mindfulness - the art of paying attention. It is a good time to get the director involved in our lifestyle changes, inviting in some real perspective. What is our diet doing to the holographic field? What are we getting from our exercise routine or lack of it? We can fine tune this process by calling in the director. This is a good place to mention that the deprivation model of transformation does more harm than good. Our lifestyle modifications have a timing all their own, and we will develop our intuitive sense of knowing when a particular change is appropriate.

The glands and organs associated with this chakra are the reproductive organs and ovaries or testes. Bringing balance in our desires will reflect in a healthy attitude towards sexuality and reproduction. We correct the imbalances in hormone levels in this process, smoothing out our moods and menstrual cycles and bringing our sexual desire level into harmony. Our dramas around desire are usually of great interest to us and are closely tied to the emotional work around jealousy and envy which we have already healed. This will make the work go more smoothly but it is never easy work since those who we call in to help us are generally very close to us.

It is surprising how much resistance to change prevails in our society. When we do not grow together with our partners and friends, it is hard to let go and move on. If we and those close to us have invested heavily in the status quo, this work will undoubtedly rock the boat. It is especially important to let the director do the work here and pull the emotionally unstable subpersonalities out of it. We can be working on their healing and maturation in other ways while the director sends in more stable subpersonalities to do the acting. The director sees the bigger picture and by withdrawing the desire emotion, can facilitate change without risk to the hologram. In new relationships, the lack of fear and desire will call in balance and growth.

Anger. Anger is the major work of the solar plexus chakra. Our astral body is tied in knots with anger and it grips us right down to the physical in the solar area. If we have been working on anger issues during our physical and etheric healing, what we are left with are lingering connections to the South and West and raw feelings of anger which still torque us out completely. For some of us, anger is our weak rung, the trigger that sets off a part of us that we usually end up hating. Why do we do it? Again, we need to isolate the subpersonality who is generally responsible for this one. Also, if we haven't determined it yet, we need to get clear about whether we withhold anger, explode with it or are pretty well balanced. We may need to go back to the bomb factory to get a handle on this, then call in some assistance, some drama, and see which subpersonality goes out there to deal with it.

How do we feel when Spike explodes? What happens when Cloe or Julia get into the act? What does our physical body tell us about the way we handle anger? We may feel fire inside, rising to our heart and head or over to our stomachs to make us sick. We get a cold sort of sick feeling in the pit of our stomach which may link it with an underlying fear issue. What does the dramatic encounter make us do? Do we switch subpersonalities from Spike to our impulsive Cloe who runs out to buy a new outfit or a new gadget to make us feel better?

This pulls the energy down to the sacral chakra and feeds the *ukhupacha* that way. Does our anger cause us to lash out and hurt people because we don't trust them? This is pure solar plexus chakra experience. The creatures of the *ukhupacha* love it. It is direct feeding and it stirs up more emotional drama for them to eat. We need to experience these feelings to know what anger does to us. We need to observe the behavior of our subpersonalities to determine who is out of control. This can be a subpersonality in need of nurturing attention or a subpersonality who has been running the show, the principal actor most of our lives.

To heal our astral hologram, we call in the director again and get a grip on the drama. We know who we are sending into the bomb factory and can experiment with alternative subpersonalities. How do they handle the situation? Our dominant subpersonality will be subdued if we give it other tasks to perform, like organizing projects or routine bookkeeping. If we keep it out of crisis situations while we learn to exercise our directing skill, it will eventually balance itself. If we cannot express our anger, we will need to nurture this repressed subpersonality, allowing expression in healthy ways. In the meantime, we can send someone competent out to do the acting, perhaps a teacher or healer subpersonality.

It is difficult to disengage from anger related drama, but, with persistence, we will begin to see through the illusions it creates and find a place of peace and trust within ourselves. Getting in touch with this will save our digestive tract and bring the liver and gall bladder into a balanced place. The pancreas, gland of this chakra, can find the healthy rhythm or secretion necessary for optimal metabolism. This will ease up the stress on the heart and digestive tract. Eventually, we will gain so much skill with the directing that the least little hint of an anger situation will cue the director via an impulse in the solar area. The entire thing will be avoided. We will still know anger as a normal human emotion, but it will not throw us off balance.

Greed. Coming into a place of observation with our greedy subpersonalities should be relatively easy if we have cleared the garbage generate by the first three negative emotions from our astral hologram. It will also be a great assistance to us when we begin doing the work of the heart in the East. When we call in the drama around

of our earthly lives is lifted for us. The process of becoming humble is one of lifting the illusion while still in the earthly realms.

Ignorance. The astral hologram is clearing as we arrive at the brow chakra. In fact, there isn't a lot of drama around ignorance until we begin the spiritual quest and summon the drama to us. The drama will be hosted by those who think we are crazy, certain we are in a cult of some kind, who question our beliefs and cause us to question what we are doing. Some of the dramas will be associated with the family and social nuclei while the rest will be interpersonal challenges from others walking our path. When we get a little spiritual work done, the vultures begin landing, wanting what we have. It can put us in really uncomfortable positions unless we can find a good subpersonality to handle the job. The director will undoubtedly chose the subpersonality with the most maturity and healing capabilities.

The further we walk on a path the more we invest in it. Unfortunately, we can get in some pretty stuck places if greed and pride get in the way. We need that open heart and sense of humility to get up to the higher center work. Until we arrive there, we will be plagued with the challenges of ignorance. If we can begin to look at the other actors on the stage as gifts, mirrors of our own insecurities, some real headway can be made. It is noteworthy that the brow chakra is associated with the pituitary/hypothalamus complex, the major gland regulatory center of the body. It holds the body's knowledge while the brow chakra and mental-3 hologram hold the key to true wisdom and unlock the gate to the spirit connection through the crown. As we complete the cleansing of the last negative emotion from the astral hologram, our director graduates from training and begins to put us in touch with trust and peace.

CULTIVATING TRUST

Eventually we will wonder who the director is and what is really going on with the subpersonalities. Our director reaches a high level of expertise as the subpersonalities gain more and more balance and maturity. We need to be actively involved in this process. We might even picture our subpersonalities as having definite directions in the medicine wheel. The director sends them out to do our work and as the director engages the spiritual path more and more, the actors facilitate the clearing of the fields by engaging the drama in a balanced and productive way. This accesses the feeling center at the solar plexus and opens doors to true intuition.

What is happening to us is the integration of personality, the realization of each subpersonality's true potential and balancing them with each other. It is like post-graduate method acting. It is really making the most of the personalities we have chosen to have. Who is the director? The director is who we really are, a kind of higher self that, until now, has been just a friendly reminder voice. The director sends out the subpersonalities to do the work based on the big picture of the soul life. The director accesses our superconscious self. Now we can see that the North direction work is an essential part of becoming who we really are. It also loosens the grip which the *ukhupacha* has on our lives. That is why the solar plexus is the center of personal power. The North is all about getting in touch with the real us. We can go through an entire incarnation here without knowing who we are. We can also see now why we cannot turn around from this place and re-enter the darkness.

It is at this stage of the work that we quit feeding the creatures of *ukhupacha* emotion, their preferred nourishment, and they begin letting up on us. The shift in our lives is so noticeable to those around us that they begin asking us questions about what we are doing. That is why the North is said to be the home of the sage and master, the teacher. The best way to understand what you have been through is to help others find their own path. It is very rewarding to be engaged in service work. It helps to cultivate the trust that must replace the anger which had lodged in and blocked the solar plexus chakra. If we cannot trust another, it is most likely that we do not trust ourselves. If we can truly become the director, trusting ourselves comes naturally. When we manifest trust in our astral hologram, trust builds in interpersonal relationships and an aura of peace envelops us. It is a nice finish for a lot of hard work.

After completing this work, we can be very clear about emotion as it enters our field. If we lose a loved one, we can feel and express our grief as a heaviness, a pain and sorrow in the lung area.

We allow ourselves to feel the grief for it is a very special human gift to do that. But we do not harbor it. We let it go in good time, clearing our fields of it as we allow the soul of our loved one to continue on its way. There are no real partings for the intent of our love permeates all dimensions and realities and we remain always connected. Usually when our loved ones pass over, we are grieving for ourselves, for our own loss. If we have walked this medicine path, we are past the suffering, violence and emotion and feel a sweet sort of grief for our own inability to communicate and perceive the other side.

EMBRACING *WAKA*

Our journey into the North has brought us into the feminine, *waka*. We may be struggling with the integration of our feminine side for years to come, but we have made the moves to bring ourselves into balance. With trust, we have added a soft gentleness to our lives and we are learning to be of service to others who are searching for meaning in their lives. The complete integration of the duality is a realization of human potential. Within the confines of what we consider the self, this is as far as we can go. Further work will lead us outside our selves to co-create with others and outside the human experience to work in the spirit. We have made our own journey to Lake Titicaca. It may not have seemed like much fun at the time, but once the work is done its significance hits us. This is a major achievement. The integration of personality balances the ego which is expanding like a cosmic egg around us. It is growing out into the mental holograms where it will assist in the full cleansing of M-1 through M-3. With this expansion comes increasing power and knowledge, the characteristics of the shamanic path. The tendency towards arrogance, aloofness, is offset by the true feeling of trust and peace that we have cultivated, so we aren't as difficult to get along with as our warrior.

Personal power is about knowing who we are. Acknowledging that we are male and female, the director instead of the actors, and a server rather than a doer are all important steps towards acquiring personal power. It puts us in a place where we can begin calling destiny into our lives with pure intent. In particular, we can call in the careers which will allow us to fulfill the purpose of our soul. With the North work, things really begin to happen for us and we will have accelerated this with any sincere acts of surrender in the West. We have the ability, no, the duty, to call into our lives what we need to fulfill our purpose. And we don't really have to be in touch with that purpose yet to do it. The more we surrender to the life of the soul, the fewer choices we will have to make. Everything starts falling into place. Following the soul's path is following the bliss. Once connected, it will be anything but boring, and never painful. The pain is in the *ukhupacha* and we are freeing ourselves of its grasp. Our dice are really getting light now and we almost never cringe when we throw them.

We can see that this path looks like no other wisdom path for it asks us to develop ego even as we free ourselves from the shadow side of life. We will work with the power and knowledge by reaching outside the ego, going beyond the human experience. As long as we are "in" ego, we are serving ourselves. If we can step beyond it, we can serve the Source, fulfilling the purpose of our soul by sacrificing our ego. Our kundalini is building through the holograms rather than rocketing up the spine. Our energetic shifts are subtle and will not harm us physically. We will come by our visions naturally as we master the energy of each holographic field. Coming into vision without the mastery of the energetic fields greatly diminishes the usefulness of the gift.

MANIFESTING *LLANKAY*

We have come from South to North around the medicine wheel, moving up the base, sacral and solar chakras and out through the physical, etheric and astral holographic bodies with our clearing. In the process, we have experienced tremendous growth and increased awareness, consciousness. Yet, we are still within the earthly realms of *llankay*, the manifestation of will. The work of the North completes the healing of the will centers and gives us the grounding and personal power to manifest in our lives. For the shaman, this is the only way to begin this journey. Will is the power piece, the earth connection, and it fortifies our reason for being here, our soul mission. It allows us to get things done.

Shamans are not contemplative. They bring spirit into action by mastering all parts of the *kintui*. This is the gift of shamanism, to connect us to the earth. Our mission on earth requires that we connect fully with the spirits of nature, that we master this realm and serve the Source with this mastery. We master the natural by engaging the human experience, raising our consciousness as we develop a more symbiotic relationship with the *ukhupacha*. We become *Huascar Inca*, and guard our own gates. After we have mastered the *llankay*, we are in a good place to work with *munay*, loving power, as we begin to open our hearts. All other wisdom paths attempt to work from the higher centers down and do not make the connection with the earth. In fact, it is often considered unwholesome to do so. It is too 'ungodly' for a spiritual path. These wisdom cultures serve the Source in a different way and the earth needs both at this time. With the loss of indigenous culture, there are fewer people holding the earthy vibrations and the planet is de-stabilizing. Part of the shamanic path is to anchor in the *llankay*, listen to the earth, and steward her future. Our work is out in the world, manifesting a new reality. To do this, we need the next step, *munay*. Using the power of our purified *llankay*, we will be able to manifest the *munay* needed for global healing.

Shamanism has not been accepted as a spiritual path because we have been hesitant to fully embrace the shadow and step out of the *ukhupacha*. We have done well at acknowledging that it exists but, in our desire to get on with more lofty spiritual pursuits, have closed the door to the work of *llankay*. This is denial. We are experts at denying that which we fear. This perpetuates the *ukhupacha* cycle pulling us back into the South. As a result, our society as been locked in the manifestation mode for some time. We pull our mental activity down into the first three chakras and have built our reality out of heavy vibrations. We are great at manifesting, creating things from matter. We know how to take things from the earth and turn them into useful tools. We do not know how to give things to the earth that are useful to her. This is true *llankay* and we are afraid of it. What we are doing is creating illusion.

After we have cleared the first three centers and their holograms, we are in a place to understand true *llankay*. Our rituals take us out into nature not only for our healing but for the earth's. We can begin to feel the energies of the rivers and lakes, the different plants and stones, and we cease frightening or being frightened by the wild things in the woods. Nature responds to our embracing of *waka* by embracing us. This is a softening process that is already working on our heart chakra and will support us throughout the East direction.

Trust and peace, the hard-won rewards of our journey through emotion, are reflected in a brightness in our eyes. This is intensified by being in nature, the breathwork practice and our aerobic exercise. We are healing ourselves at a cellular level and it is reflected in the eyes and the glow of our skin. When we are in the deeply introspective parts of our work, this brightness goes within, only to re-emerge upon the completion of the processing with greater intensity. Others are drawn to us, pulled by our holographic energies, and take comfort just being with us. Our energies are helping to balance their energies. What is happening also is the manifestation of trust and peace.

Again, our vibration makes a subtle shift as our awareness enters the astral hologram. We are mastering our own holograms by learning how to shift our consciousness from one to another while sensing the vibrational shifts. It is crude at this stage, but heartening. We can literally look out of the eyes of the physical, etheric or astral body at this point. No wonder the eyes, themselves, reflect our new level of awareness.

We have, no doubt, acquired a whole new set of friends and our relationships with old friends and family have shifted into healthier places. Some friends have fallen by the wayside as we have moved forward on our path. They are watching from a distance. Those who serve the *ukhupacha* with negative emotion by stirring up drama are no longer able to tolerate our presence. We no longer caretake but seek out ways in which to serve, to teach, to enlighten others. We are cultivating wisdom, the gift of the North, and may also go back to school to pick up additional skills. We are homing in on those careers of destiny and are using intuition to guide us.

Intuition is also associated with the solar plexus chakra. It is that feeling center we were talking about previously. When we have really turned our negative emotions into the positive or purified emotions, we begin to activate that center so that intuition doesn't come in flashes but is part of our everyday life. It expands our feeling center and shifts our reality beyond illusion. We will continue to cultivate intuition as we journey throughout the *hanaqpacha* but acknowledge its awakening at this point in our journey.

Opening of this feeling center is a good focus for our meditations at this point. Since we are working with emotion, we can exercise feeling in meditation and in nature to assist us. The North direction is energized by the element of fire, hence the solar chakra, fire of the sun, and the dragon archetype, with fiery nostrils. Our rituals center around fire and we find comfort in candles on our altar and around our house. We take ourselves to the fire and bring it into our chakras and as we cleanse the astral hologram, we clearly begin to feel that the energies of our body match those of fire. With our intent, the fire spirits come and make the fire friendly and we are able to put our hands directly into it and draw it to us. This is good for we are hungry for this energy.

This carries over into our eating habits as we find ourselves seeking out foods that contain more fire, more sunlight trapped within. Our diets become much more plant-oriented and we find ways to obtain protein from plants, such as grain and bean combinations, nuts, seeds and so forth. Eating becomes an adventure in mindfulness, and needless to say, we don't find ourselves in fast food restaurants. By this time, we are also realizing that it makes us pretty sick to go to shopping malls and sporting events where large numbers of people and high degrees of visual stimulation prevail. Television, abrasive music, and emotional drama have fallen by the wayside, too.

Moving through the emotional work brings us beyond the point of being sucked into the glamour aspects of the spiritual path. Because we have cleared and anchored the *llankay*, the intuitive center is opening, and we are not easily manipulated by spiritual emotionalism. We can even feel the effects of it twirling around in our solar plexus. Our awareness is such that we simply acknowledge what it can do and twirl it right back out there with our intent. This is personal power. When we experience something manipulative it makes us feel icky. That is the "feel" signal for manipulation and control - a tug in the solar plexus area. Since we can really "feel" it now, we can just say no. This is true not only of spiritual manipulation, but all forms of control.

At this stage of the path we seem to attract spiritual emotionalism to help us exercise our personal power and to assist us in opening the feeling centers. We are so familiar with the *ukhupacha* that the everyday control dramas just don't do it for us anymore. We need the subtle spiritual dramas to fine-tune our skills. Needless to say, with our subpersonalities coming under the wisdom of our director and our consciousness raising once again, we no longer engage in manipulation ourselves.

It is clear now why the soft approach to spiritual awakening isn't what this path is about. It is a journey of individual duration and content. To hold the belief that we can attain enlightenment on earth without the hard work and pain of healing our lives is delusion. Even those who have had near death experiences must heal their lives. However, they have been gifted a journey beyond the *ukhupacha* which motivates them to swiftly complete the work. Until we have done the work and are clear of it ourselves, we must believe that it is illusion that we can move beyond it. With the completion of the *llankay*, we invite the energy of *waka*, of internal balance, into our lives and begin the work of opening our hearts to unconditional love and compassion.

8

EAST:
CRITIC

From our place of emotional clarity, we begin to see life as it truly is, and it rocks our world. If our intention is to come into the East and open our hearts, we will have to replace dysfunctional systems with new paradigms. We need to become fully empowered human beings if our intent is to bring spirit within us. It begins with the heart work, which opens the door to spirit. Spirit cannot be sustained with paradigms based on good and evil for spirit does not make those distinctions. Spirit is the Source within us and the Source created all things for a reason. We have come a long way with the *ukhupacha* and are beginning to recognize that it is our own limited vision that sees it as shadow. Now that we are beginning to transform shadow into light, we are able to move with the Tao, yin and yang.

We will have to look at the way we make choices. This involves two big pieces of work. First we must look at the system of hierarchy which our society has created to sustain the good-evil paradigm. It robs us of our personal power and traps us in a state of need. That fosters the second part of our work which is centered around selfishness and greed. We are made to believe that the object of life is to be successful, and that to achieve success we must climb the ladders of hierarchy. Our hearts won't open while we are enmeshed in these systems. We are engaging the work of judgment becoming non-judgment, and it is difficult even to conceptualize an outcome. This is higher-level surrender work than what we are used to, but we've been through basic training, so it is not an impossible task at all. There are many gifts in the East awaiting those of us who choose to free ourselves from the last gripping hold of the *ukhupacha*.

We have, in the first three directions of the medicine wheel, cleared the physical to astral fields and come into *llankay*, the will aspect of *kintui*. When the work of clearing is truly complete, the will is a great tool for us. But, if we stop at this point, it can be used in greed and self-service. We literally sell-out to the creatures of the *ukhupacha*, and even though we have done a lot of self-healing work, we can use the will in a harmful way. That is why the work of the East is so important. We need *munay*, loving power, to exercise the will in an impeccable way that serves the Source.

"JUDGE NOT, LEST YOU BE JUDGED"

Getting clear of the drama, moving past emotion, changes our lives forever. It is so empowering that there is a temptation to stay in the North and bask in personal power awhile, maybe a long while. Movement into the East is intentional and so is the work we do here. If our intent is clear about doing the work, it was probably already presenting itself to us in the North. If we have moved into any teaching work that involves integration of the spiritual path, we open ourselves to an enormous amount of criticism from others. No other form of teaching gets the critics as riled up as personal growth and spirituality.

When we consider it, there is no formalized education for wisdom seekers. Because the movement towards spirituality is pretty intense in our society now, we find ourselves supporting whatever we believe in at the moment, and we get defensive if someone disagrees with us. We are also fickle. We are experiencing the trial and error formation stage of a new wisdom culture. It's like going into the fast food center at a major mall and being bombarded by fifty different choices for our spiritual diet. Today we try Zen, tomorrow we'll find our star connection. In between, we see psychics and wear a lot of beads and feathers. Whatever we are into at the moment gets our support and we bash everything else. This is all about judgment.

If we do get hold of some wisdom and begin to share it with others, we will be criticized and challenged. Sometimes it may feel like we are running for president and our entire lives are up for review. This powerful need to criticize is a very interesting phenomenon in our society arising from that ingrained belief that we must be perfect. Since we obviously are not, we expect others to be perfect instead, especially those we want to guide us (give our power to). In other words, we want them to do the perfect part for us so we can continue to feed our self-interest. We can get so caught up in our criticism of others that we destroy their lives. If we are on the receiving end, our lives will be destroyed unless we destroy our lives first, by doing the work of the East. To get to a place of clarity in our lives, where judgment does not affect us, we must first do our own work around it. It makes perfect sense, when we call in this energy, that the first thing that happens is judgment against us. We're off and running.

And what do we do? Call in the director. And the place to start? At home. We begin by listening to the dialogue going on between our own subpersonalities. Now that they have quit instigating emotional drama, there is the realization that, as a result, they regard the drama from a place of ego. When criticism is leveled against us, the subpersonalities take it personally and sling mud right back at the offender. It's an ego exercise which is launched from emotion, most always anger. Let's remember that anger has not vanished, but that we have learned to release it, not let it control us. We release the anger by mudslinging. What is really going on? We have called in our critics to help us with our work. They are mirrors of our own opinions. We need to listen carefully to them and observe their behavior. This can only be done from the director's position. If our director has really taken the work seriously there has been the realization that the directing is done outside of ego. The director is accessing the higher center, outside our "self", and even though we don't know how to bring that aspect of who we are into focus, or even into this reality, it is a piece of our future which can work for us now. This is the perspective we need to do the East work.

We look in the mirrors. Remember Cloe? Cloe is out there minding her own business, teaching a few people how to help themselves, when she is attacked. It isn't a direct attack, of course, that would be too easy. She hears, through a friend, that a former colleague is spreading a rumor that she is sexually promiscuous. Cloe is shocked. Her first reaction is to call the person up and confront them. That is the old Cloe reacting, the Cloe who moved from gossiping about them in return to direct confrontation. But she has grown some through the North work and decides to hold off a bit and do some work around it. She acknowledges that this person knew her before she started to walk the *kaypacha* medicine wheel. She reasons that this person is likely jealous of the work she has done because she is in a clear place emotionally and word gets around fast. Her third realization is that in the life she has let go of, in the past she has released, she did not understand anything about having a meaningful relationship and, in her search for herself, did have quite a few. Cloe has come a long way. She asks the director for assistance.

The director stretches Cloe further. It is true that she had quite a few relationships which were released during her South and West work. She has changed her life and is no longer looking for someone to take care of her. Why are they coming up again, in this way? This doesn't have anything to do with the relationships, neediness, or being promiscuous. The director asks Cloe to look in the mirror. Mirror? Her former colleague is the mirror. Now Cloe has her hands full. The director asks her to go back through her life again and remember the many times that she had gossiped about others. She remembers the unkind things she said, the confidences she broke, and a few borderline malicious pieces of gossip she instigated or passed along. Ouch! What does she do with this?

The director asks Cloe to initiate work around forgiveness. First, she is to forgive the present offender. This immediately takes the energy out of the character assault and gives it back to her former colleague. It's a kind of mental plane martial art and it defuses the entire situation. The colleague doesn't need to know anything about it either. Next, Cloe performs little rituals forgiving anyone else who has ever said anything unkind about her. Often times we don't even need to hear the gossip for it to be cluttering our M-1 holograms, the level of emotional ego.

The second part of Cloe's work requires that she take the memories of hurting others which had already come up for her and perform meaningful ritual, asking them to forgive her. She cuts out little red hearts and puts their names on them, focusing on the issues for which she wishes forgiveness. She imagines that even if what she had said was true at the time, each person has had as much time as she has had to do their work as well. She now knows that it was inappropriate not only to share opinions of others but to <u>have</u> opinions of others. How could she have known what is at the core of their being, then or now. She cluttered their M-1 holograms and is asking for that clutter to be returned so that she can dispose of it in a loving way. She draws the clutter to her with intent. She puts the little hearts in a basket on her altar and sends the people love often. An amazing thing happens. As soon as she clears a few memories, more memories surface with more opportunities for forgiveness. She continues until the memories cease.

This is a powerful exercise in forgiveness and she is an expert when it is completed. She is also more fully potentialized as a subpersonality. Each one of these exercises must be done from a place of unconditional love, with no expectation of benefit from the outside. Each exercise pries the heart open a little further. Cloe realizes that her past really is gone and can no longer harm her, that anyone who assaults her character is only hurting themselves and those they involve in the assault. She holds them in her heart, no matter what they say. Furthermore she regards them as a gift to help her see herself more clearly. Eventually, when she feels very clear about the work, Cloe has a little ceremony and burns the red hearts. She takes the ashes to her favorite hilltop on a windy day and asks the wind, the heart chakra element, to disperse them. She calls in *munay* for herself.

This is just the beginning of the work as each of our subpersonalities is challenged in the way appropriate for them. There are several things happening at once here. Each subpersonality is in a tremendous growth situation, rapidly potentializing and integrating the aspects of ego. At the same time, the emotional aspects of the ego are being met and released. We are growing away from reaction and with the expertise of the director are coming more into an intellectual reaction to the drama. The third thing happening is the gradual opening of the heart which really stabilizes trust and peace, gifts of the North.

When we are involved in the work of forgiveness it can be overwhelming, but we find ourselves becoming very dedicated to the process because it feels good and makes sense. What we don't want to miss is the opportunity to forgive ourselves. We have not been perfect and it's okay. We were not born on mountain tops in Q'ero like Inkari. We decided to do this the hard way, to learn and grow from the earthly experience. Often, we have not had an appreciation of ourselves. Now we are changing so rapidly it is hard to know what to appreciate. When we started this work we were a group of subpersonalities who not only denied each other, but were imbalanced, argumentative, and immature. Now that we are becoming integrated, we have more of a sense of what self might be. Yet something is urging us forward, hinting to us that we might be much more than we think we are. So maybe we are learning to be flexible in the way we think about ourselves and, like kaleidoscopes constantly changing, we appreciate our own growth and diversity. We are beginning to cultivate self-love.

SYSTEM BUSTING THE HIERARCHY

This is a great place to be - no longer projecting outcomes because we finally understand that the outcome isn't nearly as important as the process. From this vantage point, we can proceed further with the East work and look at the whole concept of choices. We are taught that to make a choice is to decide between two or more things based on what we might think the outcome or benefit will be. It implies that one outcome is better than others and that the things we decide against are not as good as that which we choose. Says who? This is judgment, our need to control the outcome. With respect to the life of the soul, such choices are being made in complete ignorance. These are the *ukhupacha* exercises that lock us into discrimination, comparison and criticism. It is that hierarchical system that we were born into and perpetuate every day of our lives.

How do we bust this system? We'd like to reclaim this aspect of our personal power, but how do we do it? Instead of storming the gates of Troy, we need to see that there are no gates. It's an illusion. We have created hierarchy out of nothing and we can just as easily destroy it. What limits us is our concepts of time and space. If we believe in linear time, we are going to project outcome. If, instead, we give ourselves to the cyclical patterns of nature, polychronic time, we will understand the meaning of "what goes around, comes around". There is a time, a reason, and a season for everything. If we do what feels right at the moment, coming from the true feeling center, it is never a wrong choice. There may be a gift, a great lesson, in adversity. Who are we to limit our lives and experiences because we fear making a mistake, not being perfect? Bringing choice into the feeling center anchors it in the *kaypacha*. Here, it is based not on judgment and opinion but on discernment, feeling what is right for each of us.

This idea of transforming choice, of side-stepping that input of rational thinking based on ingrained belief systems, requires an act of surrender. It requires that we surrender to what is our higher purpose, the goal of our soul, and trust that our soul, in touch with the Source, will know what to do. It's awesome surrender. We are not in touch with our souls at this point, so it is an act of faith, faith in our self and in our path. This is how a baby sister eagle takes her first flight from the nest. Her wings just seem to know what to do next.

If we can implement this in our lives, it brings us into true freedom. We eliminate a complex layer of stress and what is called in is exactly what we need for our growth. Its not like we're novices at this either. We're in the East. We have already busted open our systems of co-dependency, addiction, suffering, violence and emotion. This is true empowerment. We have laid aside the judgment of others and those who judge us and now we are taking it to a new level, the infrastructure of our lives. Turning ourselves over to a higher purpose just does not support making comparisons. What would we imagine we are doing in comparing our soul to someone else's? How ridiculous. We don't even know what a soul is, but we have an idea that it is light and energy and love vibration. When we are out there riding the wave, how could we be different from the next soul? We're all the same "stuff". It is when we descend into matter, into the *ukhupacha* that we start to see differences, begin discriminating, because the veil of illusion drops before us. Elitism has no place in the medicine wheel. On the other hand, discernment is something we must cultivate.

This idea of polychronic time makes a lot of sense, too. If we believe that time is circular it means that we can live for the seven generations to come at the same time we live for the seven that have been. In this way, we might go back at some "time" and repair the damage done to mother earth, to put all her minerals back in place, to clear her air, and reclaim the garden. We are locked into this dimension by the illusion we have created and are greatly limited by it. We will not be able to understand the possibilities unless we learn to bust systems in our own lives, a microcosm of the earth's existence. Then we can take our expertise out there to reconstruct the past and see into the future. Let's start breaking out of our limitations, right here and now.

Good and evil. First let's accept that there are positive and negative things going on all the time. Sometimes we call the negative into our lives to learn from it. That does not mean it is evil. In fact, it is good if we learn from it, isn't it? There it goes, yin becoming yang right before our eyes. This means we can be losers and still be winners, winners and really lose. The only thing we don't want to be is asleep, for then we cease moving with the Tao, the yin-yang, and we are no longer in the game. It doesn't mean that we try to "fix" the negative people who have helped us do our work. We let them become whatever they will become. We send them on their way with acts of forgiveness and unconditional love. If we do not learn to do this, we will be lost in this hall of mirrors forever.

Family nucleus. We have to start system busting in small ways and work ourselves up to the big systems. Let's begin with the family nucleus. If we have been doing our work with good intent, the control dramas at home have been eliminated and everyone is waiting for the next ax to fall. It is, of course, the ax of hierarchy, system busting the pecking order. Visions of children running the home pass before us as we try to calm ourselves and look to the East.

We see a family sitting in a circle with a talking stick. They are having a family meeting. They are discussing what has happened over the week, how they feel about it and what they would like to do next. Each person, little and big, gets an opportunity to speak their truth, to be heard, without interruption. The children learn to express feelings, are honored for speaking their truth and for being heard and at the same time they learn to sit in respectful silence listening to the voices of others. It is a powerful tool and children love it. The stick itself can be made as a family project. Good intent is put into every part of it. The parents still make the major decisions for the family, trying to impart the larger picture in their speaking, but they know how the children feel and take that into consideration. The children don't have to act out trying to be heard or empowered and they are not as apt to interrupt others when they speak. Who could argue with any of this? Often the parents will want to take the children's considerations very much to heart and do what they would like. Family rules can be made in this way and since the children helped to make them, they have an investment in keeping them. Crisis situations can be handled without chaos. The object, overall, is to activate the feeling center in all family members and learn to make decisions from the heart.

When these children go out into the world, they will not accept the dominant systems of our culture and things will begin to change. If we can further support the work at home with a similar school environment, they will not receive mixed messages about adulthood. We may have to create our own schools to do this. Imagine the kind of world we could live in if understanding how the wind speaks had a value equal to that of mathematical theorems. This is system busting at its best.

And what starts in the home will begin influencing our lives everywhere. Our children will begin teaching their friends and teachers and they will come to us asking questions. This is grass roots wisdom coming into a culture badly in need. We will support the children with adolescent rites of passage into adulthood, so that they can leave childhood behind in a defined and empowered way. We can find support outside our own homes to share children with other adults, a small step towards community child rearing, the great big system buster. When we hear of another parent having problems we make the suggestion of the stick, telling them it really worked in our family. The talking stick is an appealing tool because it is based on Native American ideas of democracy, the very ideas which inspired our founding fathers. We have been here long enough to be integrating the wisdom that dwells in this land. It is no mistake that we long for that knowledge. We just need to learn now to listen to the wind ourselves.

System busting our lives. Right now, we need to move, with this work, in and out of the reality of our culture. We can learn to be invisible in future work. It means giving up the notion of ever "being" anyone, of investing in hierarchy, and it may not be for everyone. Right now, we need to look for small ways to break the systems we are trapped within. The East is the place of vision and it is a good time to tap into our inner wisdom. Opening our hearts means we can no longer live with hypocrisy, criticism, greed and self-service. That pretty much means we can't live in our culture. We have probably already said our good-byes to organized religion, and aren't plugged into any of the mind-control systems of our culture. We are really conscious now and are looking for ways to support our spirituality in our work and play. Moving past judgment means we no longer criticize that which seems intolerable to us but look, rather, at what seems intolerable within. This path is getting a lot narrower than it originally looked. It looks narrow because it is nearing a point of expansion but we must leave behind the last of our baggage to get through the gate.

Let's think again about how we identify ourselves. It is through these subpersonalities and the way they project us to the world, the "I think", in thought and action, part of ourselves. We imagine that we are these subpersonalities. Now we know that there is someone in us that has the world view, a perspective we never had before, and that is the director. We have been shifting our identity as we potentialize our subpersonalities. We are meeting the world more and more as the director, speaking and acting through the subpersonalities. The more potentialized the subpersonalities get, the more integrated the personality. To let go of judgment, opinion and criticism is not to become personality-less, but rather to become balanced within our personalities. We have tremendous individuation, utilizing that which is unique about us to the maximum good. At the same time, we operate from a place of personal power. We know who we are. We are a skillful director of unique, integrated personalities. We chose these personalities to assist us on our journey, not to control us and run our lives amuck. Finally, we feel like we may be in the drivers seat, or at least have the keys in hand. Our dice are no longer loaded against us and we are experiencing the results of the throw with an attitude of acceptance and surrender.

THE TRIBAL MIND

We have dematerialized our former values out of necessity. We have simplified our lives to accelerate our spiritual growth and we are getting very little support for what we are doing. What we need to begin working with is intent. Intent becomes our most useful tool, gathering power with each holographic clearing. We can call anything to us and the clearer we are, the more clearly we are heard. What we would like to call to us are the like-minded people with whom we can form a support system. So, we are busting systems and creating new ones to replace them, but this time they are not built on illusion and are kept flexible and free of judgment. We sit in circles with our talking stick and begin laying the foundations of a new reality. This is community, the call of the East, and with community intent we begin to shift into our destiny.

At first, we must call to us the small circles to support this work. This may already be in place for us. This is difficult work to do alone and working in a small community gives us the opportunity to exercise the opening of the heart. Perhaps our second step will be calling together enough people of like mind to begin the system busting steps of progressive schooling for the children and evolving new parenting paradigms. As a community, we may be more drawn to devising ways to survive in the larger community through co-creative enterprises, a healing center, a co-operative and restaurant, a pre-school or drop in center based on the medicine wheel. We may want to support the spiritual practices of movement, breathwork and meditation with a community. As community, we will find that our pooled talents will lead the way into these ventures. These activities will arouse the interest of others in the larger community and draw the right people to us. Our approach must be gentle, with great patience, open to seeing the initial changes as a flow of energy rather than startling material manifestations.

Care must be taken to enter the larger community with love and compassion, being almost invisible, to avoid backlash. System busting is frowned upon by the hierarchy. Within our enterprise we are careful to sit in circle leading from a council where every voice is heard. We share our ideas and dreams as collective vision. We are supporting a new way of life, and like a young tree, it is growing and blossoming in the center of chaos without anyone paying much attention until it is spread like an umbrella over the whole community. Those disenchanted with the hierarchy in their churches will be drawn to us because the learning is horizontal and we do not judge. Parents will be drawn to our teaching style because we do not pigeon-hole and cattle herd the children.

These are all acts of co-creation, intentional community. In the North, we embraced the duality within, and here in the East we go outside ourselves to co-create with others. This is vision in action and it will change the world. We can see now, from this vantage point, why it was so important to do the work of clearing our holograms and opening and stabilizing the *llankay*, the will, before coming into *munay*, or loving power. We have opened ourselves to something greater than ourselves with clarity and intent. The fear, anger, criticism and emotional drama are behind us and our hearts are opening as we engage in this work. When we sit in council, work, breath, and meditate together we begin supporting a new level of experience, the tribal mind. If we begin to share our dreams we will find that the dreamstate is very much involved in this also. We are, in our acts of co-creation, merging the mental holograms of the community and we begin to know what the collective mind thinks.

In aboriginal cultures the tribal mind was tended by the shamans. Now, we are all being asked to be shamans, to live in the tribal mind, expanded consciousness. We are being asked to cease living for ourselves and begin living for communities that steward the earth.

This is the vision of the East and the mission of mankind. It cannot be done without an opened heart and cleared holograms. We cannot bring our baggage into this place. It would not be tolerated in this system. We see that we have system busted to create new paradigms, new systems which support conscious living, which are more flexible and useful. And we will continue to bust these systems so we don't ever get stuck again. As we do further work, this collective mind will be strengthened and explored and becomes the vehicle for global transformation.

We will be drawn to live in community as well, to hold a resonance with the work that will support our journey into higher consciousness. These acts of co-creation are wonderful ways to begin exploring those possibilities and to fully open the heart chakra before community living is attempted. The combined talents of those forming these communities will ensure self-sufficiency. Tribes that come together in their gardens or farmlands bring the energy of consciousness into the food they eat, the medicines they prepare, and the beauty that surrounds them. To meditate in a meditation center is a start, to take it into the garden is to fulfill the dream of the earth. The spirits of nature will be called into our lives and vast areas of learning will open for us. A self-sufficient community holds a vibration, a resonance, that sustains its members. Those who must go out into the larger community to teach or work will regain their balance when they rejoin their tribe. The tribal mind goes with them on their journey and draws them safely back home.

Stewardship of the earth is the greater vision of the East. It is a tall order, especially for a culture that has supported just the opposite. Again, it can only be done from a fully conscious place. We have been like adolescents in our relationship with mother earth. She has been a patient mother waiting for us to grow up, to become adult, but her patience is now running short. The phoenix that lies within her, buried in the ashes of destruction, is about to undergo the final steps of transformation from this death. The wings of the phoenix will begin to beat and she will rise again to summon her destiny. We'd like to be in a good place when this happens. Fully conscious is where we would like to be. For to survive this transformation, this cosmic transmutation, mankind will be asked to transcend consciousness, to enter the *hanaqpacha*, the world of higher consciousness. All of the work we have done in the *kaypacha* medicine wheel is preparation to be open to this, not an end in itself.

We have, with the clarity gained doing this work, the power to move energy with intent. This must be done with impeccability, with absolute purity of intent. Anything less will bring us destruction. These are skills we need to practice in community, to support ourselves with the tribal mind while we learn to differentiate the energy we begin to move. At this point it is an exercise in good intent, and a way to access the feeling center and explore the power of pure emotion. All of this will grow if we chose to take this work further.

MUNAY

Unconditional love and compassion have been nourished from a place of growing self-love. Through acts of forgiveness we have come to clear our M-1 hologram and open our heart. This gives us access to *munay*, loving power. This aspect of the *kintui* builds upon the *llankay* or will aspect. We continue to open our feeling center in the solar plexus area while we are opening higher centers. We explore and develop the pure emotions there and learn to differentiate feelings from thoughts about how we feel. Opening the heart center helps us stabilize the will aspect of *kintui*. The loving power is the guide for the right use of will. Without the open heart, our will center and feeling center can be used to support greed, arrogance and ignorance, the negative emotions of the higher centers, all parts of ego and false identity.

The work of the heart, the East, is to transform greed into unconditional love. Our acts of forgiveness and unconditional love empower us by clearing our fields and drawing our displaced energy back into our own field. We can see that having trust in place in the solar center greatly facilitates this, as does the non-attachment and mindfulness cultivated in the lower centers. This is an ongoing process. To think we are ever done is to abandon the process. Done is an outcome.

Circles have no beginnings or endings, but they can spiral upward towards the Source. So working with greed is working around the concept of service. When we are unconscious, we are serving the creatures of the *ukhupacha*. When we wake up, we begin serving ourselves and our own potential. At some point, if we are to seek higher consciousness, we must shift the service to the community. This is preparation for fully shifting to service for the Source, the soul's purpose. The East, opening the heart, is very much about shifting consciousness to the community, the tribal mind. As we begin to serve others, we learn that love supports us in a way that self-service and greed could not. We are encouraged to open our hearts further and completely abandon self-service. It is another big surrender, but it is built on a firm foundation, the trust and empowerment of *llankay*. All of this work is preparation to pass through the narrow gate to meet our soul. We will never pass through that gate unless we have cleared the first four holograms, opening the feeling center and the heart center, fulfilling the first two aspects of *kintui*. There is no way to cheat, talk our way through the gate, or fly over the top. It simply will not happen that way as long as we inhabit our bodies and live on the earth. We must do the work of preparing the temple before we invite the holy spirit to dwell within.

We have learned to use our intent to call in and support community, the tribal mind. When we are in this pure place of the heart we can, like Inkari, call in the loving human being who will find a place within our hearts. Inkari and Qoyari called each other in an act of co-creation. We are now in a place of such clarity that we can call in another who is also this clear. These relationships are not karmic, have no suffering, violence, emotionalism, or judgment. Here is the possibility to bring the divine vibration into relationship, to love within the holograms and co-create as partners in community. This is the call of the soulmate, those whose yin and yang fit perfectly together, those who already embraced their own duality in the North. It is a coming back to the Tao, to wholeness. It needn't be done with a sexual partner either, though it is generally male and female (on the energetic plane) to bring yang and yin to fruition. The vibrational sharing with the co-creative partner will support us through our higher work. Our co-creative partners may be working partners, those who share our vision and compliment our own integrated personality. We need only call them in with pure intent from a opened heart. This is fully conscious choice - using *llankay* and *munay* to manifest vision and destiny.

As we come into full consciousness, we undergo another vibrational shift. It is subtle now that we are cleansing out in the M-1 hologram, but it may be felt as a gentle whirling in the heart chakra. Until we are comfortable with this openness, we will be aware of the vibration there. We have removed the emotional aspect of the ego by releasing judgment and transforming greed into unconditional love. We have further empowered the director who holds the key to the larger picture. We find ourselves more and more in the role of the director, not actually in personality, but in a place of observation and perspective - center. This work has also removed emotionalism from the spiritual path, an absolute necessity for facilitation of work at higher levels where there is no room for impure emotion.

Our daily practices include work with the wind, the air. If we are to listen to the urgings of our soul, we must practice by listening to the speaking of the wind. The wind is cleansing the mental planes as well, and brings the entire multidimensional self into balance. We are making food choices from our feeling center and no longer need assistance with dietary regulation. As long as we listen to our bodies, they will gather what they need to sustain life at this new vibration. And the food choices are likely to be of an airy, highly energetic nature. We continue with our movement and breathwork practices and ritual around fire to sustain the cleared holograms of the lower centers. South direction work does not end for us, but it is lessened. Our past is immediate, and it never has to clutter connection to the soul through our energetic field. We recognize when we have hurt someone's feelings, honor the place they are in, and ask their forgiveness immediately. It costs us nothing. We are coming into a very nice place of balance and enjoy good health all of the time. Because our nature has become more air-like, we feel lighter, react less to pain, and have

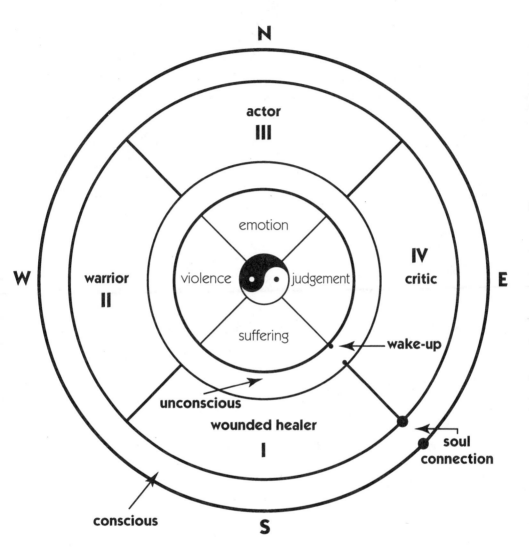

VII. The completed *kaypacha* medicine walk which allows consciousness, the cleared chakras and holograms, and the fully integrated personality.

come to know a feeling of real joy which emanates from the heart center.

We have completed the *kaypacha* medicine wheel, an awesome amount of work. Our dice are no longer loaded and we are coming into vision in a very stable way, from the heart center of mother earth. Like eagles, we are called to higher consciousness. We are asked to do additional work to bring the vision of the Source onto the planet. It is our choice. We are still living in the pre-meditated world of consciousness, learning to let go and invite in the director. Not until we are absolutely sure we are ready, will we walk up to the gate at the end of the narrow passage. For this gate closes behind us and, as we already know, there is no turning back.

Huascar Inca stands ready to assist us. *Huascar*, the once fearsome guardian of the *ukhupacha*, has become our greatest ally. He has beckoned us within, and we have seen the illusion of the *ukhupacha*. With our new vision, we see that we are standing in the garden, that we have been all along. From this place of balance, we honor the four directions.

> *We see beauty before us.*
> *We see beauty behind us.*
> *We see beauty above us.*
> *We see beauty below us.*
> *We see beauty all around us.*
> *We walk the beauty way upon the earth.*

Navaho

Inkari and Qoyari reflected universal balance in their acts of co-creation. They established the great Inca civilization in Cusco and throughout the Andes and unified all the different peoples under one language and government. When the mission for which they had split time and created the kaypacha was set in motion, they led their royal court to the old mountain, Machu Picchu, which called to them on the wings of the condor. They walked for many days along the royal road of the Incas over mountain passes and through lush valleys filled with hummingbirds and butterflies. This journey of the soul terminated at the gate of the sun the entry to the mountaintop landscape that would become Machu Picchu. The young mountain, Huayna Picchu guarded the city of light which they built upon the old mountain.

Their walk along the Royal Road, the path of knowledge, was as difficult as it was beautiful and during the walk they symbolically journeyed around the four directions, teaching the people how to mend their lives. In the designing of the city itself, one needed to descend from the sun gate to the watchman's hut. There the gate guardian assisted one's surrender upon the stone of death determining readiness to move upward towards the hanaqpacha. Inkari and Qoyari prepared to give their final gift to the people, the spiritual teachings which would prepare them, eventually, to lift their consciousness to the hanaqpacha. They led the people in a fast for forty days and forty nights during which time no fires could be lit. They were awaiting the time of Inti Raymi, the Festival of the Sun, when matter and spirit fused the young and old in the ascending soul. The intention of this festival was to return to the shining consciousness of the Sun.

During this time of waiting, the royal lineage of the Incas was established, a call to perfection which required austere discipline. In bestowing Inca, Inkari defined the path home to the Sun as one of embracing the radiance of the spirit, of sacrificing the soul to the spirit in divine manifestation. When the time of preparation was complete, there was the great festival of Inti Raymi with dances of the sacred bird, divination by the oracles using the coca leaves, offerings of kintui, and the mastay, the magical ordering of the three worlds. The origins of these last offerings was the fire of their return, and Inkari and Qoyari took their leave of the people. They walked to a mystical forest jungle of warm earth which was a privileged place in the eye of the Great Mystery.

Before they left the people at Machu Picchu, Inkari and Qoyari promised that they would return, at the end of time to lead the people into the hanaqpacha, the age of Pachacuti, higher consciousness.

9

SOUTH:
HEALER

Inkari and Qoyari did not lead the people directly into the *hanaqpacha*, for they were not prepared at that time. We are still not ready to enter the gates but are beginning to work within the energy of the *hanaqpacha*. Their journey to Machu Picchu is symbolic of that quest for higher consciousness that defines the spiritual path and there is a definite shift in focus as we do the work of this medicine wheel. We are still living within the *kaypacha*, the age when time was split to do the work of this reality. But we can already feel the intensity that is marking the end of time as we know it. Everything is in acceleration as we race to the end of time. If we have been able to do the work of the *kaypacha* medicine wheel, we will not feel the panic that will accompany the shift into the future. It puts us in a good place to tackle the uplifting work of the higher centers.

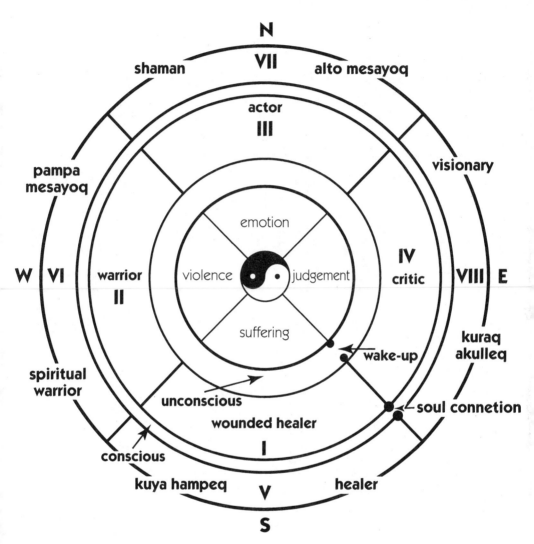

VIII. The *hanaqpacha* medicine walk superimposed on the *kaypacha*. Conscious living allows us to walk the wheel again, clearing chakras and holograms V-VIII. It is in this walk that the director transforms into the illuminated director and we begin to access the superconscious. This is the priestly path and the initiatory steps in the Q'ero priesthood are shown.

Like Inkari and Qoyari, who began their trek upon the Royal Road in Cusco, we take off from the East direction on our own journey. And we have much work to do along the way, releasing the last of the suffering, violence, emotion and judgment which we have extracted from the *ukhupacha*. *Huascar Inca* is our guide, for he is the guardian at the death stone and we cannot enter the city of light without his approval. Our journey takes on mythic proportions as we travel through lush valleys and over snowy mountain passes. It is the journey of embodying the spirit, but our first task is just to get to the sun gate at the end of the Royal Road. It is at the sun gate that we touch our soul, and begin the upward journey to the light, the path of spiritual evolution through the higher centers. We find ourselves living partly in this reality and partly in the myth, dimensions that seem familiar to us for the archetypes are beginning to find places within our consciousness. We are opening ourselves to the magic of the path.

THE ROYAL ROAD

We begin our journey from our newly opened heart. We find that it opens and closes and it takes some conscious effort to keep it open. So, a big part of this journey is about keeping our hearts open and sharing the love with others. We have, as our goal, the sun gate, the point above the shimmering city of light where we are open to the vista of Machu Picchu. It is at this point where we have the momentary vision of the *hanaqpacha*, the world of spirit. Once we have begun our descent towards the city, we lose our perspective. This gate of the sun represents the point where we touch our souls and are given the insight of our purpose here on earth.

The road up to the gate is long, winding and gets narrower as we near it. We saw this coming. We are not finding much room in our lives for things that are not essential and spend our time in mindfulness exercises. We are needing to differentiate the various feelings in the heart chakra by making the essential connection to the feeling center below it. We can feel our reactions to people and events as a whirling in the heart area, as if that eagle were flapping its wings right in our chest. This is frightening at first, but then very powerful as we understand and accept it. The feeling center is becoming very sensitive and our intuitive capacity is increasing rapidly. For a narrow path, there certainly is a lot going on.

With all of this action in our chest, coupled with the higher vibration which is present especially in meditation, we can experience a build-up of heat in the area around the sternum, above the heart. This is actually the place of the thymus gland, the gland of the heart chakra. The thymus is the gland of immunity in children, shriveling as we grow older. We feel like it must be growing very big with this build-up of heat. It really is regenerating, but at the holographic level. And the build-up of heat is the trapping of energy. If we rap sharply on the sternum when this happens and take deep breaths, it dissipates. Sometimes we need help from our gifted healers to move this energy. What is happening? We are climbing up to the sun gate and our energy is gathering there so that our soul will be ready to greet us.

This point above the heart is the place within the hologram where the soul may enter and connect with us. The soul is always with us but not in a conscious way. This is a conscious connection. It will not happen if we cannot keep our heart open, so our preliminary work is with the heart energy. The work usually makes the heat build-up more intense. We need to find our unique way of dissipating this and maintaining our balance. It is harmless, but those who are not prepared might mistake it for anxiety or panic. It is nothing like that, but the very real prompting of the soul. It is a great affirmation that we are on the right track.

And so we hike along the trail to the sun gate, delighting in the surroundings, joy in our hearts, and, low and behold, we are met with more old baggage. At this stage, these remnants of the South direction work are likely core issues, ingrained belief systems, and we will find the right combination of bodywork and ritual to release them. We are letting go of the core belief that we need to suffer. It isn't anything that we can consciously put our finger on either. It is at the core of our being and it is wrapped around us like a straight jacket. Our culture is so attached to suffering at the core level that this one belief may take most of our trek to dispel. Once removed, we feel one hundred percent lighter and have even more room for joy. We are back in the South now and are finally understanding how tightly we were held by the creatures of the *ukhupacha*.

When we finally let go of that core belief, a little miracle occurs, and the illusion of the *ukhupacha* can become clear to us. Perhaps we are on a high mountain pass and can see for miles around us, jungle below, snow capped peaks above. We have enough perspective on the top of this peak to realize what is really important. We linger there for a short time to take stock of the journey thus far. We are given insights into the integration of subpersonalities and see ways to finish potentializing them. For a moment, we are totally conscious of being the director who is connected to something bigger than we are. These affirmations are priceless gifts to us after all of the hard work we have done.

As we trek through the next valley we find ourselves back in our subpersonalities, cleaning up bits of violence, emotion and judgment that bubbled up when we released the suffering once and for all. The subpersonalities begin to behave with such maturity that the comings and goings between each subpersonality and the director reach a subtle level. We feel a little hum of integration and, for a moment, a bit of invincibility. Those we call in to help us with our work are outrageously obvious to us now. The work itself can be comical because of this. How could we have been so caught up in the illusion, we wonder? How do we know we are not now in a far greater illusion? We don't. We must trust those moments when we are filled with insight and the feeling that this is so right.

Finally we are at our last vista, our last place of vision, before we sink to the floor of the deep, lush valley. Our heart is pounding and the heat is burning holes in our chest. We rap on the bone and we breath. "Unlock your mystery bone. Carry me to my destination. Let me touch my soul", we chant. It seems a million steps down into that valley and a darkness descends over us as we trek deeper and deeper into the jungle. We know this is right. We are flying down the huge steps, feeling like the condor soaring from the mountaintop. At last we are at the valley depths and look up before us. We cannot see the sun gate for the trail twists around the back of the old mountain, Machu Picchu. It is narrow and treacherous in places and the dense foliage blocks our view at the same time it wraps us in its earthiness.

We have brought with us only the essentials, the bare bones of existence in a pack on our back. We take the pack from our back and unload it, laying everything out on the stone wall next to us. We have a parcel of food, a canteen of water, matches and kindling to start our nighttime fire, and the feathers of the spotted eagle to bring wind to the fire - earth, water, fire and air - South, West, North and East. We have brought with us the *kaypacha* medicine wheel that we have just walked. What is this funny sensation in our feeling center? We turn around as an energy hits the back of our heart chakra and there is *Huascar Inca*, arms folded in front of his chest, big grin on his face. He looks down at the stone wall and then back into our eyes. We explain that we have come so far not only along the Royal Road, but all the way from the *ukhupacha*, that we have brought with us these momentos from our journey. Our eyes glow with our accomplishment. We really have come a long way.

Huascar shakes his head and begins to explain to us the great gift of *ayni* which Inkari originally brought to Q'ero. *Ayni*, reciprocity, is the give-a-way or sharing of our wealth with mother earth, father sun and all those around us. It is a giving of ourselves, a sacrificing of identity, to seek reunion with the Source. We have much to be grateful for at this point in our journey. We look down at our four possessions, the gifts of the *kaypacha*, and understand that we must leave them behind as *ayni* if we are to go one step further on the path. We should be used to surrender by now, but it still seems difficult. We must go up the mountain empty-handed, with no expectation, seeking our soul and the next level of the medicine wheel. We leave our offering at a makeshift altar and turn to face the mountain. We take with us an integrated personality and our guide and ally, *Huascar Inca*.

THE GATE OF THE SUN

There is no way we could have made it up the mountain with that pack. By the end of this climb we are on our hands and knees, gasping for breath. The stone steps are moist and we don't notice their hardness. *Huascar* doesn't really help us but is a pillar of moral support. We have been through a lot together. We could not have done this without trust in the feeling place and the open heart. We would be back along the trail, doing more work. As we near the sun gate, we know that we have known about this, on some level, all along. It all looks so familiar. We wonder if it is like that for everyone and without having to ask, *Huascar* nods an affirmation. It is as if we have begun a journey home and things are finally looking familiar to us. We have.

This is the beginning of the evolutionary path which draws us upward towards the Source. We have been trapped in matter for this whole life and we are now feeling the pull towards spirit. It really lightens our step. Now, there is no doubt in our minds that this is our path, jungle below, mountain beside us, sun in the sky. There is a new sense of balance between heaven and earth, one that is illuminated fully. Finally, we reach the gate, an arch with no real door, and see that we are separated from the other side by gossamer cobwebs. Could it be that we are at the actual web between the heart and throat chakra? It seems that we are. Nothing surprises us anymore. We try to penetrate this web but it is thick and will not give in to us. We cannot find a way to tear it open either. It seems unusually resistant, elastic. We reflect a moment upon the journey and admit that it all makes sense. To come here unprepared would do us no good. It is very clear to us that we cannot penetrate this web without our friend, *Huascar Inca*, unless we chose death to the earthly life.

We turn to *Huascar* and he asks us to focus on the web with our intent to embody the spirit, with our willingness to step beyond this life. As we do this, he stands before the web and draws it into the palms of his hands. We see the free gate, and he beckons us to stand beneath it's arch. As we take that step and stand within the gate, the earth begins to quake, the clouds separate, and our father the sun, *Inti Tayta*, shines upon us and through us. We see, in his golden rays, the path back home, and, from this moment on, will be in touch with our soul, the being of light/energy who designed the game board.

What does this mean? We begin to remember the game plan and to know what we really came here to accomplish. We needed to be this combination of light and air, to have given away almost everything, to make that connection. If we slip back into greed, anger, desire or jealousy, we will lose this connection and have to regain it. We suddenly know quite a bit of what's going on. We look down at our dice, which we have not let out of our sweaty grip through this whole earth journey, and realize that we can now open them up and put anything we want in them. We have the potential to change the conditions of the game, load the dice in our favor, change our genetics, our personalities, our bodies, our minds, the entire hologram, if it will assist us on our journey to enlightenment.

Huascar lets us bask in the light a moment longer while the quaking earth settles down, then commands the clouds to cover the sun again. When this happens, we see before us the side of the old mountain. We can make out the watchman's hut at the entrance to the city of light, but the city itself lies beneath the clouds. It is a mystical vista. We have not lost the golden rays of the sun that remain attached to our hologram above our heart, and can feel them warming that area of the body. We stop, briefly, at a running spring to refresh ourselves before we begin climbing down the broad steps to the city entrance.

THE SHIFTING PSYCHE

Where were we really when we were standing in the sun gate, basking in the radiance, in touch with our soul? We were completely outside the subpersonalities, in a place of center, non-ego. We fully embodied the director. When the director was fully embodied, it allowed full access to the soul, or higher self. This would happen occasionally when we had small awakenings upon the path, but this time it was earthshaking. Where were the subpersonalities? They formed the gate itself, surrounding the director in balanced integration, if only for a moment. Being in center is being outside the manifestations of ego, the subpersonalities. It can only happen when they are in fully integrated balance. This has been the work of the *kaypacha*, and we must now engage in any remaining potentialization of subpersonalities to stabilize the integration and soul connection. This will allow us to begin inviting in the spirit, the true higher consciousness. The illuminated director, through soul linkage, is accessing higher knowledge, bringing it into consciousness to guide us on the path.

Ideally, we would like to shift the "I" from the subpersonalities who have been creating our identity from the *ukhupacha* to the director who accesses something greater than "self". The energy to sustain and guide this transformation is loving power, munay, being generated through the heart by the balanced will aspect of *kintui*, *llankay*. We are now in the process of accessing *yachay*, wisdom, the third and final aspect of *kintui*.

We might benefit from the visualization of the subpersonalities forming a ring around us, a medicine wheel, our gate of the sun. This has been facilitated by uplifting them from the *ukhupacha*, bringing them into consciousness. If we are thorough in our work we will have a subpersonality to place in each of the four directions. If we are female, one will be male, and if we are male, one will be female, a result of our West and North work. Integration includes accessing this dual nature, the yin and yang. The mature director stands in the center of this wheel and the subpersonalities have learned to respond to the director rather than being out of control, out there on their own. The process of potentialization is important for it brings balance to the wheel. Each subpersonality must be visualized in a way that sets goals for it, that has it reaching for higher potential. This continues to evolve as our consciousness evolves. The only way we could have passed through that gate was to step outside the ego, to be in center. It was a lot of hard work and a little bit of magic from *Huascar Inca*. Now that we are through the gate, we can see we have a lot of work ahead in this process of evolution.

We have nurtured and potentialized our subpersonalities in a way that has expanded the ego. We have really developed our sense of self. When we are in a subpersonality, we are very much in power and knowledge. This may sound egotistical, but this power and knowledge is what stabilizes that integrated personality, the medicine wheel around us. We need the stabilized manifestation of consciousness to invite the spirit into this earthly life. We have work to do on the earth and cannot be lost in spiritual fantasy. Ego will help us meet the status quo to do the work of our soul. We will bring ego forward through our subpersonalities when it is needed, but we will not identify it as who we really are. This is the highest form of non-attachment. This separation is the work of the *hanaqpacha* South direction. During our walk down to the watchman's hut, we must take a number of things under consideration. Who am "I"? is our primary concern. Exercises that help us step into the center are very important. We must evaluate what we perceive as knowledge, the work of defining and releasing the intellectual aspects of ego.

It is no surprise that the negative emotion of the throat center is pride, arrogance, and we will struggle to transform this into humility. Because we must be fully operable in the world and are not cloistered in a monastic setting, this can only be done through this model of transformation. Potentialization and integration of subpersonalities provides us with an ego we can be apart from but access from the mature director. Our goal is to gradually shift into the center and the connection we have made with our soul as we stood in the gate of the sun is the key to making this a reality. We are already engaged in the transformation to higher consciousness, but the *hanaqpacha* work of the South and West can be considered foundational.

WHO AM "I"?

Climbing up from the jungle floor to the gate of the sun, we might have asked ourselves "who am I?" At that time our perception was limited to the *kaypacha*. We had taken the darkness and chaos of the *ukhupacha* and ordered it into the subpersonalities which we then worked hard to heal, potentialize, and integrate. If any of these subpersonalities are still dominating, it may be how we chose to identify ourselves as we climbed upward. Within the gate, our perception of self shifted drastically and we came in touch with some part of us that is much greater than we have thought ourselves to be. Yet, the experience didn't "feel" arrogant. It was something that didn't have personality and it offered us illumination through the radiance of the sun. It was like the director, but it had a deeper knowing and sense of purpose. This was the soul, our higher self, which opens to us the superconscious realms of enlightenment. We maintain the filamentous connection to the soul as we travel towards the watchman's hut. One of our tasks is to strengthen this connection, to bring it more into this reality. Walking down these steps, we may be very confused about who "we" are.

If we are living in community or have a close knit support group, we are very fortunate. This work is nearly impossible to do alone. Since ego is an outward manifestation of the subpersonalities, it is accessed easily through personal interactions. A community willing to support this work, which will hold the energy of ego confrontation within the tribal mind, is a blessing of the highest order. If we do not have this support, we could begin calling it in with focused intent.

To begin the work of the South in the *hanaqpacha*, we need to take another look at our subpersonalities and their potential. Perhaps we originally envisioned Spike as someone who could go out and fight our battles for us without getting emotionally drawn into them and drained. Spike is a warrior for sure, our male component. Now it is time to re-envision Spike as the spiritual warrior, a warrior who can step outside of time, who works with the love energy as a "weapon". Spike is our Shaolin priestess, defending us from a spiritual position, and having fun doing it. We can't imagine how this is going to work for us, but we begin setting goals for Spike that take her into spiritual realms. In confrontation, she has lately remained calm and centered, speaking from her feeling center and hold her ground with some compassion. Now she is trying something new. Spike, calm as usual, is speaking from her throat center. She is speaking her truth. How is that different from the feeling center? Rather than holding her energy steady in protection, she is projecting her energy, not in defense, but in love.

We have learned to stabilize and open the feeling center and get in touch with intuition. What is happening now is that we are getting in touch with an infant wisdom. Spike is slipping, imperceptibly, into the director's chair. She is invoking the higher self to not only provide the objectivity of the larger picture but to instantaneously and completely heal the situation. Spike's opponent can't figure out what happened but feels relieved, even joyful. Consciousness has been raised. Spike, not wholly connected to the situation, is a little befuddled by the whole thing. This is where community can help Spike potentialize herself by dissection of the event. This matured director is so skilled we can be "in " Spike without even feeling we are engaging the subpersonality. Unused to consciously being the director, we need help at first, feeling comfortable in our new role. This validates the director's position for us and gives us more tools to work on the potentialization of the director, the integration of the soul.

All of the subpersonalities must be brought to this level of expertise, their potentials re-imagined, and, in this way, we begin to learn what it means to speak our truth. We are opening the throat chakra to reveal the wisdom of the higher self. At first it is a bit chaotic, but as we actually take on the director role as a full time job, everything begins to smooth out. There is an interesting process going on here. Our identity, the personalities we were born with and have transformed and integrated through the medicine walk, is separating from who we have felt we are. Our "I" is shifting into non-ego, yet the subpersonalities, manifestations of ego, remain in a place of balance to serve. To serve what? At this time, to serve the higher self, the awakening soul. The mature director is also undergoing transformation, opening the space above the heart for the soul to enter and stabilize.

Wisdom is not knowledge. Speaking our truth is not speaking what we have learned. Speaking our truth is channeling wisdom from the superconscious, through the higher self. This is an art we must learn and practice if we are to bring it into consciousness. Wisdom has nothing to do with what we think. "I think" is how we identify ourselves. Wisdom exists outside the ego. Wisdom does not know "I", "me", or "mine". It is impersonal and transpersonal, and it knows few words. Accessing wisdom can only happen when we let go of knowledge. This sounds insane. Have we not spent a great portion of this path gathering knowledge? We have, indeed. Now we are hearing that this has nothing to do with who we really are but rather who we think we are. Thinking connects this whole issue to the mind, and low and behold, we are in the M-2 hologram, where our task is to clear the clutter from the intellectual aspects of ego. Knowledge is the work of intellectual ego. When we did the work of non-attachment we never thought of knowledge as something we were attached to, but there it is, garbage out there in our M-2 hologram. And it sticks in the throat chakra, preventing us from speaking, even understanding, our truth.

Knowledge is something we pack into our brains, like bits into a computer. It can assist us in cultural survival but it will not help us embody spirit. It can help us delineate the path, but when we reach this point, it will stand in the way of further spiritual progress. It is deeply ingrained. How do we release it? How do we survive without it if we do succeed in releasing it? Like the integrated personality, we do not need to throw it away. We need to learn to use it, to access it when we need it, but from a place of detachment, a transpersonal place. We will work at illuminating our director who, transformed from the mature director by the evolving strength of the purified emotions, will work with this transpersonal self. It is the soul, or higher self, when comfortably settled into our energy field, that lifts our consciousness into these higher realms, the *hanaqpacha*. It requires the re-potentialization of the subpersonalities, the elevation of the director, and the stable anchoring of the soul. It isn't something we are going to do overnight.

So we begin, on this journey to the watchman's hut, the difficult work of separation from intellect. It is all a matter of service. Initially, when we were in the director's chair, we used the subpersonalities to do our work by accessing the knowledge stored in the neocortex of the brain. We were still serving ourselves. Even though it is a step up from serving the creatures of the *ukhupacha*, it is still energy being pulled into matter. Knowledge is used in self-service and there is a lot of ego attached to it. Even the mature director uses the fully integrated personality to serve self. Non-ego, center, occurs when we open the mature director to illumination through soul integration and we become transpersonal. We transcend self.

Wisdom has no arrogance and can only be accessed in states of non-ego. When we channel wisdom, we can even hear ourselves saying, "where did that come from?" We are acknowledging that it is a source outside the "self". It is inspired. We can get it all mixed up with knowledge if we have not cleared the M-2 hologram of intellectual ego-related debris. This wisdom will come through us as soon as we begin having the imperceptible shifts from subpersonality to mature director. It will make us feel a little funny, like our head is fuzzy and someone else is speaking. As we work to clear the throat chakra and M-2 hologram, this will stabilize and we will know what is happening and can call it in.

If we are really attached to knowledge and our intellects and the power that they have brought us, and most of us are, we will have to ask our community to help us know when we are in that place and help us break our own pattern of attachment. We may have strong belief systems which drive us to accumulate knowledge. We need to listen for "I", "me", and "mine". We might look at this as higher center addiction. We are, after all, right back in the South and West of the medicine wheel.

SYSTEM BUSTING BELIEFS - STAGE I

To facilitate what seems an awesome task, we will need to part with a few beliefs that are going to hold us back. If there are any vestiges of suffering and the need for redemption still hanging around, they need to go first. We would not have made it through the sun gate if they had any control over us up through the M-1 hologram, so this is an easy clearing job from the higher centers.

The next belief system that must be shed is that of hierarchy. We have found this to be pervasive in our lives and to be rid of it requires the support of a community which believes that hierarchy is illusion and acts accordingly. With this kind of backing, we can reconsider how we allow the world to interact with us. The illusion of hierarchy is maintained by our service to it. When we begin to think and act horizontally, our lives begin to change. This is easiest to implement from our point in the system downward. In other words, we have the power to disassemble the hierarchy below us because we are the one maintaining it. We can still maintain a functional work situation as we make those imperceptible shifts from subpersonality to director. The illuminated director brings the wisdom to make use of knowledge and, from higher center, there is no way we can take credit for what we are doing. We live in absolute clarity that what is happening is outside the ego. We are making the shift from arrogance to humility and our co-workers just understand that it's become a much more pleasant place to work.

This will not go unnoticed by those who manage us, and we could be asked to suggest some innovative techniques as they open to a more horizontal system. Alternatively, we may lose our job. When we system-bust, we've got to be ready for anything. Oftentimes when we are knowledgeable, we intimidate people who may be trying to teach us something. What is the purpose of this behavior? It is arrogance. There is something dear to Zen Buddhism called the beginner's mind which works very nicely as an exercise to center, to be apart from ego. If we always enter a situation with a fresh open mind, ready to absorb what we can, we will never be disappointed. If we enter a situation carrying all of our knowledge stuffed into heavy brief cases, we will have no room to add more. When we empty our brief cases before we enter the room, knowledge becomes a kind of currency that slips through our fingers and facilitates growth. It is an energy exchange. That is all that it is. There is no need to hoard it. And we had best get the feel of it flowing through us in non-attachment. We have learned at the beginning of this path that the physical body is energy as well, an illusion created by slow moving energy. Knowledge moves at a higher vibration, but is still an illusion which we hide behind. As we know more and more who "we" are, we find it doesn't suit us well to hide behind false identities. Like our integrated subpersonalities, we can keep our knowledge in a place of easy access and not be identified with it.

By the same token, part of the hierarchy system we want to bust is the student-teacher relationship. To stabilize and augment the connection we have made with our soul at the sun gate, we must come into a clear knowing that we are our own teacher. All of the wisdom of the universe lies outside our grasp until we do this. The inner teacher, director, accessing higher self is the only teacher we need at this point. Anyone else in our life is just exchanging energy with us in a potentially beneficial way. And it is never a one-way street. There is no arrogance associated with this either. It is simply an aspect of us with an eternal life and no identity. No one else can know the mission of our soul, and we don't even know it until we stand within the sun gate.

If our work has not already freed us from our biological family, it is imperative at this time to complete that separation by acknowledging the earth and sun as our only parents. We are matter becoming energy and genetics has nothing to do with it. This is the evolution of our soul, but also the evolution of mankind. The family nucleus does not generally lend itself to this microcosmic/macrocosmic shift in perception. When we touch the soul and begin stabilizing and reinforcing that connection, we will want to regenerate our holograms to facilitate our future work. At this point, we can correct our genetic weaknesses and change whatever we need to. Usually our biological parents don't understand this divestment, so we keep it to ourselves. With this shifting of origins, we become something more than human, and it really facilitates the disengagement from ego by increasing our comfort level in the director's chair. The regenerating capacity of the soul is inhibited only by the ego and re-emergence of negative emotions. It is maintained by the pure emotions of non-attachment, mindfulness, trust, love and humility. Who are we? It doesn't really matter. What really matters is who we are becoming, embodied spirits, temples of the holy spirit.

CLEARING THE THROAT CENTER

Much of the work of system busting the hierarchy comes through disengagement from the system, the work we have completed in the *kaypacha* medicine walk. At this point in our journey, working in the throat center and the M-2 hologram, we must tend to the work of opening and clearing this center and holographic field. We have been learning to speak from our feeling centers after being at varying levels of openness there, but now we must clear the throat to speak our truth. We must clear the energetic pathways for wisdom to come through us. This ability to speak from the feeling center is an excellent exercise to facilitate this opening. So is toning, singing, and chanting. We will find, as we progress through this work, a change in our voice and an easy balance in projection that wasn't there before. Everyone can sing when the throat is open.

We may need to seek out some talk therapy which also helps to open the throat. At this stage of our work, we should need very little outside help with it. In our meditations, we can focus our consciousness in the throat area and ask our guides to help us with this clearing. Because we have made that soul connection above the heart chakra, we can now benefit from a very special meditation.

First we relax our body in the cross-legged position or sitting on a straight-back chair feet flat on the floor. We relax the shoulders, forget that we have legs, and shift our awareness to the spine. There we imagine a pillar of light from crown to base chakra holding us erect. We need not exert effort to maintain our position. Then we can relax the facial muscles and the jaw and allow our eyes to move freely.

In this very relaxed state, we will want to sink a dagger of light to the center of the earth to anchor ourselves to the mother. Then, opening the crown of the head, we invite in the white light from the Source through our *wiracocha*, the eight chakra which hovers above the head. White light fills our head and images may flash before our inner eye. We focus our intent and pull the light down to the throat area, feeling the sensation of energy there. We can stay in this place for some time, asking for help clearing the M-2 hologram, a high vibration surrounding and penetrating through us.

Repeating this meditation everyday while we are in this transition will open the throat and facilitate the downward flow of spirit. We are engaging the first stage of spirit embodiment and meditative support becomes essential to the path. Spirit is yet another element of our full integration of human potential. We recognize the director as an intermediary between the earth-related business of the personality and the higher self, or soul, which is accessed through the transpersonal, egoless state. When our director undergoes transformation through the process of soul anchoring and re-potentialization of the subpersonalities, our vibrational state is elevated. We can imagine our structure becoming even less dense from this evolutionary process. We are creating "space" and vibration which resonates more and more with the energy of The Source, and are able to accommodate increasing amounts of this energy within our holograms. This is spirit moving through us.

If we are living in community or are teaching in circle, we will naturally be exercising the use of the transpersonal space by allowing the director to access the higher self. These can be very rewarding exercises for everyone involved as the wisdom channeled is usually of great benefit to all present. Those who have chosen the service work of clairaudience as part of their soul journey will begin to come into their work in this way. We can begin to experience and work with telepathy. The element of the throat center is the ether, the ch'i substance which is gathered from our surroundings. To work with this element in ways beyond the movement, breath, fire and wind already integrated, we must make use of the hour of power. This is the time of day a half-hour on either side of sunrise or sunset. In this very special light, we can gather the ether and learn to shift our perception. In this way, we prepare the way for vision. This is also a very powerful time of day to do our meditations and circle work in community.

We see where we need to move the ego outward, to take it into the realms of non-attachment in order to invite the spirit into the body. There are many good exercises for releasing knowledge including writing it in journals, or on computers, or putting it into book, tape or video form. We release it, just as we would dump the contents of those heavy brief cases to invoke the beginner's mind. The soul is the guiding force and our practices reinforce and stabilize that connection above the heart. This journey from the heart to the throat is one of anchoring the soul piece, which is the essential source of light needed to complete *kintui*.

The vibrational shifts we experience now are the energies of spirit attempting to make a home within our higher centers, occasional spinning energy in the head, tickling at the brow chakra and pressure at the top of the spine. Subtle cranial bodywork techniques may help us with this integration as well as balancing of the thyroid and parathyroid energies, for these are the glands of the throat chakra. We really need to exercise some care with the work and not try to rush into that which lies ahead. As we work through the opening of the higher centers, laying a good foundation is especially important. One therapy which is particularly useful during the South and West work is ear coning, a gentle vacuum cleansing of the ear which removes excess wax, fungal and bacterial debris. This ancient method for ear cleaning, available in some alternative health centers, has the potential to clear the energetic channels of the higher centers. Like all bodily cleansings, it is important to use moderation and gentleness with the ear cleaning. After an initial clearing, treatments should be few and far between. Most of the work of the *hanaqpacha* South direction has been, as expected, on the mental plane with separation from knowledge, the ego intellect, being the key. The ego work continues as we move upward, but in our culture, the heart and throat areas present the most intense work.

KUYA HAMPEQ - THE HEALER

In the Andes, there is a defined path in the priesthood, the training of the shamans. It is a hierarchy only in the sense that there are levels of consciousness. All learning is horizontal, but it is an apprenticeship path, a wisdom path, that circles the medicine wheel. The very first steps of this path include an immense amount of service work. The apprentice also begins the training in divination using the coca leaves and the use of stones for healing. Our cultures are very different, but the path is all the same. We step upon this path as we enter the *hanaqpacha* round of the medicine wheel. Because we have mended our lives, we enter as healers. We cannot be healers until we have healed ourselves. Our beginning work, touching the soul piece, is akin to the work of the stone healers and coca leaf readers. When we have grasped the work of non-ego and are really able to be in center, we enter the stage comparable to the *kuya hampeq*.

The *kuya hampeq* continues to work with the stones but becomes merged with the energy of the plants to become a plant healer, the herbalist or doctor of the Andes. In our lives we can think back to the wounded healer work we have done in our *kaypacha* medicine walk and imagine what it would have meant to us to have walked into the office of a doctor or healer of any sort, who had done the work necessary to enter the *hanaqpacha* medicine walk. This true healer, clear through the M-1 hologram would be actively working on the M-2 plane, releasing the ego. Here would be a person with an open heart, connected to their soul. We think what it would have been like to be in their presence and consider that it may well be our calling to be this person we imagine. In the Andes, if you are called to the priesthood it takes you to the work of your soul, whether it be the coca leaf reader or the master shaman. We must continually remind ourselves that there is no hierarchy.

10

WEST:
SPIRITUAL WARRIOR

As we near the watchman's hut, we see the ominous slab of the death stone before it. We are walking into the West, the place of death and transformation and we know deep within that we will not be able to make it through the city gate without surrendering something. We haven't much left to surrender, so we walk lightly up to the path along the hut and see another gossamer web stretched across it, blocking our way. We look back at the death stone and see *Huascar Inca* sitting upon it, looking right at us. He motions us over and we sit beside him, ready to hear what we must do. According to *Huascar*, we have much to accomplish before we are to enter the city of light.

It is time for an in-depth life review, a little death experience. We take the time to touch our past and see that all the wounds are healed, that no Band-Aids remain patching things up. We search again for the meaning of the patterns and events in our lives and the way they challenged us to do this work. We may even be compelled to write something autobiographical to sum it up in a tangible way. What we are doing is getting in touch with the game plan with new perspective, having soul contact. We assess the integration of our personalities from the place of center and adjust anything that seems imbalanced there. Practicing the imperceptible shifting from subpersonality to director helps us stabilize the integration. We can call in whatever seems appropriate to perform these exercises. Our next level of practice is shifting from mature director to transpersonal self, still a sporadic and awkward process. Some real attention will need to be focused here before we can move through that gate.

Because we are in the West, we will be doing the deep healing around violence and addiction that will help us move beyond this point. We are shifting our consciousness to the brow chakra and M-3 hologram, the causal-self plane, which are cluttered with the spiritual aspects of ego. Thinking about this for a few minutes, we realize that this is where the work will become very difficult and that there will be some high stake system busting to accomplish if we are to clear this field. Our soul is beginning to come into a little power at this level of consciousness. The soul itself is looking at its agenda in this life and the pattern of game plans over lifetimes. We look up at the gossamer web across the path and then at *Huascar Inca* beside us. We might as well get comfortable. We are going to be sitting on the death stone for some time.

SYSTEM BUSTING BELIEFS - STAGE II

When we look for clutter in the M-3 hologram, the plane of soul-self connection, we see the spiritual aspects of ego, and it will be very different for each of us. It will depend a lot on how our spiritual core formed and was nourished through our lifetimes. Our culture is currently involved in a spiritual quest that has taken the spiritual path to a new kind of shopping mall. There are so many things to choose from and no guarantee that any of them contain or lead to wisdom.

We try yoga. We try wheat grass and consult a psychic. We try mega-vitamins and sleeping on magnets. People are equating spirituality with native culture and native culture is screaming back that this is theft. The spiritual quest has become one big control drama. We want anything that is fast and painless. Of course, by this time in our journey, we have been through all of that and know it is illusion, but what of the path we are on. How do we know it is a wisdom path and where is it taking us?

We look down below the watchman's hut at the city gates and wonder what lies beyond. We have an idea that we have come a long way and that we know something about walking this path. We may even be awakening others to it. But when we begin to look at the deep levels of system busting, we see something very frightening. We have invested an enormous amount of ego in this path. Actually, every time we have had to release an aspect of ego, we invested most of it in this path. It has become the reservoir of ego for us. We feel it is our path. We are not so insincere as to be forcing it on others but approach that work with an open heart. We are in a good place in that respect. Are we? Why do we need to sit on this stone and convince ourselves of it?

We have busted hierarchy out in the world, but we have failed to do it within. This inner argument doesn't even involve the subpersonalities who are looking on with some amusement. This is the higher self, the soul, trying to rattle the cage of the director. "Hey director, let me in!" The director is emotionally detached and has recently come into a place of intellectual detachment, but the director has invested himself in the path. It was how he got his power. The emotionally based romantic aspects of the path fell with the clearing of the heart chakra/M-1 hologram. The spiritual elitism met its demise with the clearing of intellectual ego coming down from the sun gate. What remains to be surrendered is the need for a path at all. The director argues that we would never have found our way to the city gate without him and his devotion to the path, his hard work of evolution and illumination. The subpersonalities have to agree for they now realize how ill-prepared they were for the journey in the beginning. The higher self comes down hard on all of them. "You are children of the sun, you do not need crutches to find your way back home. Look at the sun. Look at the light. You know who you are. You are energy. There is no differentiation at this vibration. You will not enter this city of light until you are ready to become light."

The director is worried. Should he trust this higher self? What assurance does he have that this is the truth. Why are we walking this path? What are we doing with our lives? We sit on the death stone and look back at the turmoil we have caused in the lives of our families and friends. We look at the way people have criticized us for being uncaring and unsupportive at times while we have pursued our path. Was all of this just a bad joke? Have we climbed all the way to this death stone to find out we blew the whole thing? And what about all those people following us? What about those people who have believed in what we were doing? Doubt is everywhere.

We are in a really tough place here and we want to find a word to describe it. We remember the negative emotion of the brow chakra. It is a perfect fit - ignorance. We have never felt so alone in our lives, and for the first time in ages we feel a tinge of depression. Our feeling center implodes a little bit, our heart feels some anxious flutters, our throat chokes up a little bit, and a few tears roll down from our eyes. "My God, my God, why have you forsaken me?" Whoa! Where did that voice come from? Has someone walked this way before us? We look around and see no one but *Huascar Inca* who has a smirk on his face. Our higher self had reached up into the collective unconscious and grasped for us an archetype, a model of surrender. Not only have we validated access to the collective unconscious, beyond our own superconscious, we have merged our path with that of the Christ archetype. But we let go of that belief system years ago. What is going on?

As we sit on that stone, the higher self keeps one hand on the mouth of the director to silence him and, with the other, reaches up into the collective unconscious and begins bringing down the archetypes of death and transformation for every culture that has ever existed upon the earth. This is, without question, the most astounding thing that has every happened to us, and our subpersonalities circle around us in rapt attention. Eventually the director gets a knowing look in his eyes and the higher self releases his mouth. It is as if a beam of sunlight has embraced us and a great knowing has entered our lives. We are a part of something so much greater than we had ever imagined that tears of joy run from our eyes and pool out onto the death stone. We understand in that moment that "self" has no meaning whatever. Alone is what "self" can feel. We will never be alone again. We feel our entire holographic body shudder and watch the words "I am" travel out towards the sun. In our next shudder we free ourselves from need and want, and like a kite tail hitchhiking with them, addiction, fear and violence. With each release we can actually see more spirit come into our field. We are filling the holes in M-3 with the vibration of the sun. The last of our core beliefs - that we need anything in this life to cling to as a form of identity, including this path - shoots out of M-3 like a rocket. Who are we becoming now? Light. We have healed our soul and we have done it without any assistance. *Huascar Inca* reaches over and takes us in his arms. A job well done.

THE DEATH STONE

Have we ever really known what death is? We don't talk about it much in our culture because we fear it. It is, for us, a separation from this life, from all that is familiar and secure. It is that fear of loss in the base chakra that keeps us anchored to the earth at the time of death, reluctant to let go of the lifeline. But we have done our emotional work and sit on this death stone in touch with our soul. We have just undergone a complete life review and have separated ourselves from the last of our identity, the ego pieces which were holding us back. We are conscious of the fact that we are in a place with no "I", no self, yet we can pinch ourselves so we are somehow surviving this situation. There is a real sense of detachment from the world, even though our community and co-creative partners may be right beside us. It is a bit surreal. We feel empty as well, as if we know nothing and have no path. Well we don't. Yet we are held in the embrace of some benevolent energy, perhaps the soul allowing spirit to move deeper within us.

Is it possible to die and keep on living? It seems so. We don't feel like the process is complete, as if we have experienced the death part but not the transformation. We are caught in a place, a no man's land, but it doesn't feel so bad. What we are thinking about is this shift from the director to the fully illuminated director, through the higher self, the soul. We are clearing a path of entry so that we can have some control over the comings and goings of the higher self. It is really the director who has to do this surrender work.

Our thoughts turn to service. We have previously made a transition to community service in the East direction work of co-creation. This West energy is urging us to surrender to serving something greater than that. The soul or higher self which accesses the superconscious and the transpersonal is asking us to fulfill the purpose of our journey here, our service for The Source. This doesn't mean that we will cease serving the community, but we will shift into the transpersonal in the way we manifest that service. We have a sense that this is what the soul is pulling us towards and it feels good to us in the feeling center and the heart center, so we intend it with the full force of our being. This represents a shift in the motivation of our work, certainly a transformative step in our process of embodying spirit.

We are, in actuality, integrating the soul by surrendering to the transpersonal self. We might imagine our subpersonalities around in their supportive positions with the director in the center. From the director upward, we extend filaments of light to the enlightened or illuminated director. Surrender is the tool of filamentous connection. If we step back into any manifestation of ego, we can weaken and break this link. We have a feeling that this illuminated director, through the transpersonal self, sits on the edge of a vast expanse of super-consciousness from which it could draw wisdom into our conscious realm. If, in our journey, we can find a way to strengthen that connection, we may be able to spend time in the superconscious, the place outside of time. We see pretty clearly what the act of death and transformation means.

We are also aware that we can chose to die at this moment. We have come to a clear place with our life and anything more that we do is the work of higher self. We have cleared the karma from the previous lives which we had put in our dice, and all karma that has come to us in this life. We have healed our lives and assisted many on the path we were walking. It is our choice to go or to stay. It is the last conscious choice we will make. This is conscious dying, to bring choice to it, to exercise a higher intelligence about it and to know it is no different from life, but an energetic shift to spirit. Rather than embody spirit in the human form, we would choose to be pure spirit. It is just a de-materialization process. Sitting on the death stone, making our final choice, we understand the experience of near-death. It takes you to this place of choice. And like those who return, we hear the voice of the soul tell us we have greater work to do on this earth. The soul had made this choice before incarnation.

However, we must complete the process of death and transformation, the whole reason we are sitting on this stone. The stone itself invokes this experience within us. We are conscious of the need for ritual, to die to all that we were and walk away a new being. *Huascar Inca* assists us as we lay, face up, upon the stone. It is the hour of power and the sun is setting in the West. *Huascar* stands at our head and sends our soul on a mission with the setting sun. It is to merge with the sun, our father, and return at dawn to re-incarnate within us. We are, in this ritual, surrendering to the mission of the soul and strengthening its connection to the Source. We have complete trust in *Huascar Inca*. We have come a long way together and he is now our greatest ally.

We are lost in this in-between place for that night, aware of the spirits of nature, dimensions and realities we had never dreamed possible. We are not asleep but are deeply in touch with the hypnogogic state, the place of slipping into sleep. We travel in landscapes of great beauty and bone chilling horror and it doesn't seem to bother us. We are being challenged with everything and we are in a place of complete balance and trust. Yet, we are not really with our soul. We are deeply connected at this time with the earth and the jungle animals come to our funeral bringing gifts. We realize we are they and they are us and we embody within our first four chakras the serpent, the jaguar, the dragon and the eagle. We feel completely connected to the spirits of nature through them, to the *ukhupacha* that no longer controls us. What a treasure we hold within.

As the dawn approaches, we hear a distant thunder and soon great storm clouds appear overhead. We cannot move, cannot run to the watchman's hut for shelter. Our body is so heavy without the soul, we cannot move a muscle. It is as if rigor mortis has set in. We see flashes of lightening hit the old mountain and the young mountain, fusing that energy of the young and old within us in the path of the soul. *Huascar* leans forward, arms outstretched to gather our incoming soul as a bolt of lightening strikes us right above the heart. Our physical body, so heavy a minute ago, is jolted from the stone, rising to greet the soul. In that instant, we see through the splitting of time the illusion of life and death and know, at last, who we are.

We slip into a deep sleep and awaken to a shining sun and the flight of hummingbirds. They are inviting us to the city of light. We look over at the path, and the way is clear. We cannot find *Huascar Inca* and sit up rather suddenly. Looking down at our body, which has an unearthly lightness about it, we do not recognize our old self. We have no mirror to see our face but we don't need one. We know, with every aspect of our being that we <u>are</u> *Huascar Inca*. We have embodied this powerful archetype during the death ritual. *Huascar Inca* is very much at home on this death stone and we move towards the watchman's hut with familiarity, though we have never been here before. On entering the hut, we find a warm breakfast and coca tea waiting for us. Sitting at the table, sipping tea, is a being of great magic and power. With a beak of gold and wings of turquoise and green, like the hummingbird's, a serpent sits coiled upon a stool, shimmering with luminosity. We have come to break bread with *Quetzalcoatl*, the Lord of the Dawn, the great feathered serpent.

Even though we could walk through the gate into the city of light, *Quetzalcoatl* cautions us that it would be premature. We are to be the watchman, as *Huascar Inca*, for a while. Our work will be that of *Huascar Inca*, to lead others through this death and transformation part of their journey. We will make many trips to the valley beneath the sun gate and accompany people up the last steps of the Royal Road. We will dissolve the web at the sun gate and allow their souls to make conscious connection. We will accompany them to the death stone and support them in the release of the self. Then, we will send them on their way, through the death process, either to the world of spirit or through transformation back into this world. We are to become a master of the two realities. And every morning, we will meet

Quetzalcoatl for breakfast and open ourselves to vision, preparing ourselves to enter the city of light.

OPENING TO VISION

In the process of embodying *Huascar Inca*, we stabilize the work of the throat. *Huascar* is the archetype of the throat chakra and while we complete the work in the brow chakra/M-3 hologram (the causal-spiritual plane), we call to us the understanding of death and transformation that he can provide. This is the essence of the West direction and the highest form of this work is the death of self and birth of the soul. It truly is a death experience and if we come to it without fear we will have no problem making a smooth transition. This process awakens the spiritual warrior who can see beyond death and help others through this process. Our own work at this point is preparation, at the direction of *Quetzalcoatl*, for our journey into the city of light, the crown chakra.

In our work prior to the death stone, we released the last of ego and ignorance and invited within us the seeds of wisdom and truth. Our task at this point is to nourish these seeds that they might grow into sacred flowers of many petals. While we do this work we are in the process of the further embodiment of spirit, pulling more of our superconscious into this reality. Our exercises are centered around seeing through the worlds, the different realities, which bring vision into our lives. To come into vision any other way invites madness and an unsettling of the heart and soul connections. Because we have come through the *llankay* and *munay* to the watchman's hut, our vision will support the mission of our soul and the soul of mankind, rather than the creatures of the *ukhupacha*. Shifts within the physical body include the complete functioning of the hypothalamus and pituitary glands. The new chemical substances secreted by these glands will stimulate the neuropeptides to help us open to vision. Our meditations can include directing energy to the area of this gland, behind the eyes. If manifestation of clairvoyance is a part of our soul journey, it will begin to come to us at this time. Vision, we must remember, is access to wisdom, not necessarily an adjunct to sight in the physical sense.

Wisdom is carried on light energy. In terms of the spiritual quest, wisdom will not enter until the mental fields, M-1 to M-3, are cleared and luminous. The entry of wisdom and what that wisdom brings to us is as unique as we are. It is the purpose of our soul and its commitment to The Source and it has no meaning to anyone except us. It cannot be written in a book. It can only be acted upon. To be in touch with it is to have made the transition from the spiritual path as we conceive of it on earth to the path of light that takes us back to The Source through the process of spiritual evolution. Teachers are of no use to us unless they can access these realms with us. Knowledge is of no use to us. Light is what we crave.

One practice that we must begin at this point, if not before, is feeding the luminous body from the sun at sunset or dawn. If we begin this practice early in our journey, we will look at the setting sun with bare eyes. We may need to partially shield it with our hands, raised palms forward to the sun, creating a space between the merged or overlapped thumbs and index fingers to hold the sun in our gaze. Gradually, we will be able to look at the setting sun without the shielding. As we continue with this practice, we will be able to take in the sun at progressively longer intervals before sunset. It is a gradual process, but we can immediately feel how the energy of the sunlight is filling our body and coursing through us. It is a powerful practice, one which has been practiced at dawn and sunset in the Andes since the time of the Incas. We must relax into it, be fairly regular with it, and, of course, exercise caution with our eyes. We are told to protect our retinas from damage by sunlight, never to look into the sun. We want to be careful to begin this practice when the sun is very low and the rays are like thick golden threads reaching to us. As our nervous systems adjust, we will know our limits. We must be careful and take into consideration that the sun is more intense on some days than others. It would be foolish for us to rush this practice or to look at the sun when it is high in the sky, possibly injuring our eyes.

The rays of the sun hold wisdom and love pulsating at a very high vibration which energize the mental planes and soul connection. When we are making this transition in the West, sun feeding is a very powerful practice at dawn and sunset, to reinforce the journey of the soul at the death stone. We can also support the West work by practicing one of the many forms of the death breath. Death should come as a great expiration, a letting go of the breath. In our culture, it is accompanied by a desperate last breath, a chilling inspiration symbolic of our grasping to life. We would like to become more comfortable with the expiration and, at first, just shift our focus to it in meditation. We may find ourselves gasping for breath, but if we have been relaxed in our meditation all along, this transition should be easy. Gradually, we become aware of the space between the expiration and the next inhalation. In this practice, we try to sustain this space and eventually lengthen it to that of the exhale and inhale. What may begin as a seven count exhale, one count space and seven count inhale will gradually become a seven count cycle of inhale, hold breath, exhale, hold the void. This practice prepares us for more advanced work in meditation and helps us relax and control the exhalation of our breath. In time, we lengthen the practice by slowing our counting.

In our normal meditation practice, we might begin to work with geometric forms, at first allowing them to appear on the projection screen of our third eye, behind the forehead. We should try all of the geometric forms and eventually allow them to perform kaleidoscopic transformations. Future work with these meditations include drawing ourselves into the form, looking for the portals into other realities. This is practice for shifting into other dimensions, work in the higher centers. We are de-materializing our reality and opening ourselves to all possible futures.

PAMPA MESAYOQ

Our lifestyles are very simplified at this point and we interact very little with the world we have left behind. Our work may be centered around the dying process. In assisting others in death, we come to greater understanding ourselves. The West is very much the place of introspection and introversion and we feel at ease with it for the moment. In the Andes, the West work represents the next step in the priestly path, the *pampa mesayoq*. The *pampa* is deeply connected with the earth, the spirits of nature and the archetypes of the first four chakras. On their journey from South to West, the *pampas* fully embodied these archetypes which symbolize the empowerment of the cleansing of the first four holograms. In their West work, they come to embody the archetype of the throat, *Huascar Inca*. The West is the home of the *ayahuasceros*, the medicine men and women who have been beyond death. These are the spiritual warriors of the priestly path and because they know the turf, they can take you out there to meet your death. When they do, they <u>are</u> *Huascar Inca*. They are open to vision, and their vision is clear. For many, this is the stepping off place in the priestly journey. Their soul work is to help those who are making the death transition, whether to spirit or in the more mythic sense of the *hanaqpacha* medicine wheel walk. They are powerful healers and masters of the death vine, *ayahuasca*.

We are opening to vision and transiting through death in a way that works in our culture. We will not be secluded in the introspective work of the West for long if we are needed in the world. The call to the city of light may come at any time for us and we take with us all the wisdom we have gained in the West. One morning, when we go to meet *Quetzalcoatl* for breakfast, we leave our dice on the table and walk with him into Machu Picchu, the city of light. We enter as the true spiritual warrior. We have completed the hero's journey.

11

NORTH:
SHAMAN

As *Quetzalcoatl* leads us through the narrow gate into the inner city, into the North, we are once again transiting the birth canal. This time, it is the birth of spirit and it is with a joyous heart that we fly along the path and down the steep stone steps. We are taken to our quarters adjacent to the main square, and begin to get settled in our new surroundings. Soon we are out in the square seeking out others, emerging from our time of introspection to find our place in the world of service.

We may be living in an intentional community at this time, which makes the emergence an effortless transition. If we are in mainstream society, we may have some difficulty orienting ourselves. Wherever we are is exactly where we are supposed to be for we are at the directive of the soul and our mission is very clear to us. Some of our time is spent in the pursuit of the shamanic life, while the rest of our time is spent in cultivating the mission of the soul. We are in service to mankind for The Source, and use our clear intent to call to us the work we intended for this life.

MASTERING THE MIND

The North is the home of the master, the sage, and part of our own work is the cultivation of mind. Our task at the M-2 holographic level was to work with the ether, the element of the throat. Our death experience in the West cleared the M-3 plane, completing the work in the mental planes of ego. Mind is the "element" of the brow chakra, and the work of clearing the mental fields opens the mind to a myriad of activities now that we are in the causal field. This causal-self aspect of the causal field links to the transpersonal self through the cleared mental field. Like all transitions from West to North, there is a shake up and re-integration process within the subpersonalities. The death of "self" has transformed each subpersonality into a more spiritual being and we must anchor the re-potentialization goals of each. They adapt easily now, being more flexible than when we started, for they are in the hands of an illuminated director.

Before we proceed with our work of teaching which will bring us to the wisdom of the sage, we need to exercise the link between the director, the soul, and the transpersonal self. Once the subpersonalities have re-integrated, the director can tend to the work of re-organizing center. The subpersonalities have a lighter and more spiritual nature now but their activity is still going to come from the imperceptible shifting of a subpersonality-director continuum. The director now needs to establish the imperceptibility of shifting to the transpersonal. When it has happened in the past it has been dramatic and confusing, right in the middle of teaching perhaps, when the higher self felt the draw to enter to assist someone who was listening. It can seem uncontrollable, out of consciousness. It is. It is superconsciousness. Now that the mental planes are cleared, we are more open to the superconscious and need to begin paving a smooth roadway between the two. This is the work which currently needs the attention of the director.

A lot of this work goes back to the practice of mindfulness and transformation of negative emotions. If we have been diligent about that, we have come into the *hanaqpacha* fully conscious. Making the transition to the superconscious requires exercises similar to those used in the *kaypacha* North, but less in the material world and more in the spiritual world. We could call it spiritual mindfulness and make it the task of the director. We can begin these exercises in meditation where the director gets some time alone anyway. We draw in the light and try to pull it all the way down to the heart. When we finally succeed in making that connection, it can be stabilized by using our earth anchor to draw red earth energy up the spine to the heart to meet this white light. Heaven and earth unite in the heart and fill the luminous field. This energy should be worked with and stabilized before the next step.

Next, we can begin to expand the mind. It is as if the white light was a great funnel coming into us and we can send the mind out to travel into it. With practice, we feel ourselves expanding, becoming a more universal mind. We must not try to grasp anything there in the beginning, but rather just float in it with conscious awareness, attention. We are learning to take our consciousness out into a greater consciousness so that it gets accustomed to the territory. It is an energetic landscape that we are exploring.

In this way, when the superconscious is accessed by the transpersonal self through the soul-centered director, we will know what is happening, will not be confused or lost, and can begin accepting what is there for us to use. Previously, we have only been able to think of self in terms of the conscious and unconscious, the *kaypacha* and *ukhupacha*, where we have been working. Now we are grasping higher consciousness, the *hanaqpacha* for the first time, and *Quetzalcoatl* is our guide. *Quetzalcoatl* is the patron of learning and civilized skills, a fitting archetype for the North direction. These are the skills of higher consciousness, which reflect those of the *kaypacha* at a more enlightened stage of personal growth. In the *kaypacha* North, we were learning to be the director in exercises of emotion. Now, turning to evolution of center, we will learn to be the enlightened director, a transpersonal human, by working with purified emotion.

Non-attachment

As we come to take a second journey through our chakras with emotion, the landscape has changed considerably. The subpersonalities are no longer acting independent of the director and have, in fact, matured into spiritual activists. We have cultivated non-attachment from the base chakra and have left our fears of loss behind. We didn't even react in a fearful way to the events at the death stone. The death experience has put grasping in proper perspective, and what really comes up for us at this point is how much our students and community members are grasping at us. The exercise is to have an open heart but not allow co-dependent relationships to form. We may have had to work through some of this when we were releasing ego for it may have made us feel pretty important to be needed.

Like a parent who cannot imagine their child surviving without them, we may foster dependency with students and those we interact with because we fear the consequences of setting them adrift. We cannot be responsible for their personal choices. We may have the perspective of a slightly elevated consciousness, but it is narrow-minded and self-serving to think that our students and associates will not survive without our presence. They may move to another teacher or another community, they may stay with us and have a breakthrough, or remain perfectly stuck where they are. If we hold them back, we hold ourselves back. Everyone gets stuck that way. If we push beyond limits, everyone gets hurt with denial and projection. The energy of the mind is fluid. The image of setting them afloat is a very good one for meditation, bringing the focus of the mind to the base chakra.

In our work with the students and associates, we will need to be firm in our unwillingness to caretake. Our actions serve them and the community as we act with honesty and an open heart. We do have perspective. We have walked a long journey, and because they are seeking us out, we do have an obligation to be of service in this way. Emotional neutrality is not the way most people want their relationships with us to go, so it will take some time to establish this kind of openness. Eventually, resistance will turn to acceptance and then to an eagerness to have the insights which can assist in their personal transformation.

Mindfulness

By this time, the practice of mindfulness will have become as natural as breathing. Mindfulness and consciousness are equivalent and our initial practice was one of just learning to pay attention. Mindfulness at this level of the work enters the realm of the mind itself. We have cleansed the senses with our work around desire, and now we are using the senses to expand our awareness. We are hearing with our minds, not just our ears. We are feeling with the etheric and astral bodies. Our exercises are conducted in daily life. In fact, they are forced on us by the increased sensitivity to all the stimuli around us. We take ourselves out into nature and feel the energy of the plants, trees, rivers and animals and are conscious of their energetic interactions with us. We actively differentiate energy patterns and keep that remembrance in the mental holograms.

Within our own being, we can touch the duality that was so difficult to bring into balance in the *kaypacha*. Here we are elevating the duality to the energetic level, becoming aware of the male/female integration and it's usefulness in our work. We focus on smoothing out any rough edges in our yin/yang transforming cycle. We may experience more equilibrium as we work towards a more comfortable fifty-fifty distribution in the duality. This involves blending of subpersonalities, imperceptible mergings that empower our dualistic nature.

Interesting work can be done with our co-creative partner using mindfulness. If this partner has come into our lives and we have grown together, we can exercise the cleared mental planes in numerous exercises which expand the mind. We can merge mental planes, explore telepathic communication, and feel the love vibration at the mental level. If we are co-creating, a powerful mental liaison can be made which we might think of as our director co-creating and drawing in the superconscious. If we had ever thought we might be bored at this level of the work, we quickly learn that it is exciting, cutting edge fun.

Trust

We have been building trust in the solar plexus chakra since releasing the anger and emotional drama from our lives. With the trust has come an opening of the feeling center in that region and much of our work in the mental planes has been the stabilization and awareness of feelings, emotions. This feeling center becomes an important relay station for the pure emotions as we link them to the higher self. The purified emotions are linking the conscious and superconscious together like filaments of light. The conscious connection is at the feeling center while the integration point is the soul connection above the heart. Here the four lower chakras and four higher chakras meet. The superconscious connection is the transpersonal self.

Flexibility becomes our focus as we work through the solar plexus area. Any rigidity will slow down the energy transmission along the light filaments. If we are not adaptable to change, we will not survive the great influxes of energy coming our way. This flexibility will be reflected in interactions with our students and community associates who will begin using it to break their own patterned behavior. There can be no hard and set rules. There is no truth that cannot, by transformation, become an untruth. We have system-busted ourselves out of systems.

Another very interesting practice can be added at this point. We are working in the mental plane and we know that the feelings are relayed from the astral body to the physical/etheric form through the action of hormones and neuropeptides. Some of these proteins are produced in chakra-associated glands while others are the products of on-site glandular-like cells. At both levels, we can use the mind in the meditative state to stimulate the secretion of these peptides and monitor their interaction at the physical/etheric planes through the feeling center. This is a beginner exercise in the capabilities of the cleared mind. We can monitor and maintain our health in precision balance. Our level of health is a reflection of our level of awareness or consciousness.

As trust is allowed to blossom and grow within us, it transforms sympathetic reactions into empathic reactions. We become compassionate human beings. There is no escaping it. Compassion comes from having walked a difficult path in life while holding those around us in our consciousness. When we go through that death of self experience, we have unlimited resources for compassion, yet there is nothing about life that saddens or disgusts us. All things are meant to be. To believe otherwise is ignorance. Adversity is the fire of transformation. We know it. We have been there. There is no remorse, no pity, in the *hanaqpacha*.

Unconditional love

The connection between the feeling center and the heart center becomes very important at this time because the director in the transforming process of becoming the illuminated director, through soul connection, is working hard to integrate the *kintui*. The *llankay* or will is made manifest in the solar plexus as a result of the coordinated efforts of the lower three chakras and their holograms. The *munay* in the heart acts as the pivot point between the *llankay* and the *yachay*, or wisdom, which is becoming manifest in the throat, brow and crown chakras and their holograms. It is in the heart that will and wisdom combine with the loving power of the purified heart center to bring *kintui* into this world. We will not change the world by changing our thinking, though that is part of what we need to do. We will not change the world by sedating and transforming our desires, but that is part of it as well. We will change the world with love. The divine vibration is that of love, unconditional love. To embody spirit, to become a vehicle through which that vibration can enter the earth and touch the hearts of all men is the fulfillment of *kintui*, the manifestation of a new reality. If that can be done, everything else will magically fall into place. This truth has always been known. This should come as no surprise to any of us.

The director, in meditation, is pulling the white light down into the heart. It has never come this far in mankind before now. In the past we have only been able to bring it to the brow, where matter meets mind, but now we are challenged to bring the light into the heart filling the mental planes with it. For the director this is the turning point in the transformative process for the heart marked the point of personality integration at the end of the *kaypacha*. We would never have touched the soul piece without a strong director to lead us up the back of the old mountain. Now we are asking the heart energy, the love vibration, to stabilize the integration of the soul which helps the illuminated director link with the transpersonal self. With this integration comes the anchoring of spirit in the human form.

Unconditional love has no strings attached. It is that part of the doctor's oath that states "do no harm". There are no control issues here, no manipulation, no thoughts of having wants and needs met through good deeds. We are doing the work of our souls now and it doesn't serve the self. The exercises to strengthen this love are those of extending the heart space around those with whom we interact. It is an energetic healing as well. Not only do we "do no harm", we try to do some good. We may not be practicing healers, but our hearts are in service all of the time. As we learn to move energy with the mind, the applications are endless. We can hold anyone in the love vibration at any distance, for this energy moves outside of time and space.

We will invite in many people who will challenge us to sustain non-judgment. We will be accused of being opinionated and critical when we are stating fact. We learn to stand steadfast in center while the hurricane blows around us. It is just wind and it further cleanses the mental planes. We become magical mirrors for those who assail us. Not only will we have clear vision about these situations, we will see beyond them and through them, offering unconditional love to shift the negative energy that accompanies them. In time our every thought, movement and breath raises the vibration, the consciousness, of the planet. This is the power of the love vibration.

Humility

In community, there are never-ending opportunities to hone our humility. If the community is holding sacred space, it is doing so in a horizontal way, without hierarchy. We have ample opportunities to perform simple tasks in mindful ways. Tasks are rotated and we do that for which we have no talent and in which we have no interest. This is good exercise to remove the "I can't" and "I won't" from our lives. With appropriate intent, all acts become manifestations of the Divine. This keeps life in perspective and sustains the clarity of the mental plane. We don't allow the "I am" to re-enter our field.

This filamentous linkage of director and transpersonal self through humility is important for the clear expression of the soul through speaking. Because we are working in the North, home of the teacher, the master, and the sage, we have called in the energy to sustain the clear transmission of the truth. We are working directly through the mental planes at the throat and, with the support of strong purified emotional linkage, we can begin to explore the transpersonal space. As the name implies, this space transcends the self. We have already experienced this phenomenon at the death stone and, perhaps, at times in the past when we managed to get our self out of the way while teaching. It is a powerful place of center in which our conscious mind plays no part. The truth comes directly through the crown chakra to our throat and the words are spoken without cognitive awareness. The words themselves are wise, benevolent, and transform those to whom we speak. This is healing through the mental plane from the superconscious. We are moved by our own words and it is clear to us that we didn't *think* them. It is a somewhat humiliating experience at the same time it is unspeakably powerful.

These moments of higher consciousness are spaced out with longer interludes of insightful conscious thought. We work at allowing the superconscious to come through, nurturing it by providing the situations for its emergence. This is the transpersonal self directing, and the work around the throat invokes similar situations to those of our initial release of self. The director must relinquish control, trusting that the connection to the higher self is stabilizing. As this is accomplished, a sense of peace comes over us and we feel the wings of freedom brush against our cheeks. We are challenged with ways to help others from a pure place without the facade of leadership.

Our intent must be impeccable and we are often challenged with the intent of others, that we might sort this out for ourselves. We need to be able to recognize the difference between information and manipulation. We have to become gifted extractors of the truth and give no energy at all to those who would use our energy to further their personal agendas.

Truth

Mastery of the mind at the level of the brow chakra brings in work of a spiritual nature. We are opening to vision and we find that vision is guided by the clarity of the mental planes. Ego misinterprets vision. The energy must be pure. We realize that the path is not important as long as it gets us to the sun gate, so we readily accept all paths as stages of an individual's soul development. We are challenged to prove that the path we walked is THE path. We know better than to bite at that one. All manner of challenge comes our way and we become the mythic martial artist yielding to the ballistics around us. We will be seduced with all manner of temptation and must continually ask ourselves if that which we are about to engage serves ourselves or The Source. If there was ever any doubt in our mind that we could call in exactly what we need to do our work, this clears it away. We respect and appreciate the power of our minds and realize that wisdom/truth can only be held in the egoless mental plane. We recognize that our subpersonalities are still with us and manifest in the world at the illuminated director's guidance as fully integrated aspects of ego. They are no more than tools to help others at this point.

As teachers, we will disappoint our students. It is inevitable. Until the students' vibrations are raised to that of the *hanaqpacha*, they can only imagine things frozen in time. We are evolving into energy itself and can rarely sustain an image or identity for any length of time. We are transmuting hourly and our students may fear change and evolution. We cannot meet our students' expectations, nor the expectations of any other living being. Likewise we have no expectations of them. We do not cling to identity and cannot, at this point, create identity for them. We will attract those who are ready to do this work and be grateful that there are many other teachers ready to work with students who are not attracted to us. Let's remember, life is a free-will game.

Grace

As the luminous filaments of the pure emotion stabilize the link between soul, director, and transpersonal self, our hearts become filled with joy. This is the spirit coming fully into matter, the anchoring of *yachay* and fulfillment of *kintui*. There is no negative emotion of the crown chakra. It awaits the purification of the causal-self plane, the work currently in progress. When this work is completed and we are really engaged in the work of the North, we live in a state of grace, and grace is the emotion of the crown. The holy

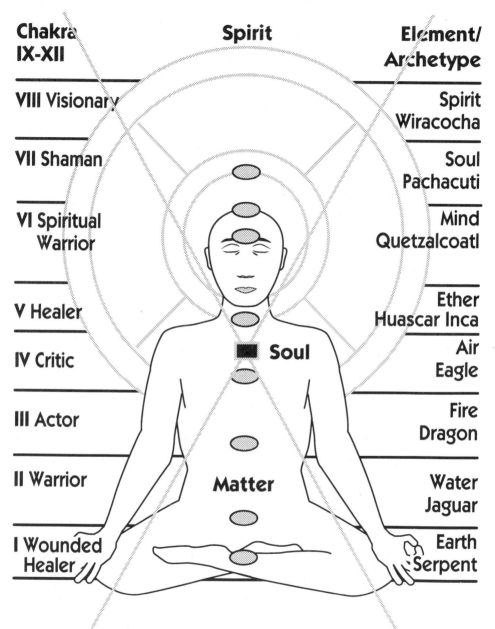

Chakra IX-XII	Spirit	Element/ Archetype
VIII Visionary		Spirit Wiracocha
VII Shaman		Soul Pachacuti
VI Spiritual Warrior		Mind Quetzalcoatl
V Healer		Ether Huascar Inca
IV Critic	Soul	Air Eagle
III Actor		Fire Dragon
II Warrior	Matter	Water Jaguar
I Wounded Healer		Earth Serpent

IX. The journey through the *hanaqpacha* medicine wheel clears chakras V-VIII after the soul connection is made. This process allows us to gradually embody spirit as we move into higher consciousness. The archetypes and elements of each chakra are shown.

spirit has come fully into the temple of gold. We reflect the radiance of the sun, our father, in soft glowing eyes, a shining countenance, and reverent step. The shifts from director to transpersonal self are imperceptible and the subpersonalities are potentializing their highest spiritual purpose.

CLEARING THE CAUSAL-SELF PLANE

Once we have made this connection of luminous filaments which links the director to transpersonal self, stabilizing the soul, we are in a unique place to begin tapping into our own superconscious. If we have done a thorough job of healing the karmic patterns which have surfaced in this life from the past lives or this one, there won't be much debris in the causal-self plane. Any remnants can be dispersed energetically, in an instant, with intent. What we can open to on this plane is the link between the soul experience and the self we have created for this life. The karma we brought into this life when we loaded our dice fits into the schematics for the game plan. What the superconscious can access is the data bank with all of the karma from all of our lives. Here we find old soul patterns that can be imprinting on this life as they did on hundreds of our lives.

Since we are, in theory, already dead, it seems reasonable to us that we should be able to access this data. Because we are also still alive, we realize that there exists a golden opportunity to disperse this karma. We are masters of the *kaypacha* medicine wheel so it hardly seems a task at all. Since we can access the overview, we can lump the karma into specific patterns and call in the work. We knew when we made the choice to stay here on the death stone that we had work to do on the earth, a mission to fulfill. We never dreamed we would have a personal opportunity to further raise the consciousness of the soul itself. This is work in service to The Source since it lightens the energy of the universe. It serves the soul and The Source. Because we are also engaged in the embodiment of spirit, the soul and Source are merging. Whereas the mind was the element of the brow chakra, the soul is the element and energy of the crown. Our task in the North is to integrate and elevate ourselves to the vibration of the soul.

The work of erasing this karma can go on for the rest of our earthly lives. It is deep-level soul healing. We don't need to rush it for it will come as we call, and we will call as we are ready. We are learning to flow with the energy of very high vibration. The superconscious also makes us aware of the intent of others and it is impossible to keep secrets from us. We have not had secrets for a long time so it seems natural. The telepathic gifts of the co-creative partner and the community are energized by our superconscious energy. Eventually, we will be one mind, but for now it is interesting experimental research.

If we have been making careful progress feeding from sunrises and sunsets, we now realize that, to a large extent, the light of the sun is sustaining us in a way that food used to. We eat little, have a monstrous amount of energy, and are not hungry. Our vibration is lifting to that of the sun, and we may be able to look into the sun for thirty minutes after sunrise and before sunset. The sun is beginning to appear less solid and we can see the energy of fire pulsating from it. The light energy pours out the palms of our hands and soles of our feet. We are anchoring the light which is exactly the meaning of being enlightened.

The death breath practice is progressing also, with more repetitions of the cycles of seven. We are becoming comfortable in the in-between space of the withheld exhale and it creates a powerful space in which to bend time. We begin journeying outward in search of our home. We don't get very far, of course, but it is opening up possibilities for superconscious death.

ALTO MESAYOQ

Back in the square of the city of light, we are engaging the path of the shaman. The shaman is the sage and master, the teacher of the community. We are aware of the mastery needed to become the shaman and do not wonder that there are few. We gather in the first light of dawn with our companions and together enter the time of a group consciousness which moves towards the integration of the soul. It will take our society time to get used to this higher vibration. We are extending consciousness beyond the historic, outside of time. Where are our role models? Where is our myth? Where are our archetypes? We must begin to reconnect ourselves with the earth in a way that honors global consciousness and the spirit. Can we listen to the shuffling of the worn moccasins that have walked here before us? Can we hear what is spoken on the wind? The shamans were the first priests and will likely be the last for they serve mankind, the earth, and The Source.

12

EAST:
VISIONARY

We move into the East as our expertise in the shamanic practices and our skill as the teacher are matured. The *kintui* is stabilizing as an energetic balance between heaven and earth. We have learned to act solely from our heart center, pulling the will and wisdom together there in loving power. We realize that this was the potential of the human form all along. The human race became trapped in materialism and lacked the insight and energy to reconnect the soul piece. The materialism was extracted from the earth mother and we were disconnected from her vibration. We can see now how we really needed that solid vibration of the mother to anchor us through the difficult work of bringing in spirit.

This integration of spirit is an ongoing process, too. We are exploring the limitless power of the mind, moving beyond the fine tuning of our own body and health into the community and the natural

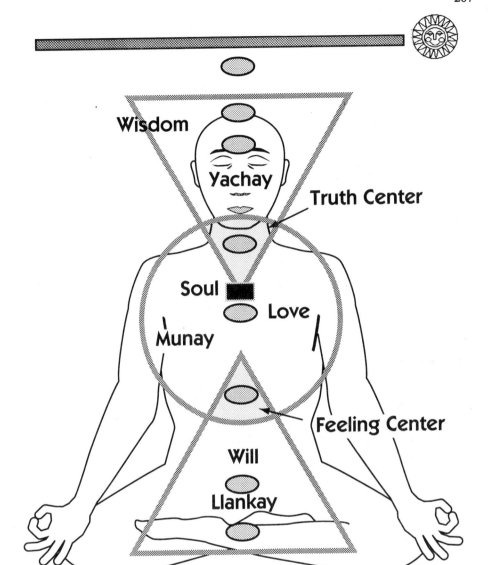

Wisdom

Yachay

Truth Center

Soul

Love

Munay

Feeling Center

Will

Llankay

X. The *kintui*, the highest attributes of mankind, are will, love and wisdom. These are realized by the clearing of the chakras and holograms. The will is in place after the solar plexus is cleared. The love is in place after the soul connection is made. At that time, the feeling center (shaded area over solar plexus) opens. The clearing of the throat, brow and crown brings wisdom into place and with this comes the opening of the truth center (shaded area at throat). With the *kintui*, we have realized the highest human potential and begin moving outside the human experience.

world. *Quetzalcoatl* represents the higher skills and has a deep connection to the natural sciences. We are learning to understand the molecular vibration and behavior of life by merging our minds with it. This is a lot easier and more comprehensive that trying to figure it out cognitively. The mind is a fluid energy that we are learning to master. As we engage the East work, we reach out beyond the *kintui*, into the *wiracocha*, the eighth chakra which sits above the head and which envelops us as a luminous field. The edges of this egg of light are not sharp, but, like rays of the sun, reach out to hold us in the cosmic vibration.

CHILDREN OF THE SUN

The luminous field, *wiracocha*, is the causal-spiritual plane. In this hologram, we are able to fully stabilize the integration of the soul and spirit, The Source moving through us. We have been working with both since we consciously connected to the soul in the sun gate. Our journey in the city of light has been one of pulling in more spirit as we have been able to make more room in our hologram for it. The soul is the being of light/energy who sat in the circle of other light/energy beings designing the board game for this life. The soul knows how to bring in spirit and in the process is fully awakening with us. Spirit is the divine vibration, the cosmic love that moves all things in the energy of creation. As we complete this integration, we become spirit and are truly part of the creative force. This is co-creation at its pinnacle. Since The Source moves, uninhibited, within us, we are serving The Source with our every breath. We are the fruition of the highest form of creation on this earth, the embodiment of The Source in a form that can move deftly in the realms of the unconscious, the conscious and the superconscious.

Our work at this time is to make the shifts between these realms imperceptible. There are many facets of this work which all contribute to the attainment of this fluidity. It is the work of sacrificing the soul to the spirit that precedes our return to the shining consciousness of the sun. The word Inca means child of the sun and the Incas were chosen to lead the people because their luminous bodies were clear and held the vibration of the sun. They were masters of the *hanaqpacha*.

Our work is to follow in their footsteps, preparing to fuse our energy with the sun.

The duality that we re-embraced in the North is moving into a fifty-fifty, male-female energetic balance. We take on the characteristic of the Tao, the yin-yang symbol. Our bodies can even shift into an appearance that is dual, though our sexuality does not change. The sexual energy is channeled into spirit and we come to know the divine vibration as that of orgasm. As the integration process becomes more complete and we become the fluid movement of The Source on earth, we allow this vibration to flow forth from us. In this way, we hold the community and the earth in the vibration of divine love. So, one of our tasks at this point is to learn to contain this and become naturally fluid with it. It does not mean we have no partner but we are likely finding deeply esoteric ways to share this vibration with them. As we become receivers and transmitters of this vibration, we realize that there is an infinite supply of divine love and the more we put out, the more comes in.

Healing in the field of the *wiracocha* is instantaneous. We heal the community when we hold them in the divine vibration. This is a simple act in which the mind extends the *wiracocha* out in embrace. Our energy mastery is at the level of The Source energy moving through us, spirit. Because we are working in this eighth hologram, the illuminated director can link into the transpersonal self at will. It is in this way that we can access the collective unconscious as easily as we have worked in the superconscious. Superconsciousness, though enlightened, is still within the realms of soul/self. It will take some practice to be fluid in this consciousness. When we first step outside self with consciousness it is both awesome and out of control. There is a lot out there and much of it is garbage. We find that a good bit of the landscape is cluttered and realize that a major portion of our work as a healer is clearing this field.

This sounds astounding, but it opens so many opportunities for us that we are immediately drawn to it. The collective unconscious is the mind of mankind. We draw from it our archetypes, or dreamscapes, and our cultural and global karma. If we have been building a picture of the three worlds of the psyche, another way to look at *kintui*, we see the unconscious mind as the *ukhupacha*, the

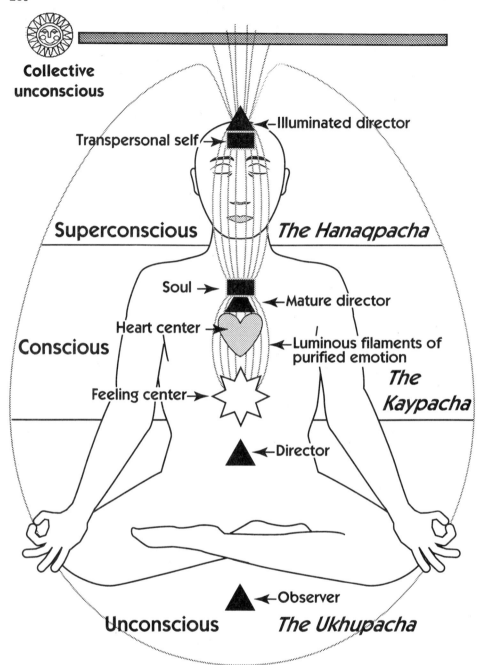

XI. The full embodiment of spirit allows access to the collective unconscious for the work of the higher self, service to The Source. The director, through complete subpersonality integration, undergoes a metamorphosis from observer to director to mature director to illuminated director. This process is facilitated by the integration of the luminous filaments of the eight purified emotions between the feeling center, the soul connection and the higher self. The illuminated director accesses the collective unconscious through the higher (transpersonal) self.

conscious mind as the *kaypacha*, and the superconscious mind as the *hanaqpacha*. They are like sections of an egg in which we stand, and the egg is the *wiracocha*, the luminous field. The luminous field reaches out to fuse with The Source, and that filters out through the collective unconscious in which our whole egg of "self-containment" floats. Like all of our holograms, the *wiracocha* and the collective itself penetrate through us as well. This is fluidity and it is the law of the cosmos. Science draws lines of separation with linear thinking. Shamans work outside of time where this thinking does not exist and does not apply.

In our process of materialization, we came through this collective unconscious and drew from it the experience of mankind that we used to facilitate our earth journey. What we gathered may have nothing to do with our own soul's past lives but is more the collective knowledge of the human race that tells us how to be human. When we die, the experience of our life that is present with us at our death, reflecting the state of our holographic fields, returns to add to the collective. We can imagine the sort of debris that exists in the collective unconscious, alongside all of the exquisite work of mankind. This access we have gained to the collective mind allows us to do some healing work with mankind for the vibration is very heavy. We can help to clear the mental plane of the human race, and in so doing greatly facilitate the raising of consciousness for all people. Here is our opportunity to re-imagine the *ukhupacha*, to lighten its vibration so we are not so trapped in matter as we continue to incarnate as humans. There is the realization that this is why we made that choice upon the death stone to stay here. This work can only be done during human incarnation, through full embodiment of spirit. This is the ultimate service to The Source in the earth plane, and it is the highest service to the earth and mankind as well.

On the personal level, we can, at this point in our work, move beyond the astrological influences that have motivated and shaped our lives. Our subpersonalities can be re-potentialized outside of planetary influences. This is equivalent to having multiple incarnations without having to go through the incarnation process of death and rebirth. This work will take us out beyond the eight holograms into the realms of the cosmos.

In our mastery of energy, we are learning to move through heavy energy and draw energy to us. In this way, we may move objects and walk through walls for they are only manifestations of energy and we are becoming fluid within it. Levitation is not difficult and we may manipulate our own image by shifting our shape. We are practicing the art of energy and it means pushing the edge a lot, realizing that our reality is what we wish to make it. Our expertise in shifting through the realms of consciousness is gained through the embodiment exercise. We have become *Huascar Inca* and *Quetzalcoatl*, and on the death stone we had the experience of embodying the archetypes of nature. In the East, we do a lot of work with this energy and in this way come to know the greater mind of nature and archetypal consciousness. We have a sense that we are preparing ourselves for something, but rather than reach out into the unknown that unfolds before us, we are content just to <u>be</u>.

BLISS

The emotion of the *wiracocha* is bliss. Bliss is being connected with the flow of the Creative Force. It is to embody The Source and manifest the Creative Force on earth. Bliss is the emotion that was with us when we were given our instructions in the circle of light/ energy beings prior to incarnation, prior to the game plan. Bliss is what associates us with the instructions and also what gives us the empowerment to perform them. They are different for everyone, so it cannot be predicted, but when we have made this connection and are "in bliss" we will find that we are working in that circle of light beings here on earth. Of course, we are minus a few bodies due to the free-will separation of some who chose to work with us in spirit only.

Bliss is the energy of the effort in which this circle engages. It is kundalini meeting Source in the composite hologram. We hold the divine vibration in the human form. Our meditative efforts, along with the healing of the collective unconscious and raising of the collective consciousness, are focused on the delineation of the work of The Source. It is a team effort now and amazingly productive. Our journeys outward are brought back to our circle and discussed. Implementation of energy flow is augmented and we move forward. We work as a team in the dreamscape also, so all energy is devoted to the work of The Source. It is very rewarding work and it allows us to interface with the community in unique ways. A community with The Source so visibly and actively working within it will have unlimited opportunities for spiritual growth, both in individual and group consciousness.

KURAQ AKULLEQ

The East direction shamans of the Andes are the masters of energy. The title, *kuraq akulleq*, actually means, *elder chewer of the coca leaves*, which implies that they have gained their wisdom with age. There are few *kuraqs* as it is a very difficult path to follow and requires the austere discipline and some separation from everyday life. They have worked through the mastery of the *apus*, mountain spirits, and are the keepers of the great mountains and the spirits of nature. They are the prophets and visionaries who guide the community in accordance with the preservation of the Divine plan on earth. Considered a necessary part of the indigenous culture, we see it completely lacking in our own. The *kuraqs* have merged their energy with that of nature through the exercise of embodiment, and, because they have, they are attuned to the consciousness of the earth, the weather, and the creatures of nature.

South American shaman's wrap their sacred objects in a woven cloth which they call their mesa, a kind of portable altar. There are two sides to a *kuraq* mesa, the representation of power, the magical and the mystical. If the shaman coming into the East has been walking the path of the magician, it is now time to embrace the mystic. And the reverse is true as well, for there must be balance between heaven and earth. The magician has worked more with nature, the embracing and mastery of the earth spirits. The mystic has followed the paths of energetic mastery from within, connecting more to the cosmic energy. The *kuraq*, master shaman, must strive to be both. There are initiations beyond that of the *kuraq*, but they are not to be diminished by the words of humans. They follow naturally if the intent is to master them. Much of that work is off the planet in disembodied states.

INTI RAYMI

As luminous beings, we prepare for *Inti Raymi* the Festival of the Sun and the return to his shining consciousness. Our practice of feeding from the sun has reached a fine art and we see our father as energy, looking right through him. We are his radiant children, the Incas, having been called to our destiny by our souls. Our *wiracocha* energy reaches out like the sun itself to warm and illumine all those around us. We have embodied our highest potential as human beings, and walk, as *Quetzalcoatl*, to *Inti Raymi* in the spirit of service to the Source.

Before dawn on the day of the festival, we climb the many stairs to the sacred plaza, and honor the spirits at a temple there before continuing on to the temple of the sun. We look down upon the main square, filled with all those gathered for this festive occasion. We kneel, facing East, upon the sacred stone, *inti-huantana*, the hitching post of the sun, and await the sunrise. We prepared to sacrifice the soul to spirit, when touched by the fire. When the sun rises over the mountain tops in the East, the golden rays travel to us and merge with our luminous body. As the crown chakra swirls with awakened energy, *Quetzalcoatl* is transformed into *Pachacuti*. We feel a golden helmet clamp down over our head and the beak of a great bird replaces our nose. The three-feathered headdress, representing the *kintui*, blows in the morning wind atop our head. *Pachacuti* is the archetype of the crown chakra, the guardian of the gates of the *hanaqpacha*, and our work there is complete. We feel ourselves merging with the consciousness of the sun and, in so doing, are given the invitation to become light.

As the sun rises over the mountain tops, we become conscious of those around us and see that there are many feathered headdresses standing at the stone. We leave offerings upon *inti -huantana* and our group descends to the main square. The fires are lit at this time and food is being prepared for the first time in forty days. We are handed coca tea and join the celebration as transformed beings of light. The first food is offered to the *apus*, *Pachamama* and *Inti Tayta*. We have learned to live in perfect ayni, honoring all that exists.

At the hour of power, in the mystical light of sunset, we return to the sacred plaza and perform *mastay*, sending *despachos* to earth and heaven to align mankind with its destiny. Following this ceremony, in the thickening light, our group sits in circle and the community gathers around us. There is music, drums and flutes, as we share *kintui*, offering the three coca leaves to each other. Blowing through the leaves three times, we send these highest attributes of man, will, wisdom and love, to their destinations on the wind. We close our eyes and look around our circle. We know we have been here before. We are sitting in the circle of light/energy beings who designed the game board. We all know this, and that we have meant to come to this moment in time. Opening our eyes, we sit in a circle of golden helmets, feathered headdresses fluttering in the solar wind of sunset. The music stops and the community awaits the blessings of *Inti Raymi*.

We feel the feathers begin to whirl on our crown chakra, and watching our companions, see the vortices of energy coming down to enter theirs. Our holograms vibrate rapidly and begin to shift as we feel the energy enter us. Our transpersonal self steps out of the way, and we feel that our entire being is sitting beside us watching this process. We are, for the moment, donating our bodies to someone who has something to say, and the process is so complete that the physical form in which we have walked the earth shifts its shape to theirs. We are in a place of complete surrender to this for it is the essence of the sacrifice of soul to spirit. This is a step beyond the death of ego, a disembodiment in service to The Source. We are not threatened by it, but open to whatever this has to teach us. For a long time, we have known that all things are possible. This experience feels something like the transmission of the archetypes of death at the death stone but without this rearranging of the body structure and the actual embodiment of another soul.

Sitting next to us is our co-creative partner with whom we have been sharing this *hanaqpacha* medicine walk. We see the beak of *Pachacuti* has transformed into the strong lines of the Inca nose, and that his hair is straight and black, his eyes warm and dark, and on his chest there is a golden medallion of *Inti Tayta*. We are looking into the eyes of Inkari, eyes we have known for eternity. And he is looking into the eyes of Qoyari whom he has held within his heart center for eternity. Together, they have always reflected the universal balance, the duality and complicity. And they had said they would return to lead the people into the *hanaqpacha*, higher consciousness, into the age of *Pachacuti*. Our disembodied self is fully aware that this is the fulfillment of the contract made with The Source before this circle designed the game plan.

This festival marks the end of time. The sun is setting for the last time in the *kaypacha*. We are preparing to shift into the *hanaqpacha*, into higher consciousness and a new reality which exists outside of time. It is the time when Inkari and Qoyari promised to return, and in sacrificing our own soul to The Source, we have embodied the gods. We were told we were gods, children of the sun, many years ago. We did not fully understand that until now. This could not have happened if we had not followed this path through the three worlds of *kintui*. We would not be able to hold their energy, the energy of the sun itself. We have come from the stars and will return to the stars. Our sun is the star of the earth and it has become transparent to us even as we have become transparent to those around us. We would never have imagined this as we trudged up the path to the sun gate. It has been quite a journey.

When we can draw our eyes away from Inkari, we look again around our circle, and see that we are sitting in a circle of the gods. We see among them Christ, White Buffalo Calf Woman, Changing Woman, White Shell Woman, Buddha, Mohammed, Hiawatha and those who are not so familiar to us but whose energy is all of the stars. As each speaks, the wisdom and vibration are received by the people gathered around the circle. Inkari speaks:

"You are children of the sun and it is your destiny to embody the gods, the energy of the stars. The earth will no longer sustain the vibration of the *ukhupacha* for she is moving into her own destiny. As we walk beside you, into the *hanaqpacha*, we ask that you not look back at this reality, that you have no attachment to it. We are taking you to paradise, a world beyond pain and suffering. This world has been around you all of this time, but you have not seen it. We have come many times to initiate you and it is now time to complete the cycle of mankind's entrapment in linear time and space. In all things, we ask you to honor the earth, the mother of your incarnation and the jewel that sparkles in the eye of The Great Mystery."

The wisdom which comes forth from the mouths of the gods shifts the energy of those gathered for *Inti Raymi*. It shifts the energy of our disembodied self as we listen with rapt attention to that which comes from our own mouth. There is no hierarchy in the sharing of this wisdom with those who are gathered around. It comes as the energy of The Source which holds all in its embrace. It is a pure love vibration without discrimination and it is received as each individual is able to carry it. For all are at different points of emergence into the light. The Source takes care that the sun shines on all of us equally, but knows that each journey upon the earth is unique.

As a circle, the gods rise to their feet and they offer *kintui* once again. All of the people share in *kintui* and chew the three coca leaves after sending the will, wisdom and love to their destiny. The people rise with the gods, leaving all that they possess behind them. The entire community follows Inkari and Qoyari as they lead them away from Machu Picchu, into the setting sun, over the drawbridge towards Vilcabamba, the city of gold.

MANIFESTING A NEW REALITY

Sometimes it is difficult to remember that the spiritual path is not a race. We use the landmarks of the medicine wheel and four directions to guide us on our path because we are rational left-brain people, always needing to be going somewhere or doing something. If we could step outside of time, we could see that we are part of a greater energy, part of the hologram of the universe and the manifestation of the Creative Force. We are limitless beings of light and this path is a process of unfolding that which we already know. A true wisdom path should guide us to the conscious soul connection, take us through the *kaypacha*, this reality to the sun gate. From that point on, we know where we're going and we can shift fully into service for The Source, whatever that might be.

We have followed the path of Inkari and Qoyari, the returning Incas. We could, just as easily, have followed the path of Christ, one of the greatest shamans to have walked the earth. All of these enlightened beings have come throughout the historic era of the *kaypacha* to show us the way to the *hanaqpacha*. There is a reason why we are drawn to this path now and some timing which we need to consider. For accuracy, we look to the Mayans who have been the keepers of time. The end of time, according to their precise calendar, is 2012 A.D. We have already entered the time of preparation. Many of us are familiar with the apocalyptical predictions in the Book of Revelations and Christ's promise to return at the end of time. The prophecies of the Q'ero, last of the Incas, speak of the end of time beginning at the June solstice in 1995. It was then that we moved into the time of preparation for the shift to higher consciousness.

Energetically, we are being pushed to do this work through planetary alignments and cosmic radiation. It is not really a tragedy that we have consumed the ozone for it mandates that we become children of the sun. We have forced ourselves to prepare for cosmic transmutation. This is destruction, purification by fire. If we are to survive on the earth we must do the work of lifting our vibration. We have, in our disregard for the earth mother, become the masters of our own tenuous destiny. There are no mistakes, only light and dark, the Tao. We have plenty of work to do in the next few years but all of the energetic assistance we will need. New realities are created with consciousness, so our first effort is to become fully conscious. Vilcabamba, city of gold, eye of the sun, heart of the Great Spirit, exists in a dimension which is inaccessible to us until we raise our vibration to it. Then we find that it is everywhere and nowhere, magic, the garden. It has been stalking us like a jaguar, an invisible presence which urges us forward on this hero's journey.

The reality we are creating is one in which mankind embodies spirit, one in which we do not get so entrapped in matter as to lose the memory of our soul's purpose. The earth is coming into her destiny and she no longer has time to raise infantile humans. We are being called upon to take care of her and ourselves so that she can come into her grandmother years and enter her own path of wisdom. It is an "anything goes", exciting future for the earth and for us. Will we miss the road to Vilcabamba because we have put off our spiritual work? The vigilant spirit will not miss the call.

WINNING THE GAME

If winning the game means getting out alive, is the road to Vilcabamba the path we take? And where does it go? If we have cleared our holographic field completely and are living in superconscious awareness at all times, we have completed the *hanaqpacha* medicine walk. We are in that magical place again, the Southeast where, as we began this path, we received our wakeup call. We came by here next and touched our souls at the end of the *kaypacha* walk. And now, here we are again, at a vibration which sustains the embodiment of the gods. Now what? Since we are on a path of evolution, clearing and extending ourselves out through our holograms, the movement is naturally outward. We have left four chakras spaced out into the universe to help us find our way home. We can think of them as being out at the sun, the planets, the solar system and cosmos, or we can come to realize that, like all of our holograms, they are right within us and all around us. The cosmos is not some distant place, it is everywhere, and like a wave in the ocean we come in and out of form from it.

So, in touch with the idea of these four chakras, we can, for the sake of our left brains, think of them as another round of the medicine wheel. We can call it Vilcabamba, or anything we want. It is a journey that is completely mythic. We have been gradually opening ourselves to those four chakras in the death breath practice. We have been reaching out to a light and expanding our consciousness even further, through landscapes that have not been described, that will not allow description. We do not need to die. Death is the greatest illusion of life. Our limited vision forces us to believe that all life is material. To die in the fear that we will lose life is to have an unconscious death. To chose our death knowing that we will live on in another form, a higher vibration, and that we will easily find those four chakras to lead us home, is conscious dying. We have been preparing for it and do not fear it. To raise our vibration through those four holograms while on earth is to sustain the divine vibration with conscious intent. It is the way we can leave this dimension alive. This is what we mean by winning the game. It is impossible to describe outside of metaphor. The work itself is inconceivable to us at this point, and requires mastery of the other dimensions. Yet, this path has been walked before on this earth, though it was not fully understood by the chroniclers of the time.

JESUS, MASTER SHAMAN

Jesus was born awake. A highly evolved soul, he walked in consciousness through the *kaypacha* without being grasped by the creatures of the *ukhupacha*. Yet he understood the dark, interior world of shadows as few people did. He entered the priestly path at a young age as well. It is likely that he was trained in the Essene community and later sent to the Egyptian Mystery School and the far East. His teachings held this wisdom as well as the Judaic and Hellenistic thought, but he was by no means a conventional person. After his years of schooling and priestly initiations, Jesus reappeared in public in the North direction of the *hanaqpacha*, a fully empowered system busting shaman. He rattled cages, challenged beliefs, practiced all of the purified emotions, and spoke of a better way to live.

In his life, we can see many of the qualities of the shaman. His personality was fully integrated and opened to the higher self. He mirrored exactly what people needed to see and spoke in parables that provoked consciousness. He bashed the hierarchy, controlled nature, and was a great magician and a mystic. He embarked on the life of the shaman when he re-appeared as the priest. His manner was that of the teacher and he employed a horizontal learning style. He even began his public life in the North by fasting for forty day and nights. In time, he moved into the East becoming a master of energy, a prophet, and a community builder. Many small communities of his

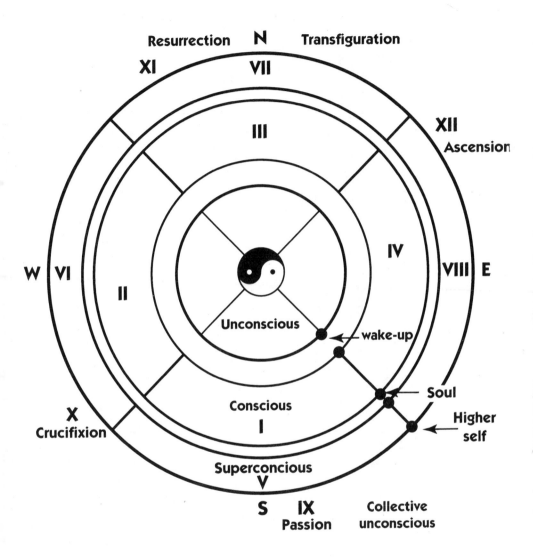

XII. The completed *hanaqpacha* medicine walk showing the potential to meet the transpersonal and begin connecting to the outer four chakras which lead us home. The relationship to the The Christ journey is indicated.

followers sprang up in the region. His activism and promotion of alternative lifestyle brought him into political disfavor, and the wisdom of his teaching became secondary to the drama around his life. He was planting seeds for the future, for our time, but it must have been a frustrating and disheartening experience for him.

With his betrayal and arrest, he moved into the work of the world above the *hanaqpacha*, walking the mythic medicine wheel. At this point, we can refer to him as The Christ, for he knew he could embody the gods. And the work he did with the gods was astounding. He was more than a master shaman when he arrived there, ready to move fully into the transpersonal awareness. He was well aware of his opportunities and had mastered the levels of energy necessary to access the four chakras connecting him to the cosmic. We have been asked to believe that he suffered and died for our sins, but he was really winning the game as few others in our history have won it.

As an embodied spirit, he walked through the South direction of his passion tapping into the collective unconscious. He *was* in touch with the suffering of mankind for he was healing the planetary mind. He was also assisting his soul growth through service to the Source. His crucifixion, accompanied by earthquake and lightening bolts, was the West work of death and transformation, symbolic of the death of "self". It allowed him to move fully into the energy of embodiment for he sacrificed his soul to spirit. He stood aside from his "self" and allowed the gods to enter and move him into the North with the resurrection and transfiguration. It was a great sign to us that all forms of death lead to transformation, that we could regenerate ourselves completely, and that we needn't die at all.

At that step in his mythic path, he was accessing the eleventh chakra - almost home. He could appear and disappear at will, move energy in unheard of ways, awaken others to the purpose of their souls and see through time. He moved through this medicine wheel very quickly for intent manifests instantly here. His ascension represented the merging with the twelfth chakra and re-emergence with the cosmic wave. He had won the game.

Glossary of Quechua and Spanish words

alto mesayoq (al-toe mess-eye-yak) North direction initiation step of the shaman, high priest/ess

apus (Ah-poos) the mountain spirits

ayahuasca (I-yah-wash-ka) vine of the dead, vision vine of the jungle

ayahuascero (I-yah-wash-karo) *Pampa mesayoq*, medicineman or woman, who prepares *ayahuasca* and takes you to meet your death

ayni (I-nee) reciprocity, sharing, give-away

curandero (ker-an-dero) spanish word for expert healer

despachos (des-pach-ohs) spanish word for the gifts given during the *mastay* ceremony, means to send off

hanaqpacha (ha-nahk-pacha) the world of higher consciousness, the upper world

Huayna Picchu (wha-na pee-choo) the old mountain, just to the North of Machu Picchu

Huascar Inca (Wash-car) gate guardian of the *ukhupacha*

Inca (Een-kah) Children of the sun; historically, the leader of the *Quechua* people

Inkari (Inn-car-ee) The first Inca male in the Q'ero legends

Inti (Een-tee) the sun

Inti Tayta (Een-tee Tie-ta) father sun

Inti-huatana (Een-tee wha-tah-na) hitching post of the sun, a carved stone at the sun temple in Machu Picchu

Inti raymi (Een-tee rye-me) festival of the sun, celebrated on the winter solstice, June 21st

kaypacha (kai-pacha) this reality, the middle world of the shaman

kintui (kin-too-ee) offering of three coca leaves symbolizing will, wisdom. and love, the three attributes of man. Also refers to the three worlds, *ukhupacha*, *kaypacha* and *hanaqpacha*.

kuraq akulleq (koo-rak ah-koo-lek) elder chewer of the coca leaves, the master shaman, East direction initiation of priesthood

kuya hampeq (koo-yah ham-pay) the healer, physician of the Andes, South direction intitiation of priesthood, includes divinators (coca leaf readers), stone healers and herbalists

llankay (yan-kai) the will aspect of *kintui*, the ability to manifest

Machu Picchu (ma-choo pee-choo) the old mountain, Inca city of light

mastay (mas-tai) an ordering ceremony which gifts mother earth and father sky with despachos delivered by fire

mesa spanish word for table, the sacred objects of the shaman wrapped in an especially beautiful woven cloth

munay (moon-I) the loving power aspect of *kintui*

naupa machu (now-pa ma-choo) the ancient times of darkness on the earth

Naupa pacha (now-pa pa-cha) the transparent beings who lived in the *naupa machu*

Pachacuti (pa-cha-coo-tee) archetype of higher consciousness, gate guardian of the *hanaqpacha*

Pachakamak (pa-cha-ka-mak) cosmic father

Pachamama (pa-cha-ma-ma) cosmic mother, mother earth

pampa mesayoq (pom-pa mess-I-yak) expert healer, West direction initiation of priesthood, *ayahuasceros* included here

Q'ero (kay-rho) Indian people inhabiting land around Ausangate, the holy mountain southeast of Cusco in Peru. Descendents of the Incas.

Qoyari (coo-ya-ree) rising star, the first Inca woman, partner of Inkari

Quechua (ketch-wha) language of the Incas and predominant language and Indian culture of Peru

Quetzalcoatl (Ketz-al-ko-ah-tel) also in Mayan and Aztec culture, feathered serpent, Lord of the Dawn, guradian of the *kaypacha*

Rhunakuna (roona-koona) the first people, unconscious man before the time of Inkari and Qoyari

Sachamama (satch-ah-ma-ma) the great serpent, keeper of knowledge and archetype of the South direction, holds kundalini within the earth

ukhupacha (oo-who-pacha) the dark, interior world of shadows, lower world, shadow side

Vilcabamba (bill-ca-bam-ba) legendary lost city of gold of the Incas

waka (wah-ka) the feminine light ray, energy of the feminine North

Wiracocha (wee-da-coach-ah) Great Spirit, but also our luminous body. Sometimes spelled *viracocha* and pronounced (bee-da-coach-ah)

yachay (yah-kai) the wisdom aspect of *kintui*

ORDER FORM

PLEASE SEND:

_____ copies of *Kintui*, Vision of the Incas

TO:

_____

Name

_____

Address

_____

City   State   Zip

I ENCLOSE THE FOLLOWING PAYMENT:

Book Price $15.95 X _____ number of copies = $_____

Minnesota residents add sales tax of $1.04 per copy _____

Shipping: First book   __3.00__

           additional books $1.00 each   _____

Total enclosed as check or money order (no cash) $_____

Makes checks payable to Heart of the Sun, Inc.

Send order to: Heart of the Sun
                    P.O. Box 495
                    Mount Shasta, Ca 96067

Orders will be shipped within 7 days of receipt.
You may copy this form.